I0014553

Propositional Logic as a Boolean Algebra – A New Perspective

Vol. 1

William S. Veatch

Website: www.mwnmathwithoutnumbers.com
Amazon author page: www.amazon.com/author/williamveatch

Copyright © 2017, by William S. Veatch.
All Rights Reserved. Moral rights asserted.

ISBN-13: 978-1979069236
ISBN-10: 1979069239

DEDICATION

This book is dedicated to the memory of my parents, Richard and Lorraine, and my brother David; and to my wife Debbie and our three children Christina, Will, and Margaret

CONTENTS

PREFACE

This book considers the question of whether we can interpret Traditional Propositional Logic using the Logic Operations AND ($\wedge$), OR ($\vee$), and NOT ($\neg$) as a Boolean Algebra when viewed in the broader context of the Mathematics of Ideas as developed in the book "Math Without Numbers – The Mathematics of Ideas – Vol.1 Foundations" ("**MWN Vol. 1**"). *See*, [Veatch 2016] in the Bibliography at the end of this book. (Capitalized terms are defined throughout the book and many definitions are incorporated by reference from MWN Vol. 1. Please use the Index at the back to locate particular definitions.)

Specifically, we explore the concept of building a Boolean Algebra of Propositions that is based upon multiple Atoms. In Traditional Propositional Logic, we assume that there is a Base Set with a single Atom, $X=\{1\}$, resulting in the Boolean Algebra $P(X) = (0,1) = ($ False, True $)$. In this book, however, we construct a new "MWN Propositional Logic" using 2, 3, 4, or more Atoms, resulting in more complex Boolean Algebras with $2^n = 4, 8, 16$, or more Elements.

We will discover that there is a Boolean Algebra of Propositions using multiple Atoms, as well as a Boolean Algebra of Logic Formulas. It is not as simple, however, as equating OR, AND, and NOT to Union, Intersection, and Complementation in the classic Boolean Algebra of Sets. As we proceed through the book, we will discover that as used in Traditional Propositional Logic, the Logic Operation "OR" is not equivalent to the Boolean Algebra notion of "Union"; and the Logic Operation of "NOT" is not equivalent to the Boolean Algebra notion of "Complementation."

In fact, we will see that in Traditional Propositional Logic, the Logic Operations OR, AND, and NOT ($\vee, \wedge, \neg$) combine two distinct tasks:

- **Set Operations:** The formation of Sets using the Set Operations of Union, Intersection, and Complementation ($\cup, \cap, \_'$), and
- **Assignment of Truth Values**: The assignment of binary Truth Values, where Truth Value = (False, True).

In MWN, we accept the Set Operations inherent in ($\vee, \wedge, \neg$), but we reject the approach to the Assignment of Truth Values. Instead, we use the MWN approach of Mapping Truth Values to Lattice Elements, where Truth Value = (Mixed, True, False, Empty). A fundamental thesis of MWN as applied to Propositional Logic is that we can apply a binary Truth Value only to Atomic Ideas: $Y = [\ 2,\ 1\ ] = [\ \text{True}\ ,\ \text{False}\ ]$. Sets of Ideas have four possible Truth Values: $P(Y) = [\varnothing,\ 2,\ 1,\ 21] = (\ \text{Mixed, True, False, Empty}\ )$, corresponding to the Power Set of the Truth Values applicable to Atoms. The basic concept is simple, but the impact is profound: a Mixed Set of True and False Atoms may not be True or False when taken as a whole.

At first, it may seem unsatisfactory to have Sets of Objects that have a "Mixed" Truth Value. Upon further consideration, however, we see that this reflects the reality of how we think. Classifications and decisions are not always black and white, but rather there are shades of gray. As we proceed, we will develop guidelines for assigning Truth Values to the "Mixed" Elements. A binary (0,1) Boolean Algebra works well for switching circuits and computer logic, but a more robust Boolean Algebra with more Atoms works better for a broader Mathematics of Ideas.

To implement our new style of Propositional Logic in Math Without Numbers, or MWN for short, we create three separate but related Universes of Discourse ("U_D"), each of which constitutes a Boolean Algebra using Union, Intersection, and Complementation. The first U_D is the Universe of Ideas that we discussed at length in MWN Vol. 1. It is not a U_D of Propositional Logic, but, as we will discuss in detail, it is critically important to understand the Universe of Ideas that forms the foundation of a Proposition by supplying the Subject and the Predicate of the Proposition. We refer to this U_D of Ideas as Order 1 or the First Order.

The second U_D is the Universe of Propositions. In this U_D, Each Atom is a Proposition, and each Proposition is an Atom. A Proposition is a statement about the relationship between two Ideas. Often in Traditional Propositional Logic it is stated that Propositions have only one Attribute, *i.e.*, a Truth Value that is either "True" or "False." In MWN, however, we identify several Attributes of Propositions that are important, including the following:

- The first Idea or "Subject" of the Proposition.
- The second Idea or "Predicate" of the Proposition.
- The Two-Set Relationship of the Subject and the Predicate, *i.e.*, is the relationship of the Subject and Predicate: Identical, Disjoint, Subset-Superset, Superset-Subset, or Partially Overlapping?
- The classification of the Proposition in Classical Logic: A, E, I, or O. (Each Proposition has two classifications: A-I, E-O, or I-O.)
- The P_3 Lattice Position of each of the Subject and the Predicate. (*See,* **Chapter 6**, for a discussion of Lattice Position.)

- The Truth Value of the Proposition, *i.e.*, "True" if the Proposition accurately reflects the Two-Set Relationship and/or Lattice Position of the Ideas forming the Subject and the Predicate; otherwise "False."

We will see that there are several different forms that Propositions may take, such as the A, E, I, and O forms of Propositions in the Classical Logic of Aristotle, or an alternative form articulated by John Venn in the 1890's that we label A_{V1}, A_{V2}, I_{V1}, I_{V2}, and E_V. Some forms of Propositions will specify the Two-Set Relationship and possibly the Lattice Position of the underlying Ideas, but others do not. The one thing that all Propositions must have by definition, however, is a fixed and determinable Truth Value. We refer to this U_D of Propositions as Order 2 or the Second Order.

The third U_D is the Universe of Logic Formulas. We start by defining "Atomic Logic Formulas" using one variable and its negative or complement: (x) and ($\neg$ x). We create a P_2 Boolean Lattice with two Atoms and four Elements, but then we quickly focus in on Logic Formulas in two variables. In this U_D, there are four Atoms, each of which is in the form of a Logic Formula in two variables: **Disjunctive Boolean Normal Form (DBNF) Clauses**: $(x \wedge y)$, $(x \wedge \neg y)$, $(\neg x \wedge y)$, and $(\neg x \wedge \neg y)$; or alternatively **Conjunctive Boolean Normal Form (CBNF) Clauses**: $(x \vee y)$, $(x \vee \neg y)$, $(\neg x \vee y)$, and $(\neg x \vee \neg y)$. In each case, we can use the four Atoms to form a 16 Element Power Set, which constitutes a Boolean Algebra using Union, Intersection, and Complementation. We will also discover that in mathematical terms, Boolean Algebras of Logic Formulas are "Free" Algebras with "n" Generators. It is well-established that every combination of logic symbols "$\vee$", "$\wedge$", and "$\neg$" involving two variables is equivalent to one of these 16 Elements, if we join the Atoms with "$\vee$" (if DBNF) or "$\wedge$" (if CBNF). We refer to this U_D of Logic Formulas as Order 3 or the Third Order.

In fact, we will identify many Boolean Algebras that are relevant to the study of Propositional Logic. For example, the Order 2 Propositions themselves, when viewed as a Subset of the Universe of Ideas, form a Boolean Algebra in the same way as any Set of Ideas. *See generally*, MWN Vol. 1. In addition, there are Dual P_4 Lattices in Order 3 mentioned above, *i.e.*, Boolean Lattices with four Atoms that represent the entire system of the symbolic logic of two variables.

Note that this is not Vol. 2 in the series: "Math Without Numbers – The Mathematics of Ideas." Rather, this is a separate book that explores a very specific issue: Propositional Logic as a Boolean Algebra. We will resume with a full discussion of Inductive and Deductive Logic with MWN Vol. 2 "Logic," expected in 2018. We have endeavored to make this book a standalone volume that a person can read to learn more about Propositional Logic, without necessarily reading the entire MWN series. Without a doubt, however, there will be times where the reader would benefit from a deeper understanding of the foundational issues discussed in MWN Vol. 1.

We refer to our system as "Math Without Numbers" or "MWN" for short, so as not to confuse this system with others. In many instances, we define words and symbols in a different way from Classical Logic or Traditional Propositional Logic, but always with a purpose.

Volume 1:

In **Chapter 1**, we begin with an introduction to the Logic inherent in Lattices. We also provide an overview of the differences between Traditional Propositional Logic and MWN Propositional Logic.

In **Chapter 2**, we step back for a moment to examine the foundations of the Mathematics of Ideas as set forth in MWN Vol.1. Of particular importance is the concept that when we create a Map from the World of Ideas to a Lattice in the World of Abstract Sets, we are asserting the Attribute Value (*i.e.*, Truth Value in the case of a Proposition) of the Lattice Element in relation to other Elements in the Lattice.

Chapter 3 looks at the definition of a Boolean Algebra and why so many scholars and logicians have focused on trying to find ways to characterize the rules of Logic as a Boolean Algebra. In particular, we take note of the fact that the Normal Form (and its four variations DNF, CNF, DBNF, and CBNF) is a characteristic of *all* Boolean Algebras, not just Propositional Logic.

Chapter 4 examines the concept of a "Free Boolean Algebra with 'n' Generators," and we see that a Free Algebra forms a good model for the Boolean Algebra of Logic Formulas.

Chapters 5, 6, and 7 examine in detail the three Universes of Discourse that are most relevant to our study of Propositional Logic: Ideas, Propositions, and Logic Formulas. We study the notion of Truth Value in more detail, including the Principle of Bivalence, the Law of the Excluded Middle, and the Principle of Non-Contradiction. We propose the following Axioms:

(1) Only Atoms have a fixed and determinable Truth Value;
(2) Sets (*i.e.*, Elements of a Power Set) may be Homogeneous, Heterogeneous, or Mixed in terms of their Truth Value; and
(3) Depending upon the context, we can create a rule for assigning Truth Values to Mixed Elements.

Volume 2:

Chapter 8 looks at Attribute Functions, Attribute Equations, and Attribute Lattices. In MWN, we use the familiar notion of a Characteristic Function to classify an Atom as either "Yes" or "No" as to whether the Atom exhibits a particular Attribute. We then generalize the concept of Characteristic Function to apply to the Sets that are Elements of the Power Set of Atoms, and refer to the generalized function as an Attribute Function. From there we look at related concepts of Attribute Equations and Attribute Lattices.

In **Chapters 9** through **12**, we examine each of the P_1, P_2, P_3, and P_4 Lattices in detail. For readers who are anxious to see how MWN Propositional Logic is applied in practice, it is okay to read **Chapter 1** and then skip to **Chapters 9** through **13** to see the MWN principles in action.

Chapter 13 looks at an example of applying our MWN Propositional Logic to the classic example of "Socrates is a man." We also look at the question of Material Implication and the long-standing debate among logicians and philosophers about the meaning and interpretation of $(x \to y)$ which is defined as $(\neg x \lor y)$. What we discover is that the notion of Material Implication, in terms of the common meaning of those words, is best understood by looking at the Logic of Lattices that is inherent in the First Order Lattice of Ideas. It is the First Order Logic of Ideas that drives the meaning of the Logic Formulas in the Third Order Lattice of Logic Formulas. This is one of the most important results of the application of MWN techniques to Propositional Logic.

Chapter 14 is the conclusion where we summarize the various examples of Boolean Algebras that are relevant to the study of Propositional Logic. We see that Propositions form a Second Order Boolean Algebra that operates in exactly the same way as any other Universe of Discourse of Ideas. We can use a Base Set of Atoms, consisting of Propositions, to generate a Boolean Lattice that together with the Operations of Set Union, Intersection and Complementation forms a Boolean Algebra of Propositions. We can also create a Third Order Boolean Algebra of Logic Formulas that also uses the Operations of Set Union, Intersection and Complementation to form a

Boolean Algebra of Logic Formulas. One of the principal differences in the MWN approach to Propositional Logic is that we use the Operations of Union, Intersection, and Complementation to form the Boolean Algebra rather than the Logic Operations of OR, AND, and NOT. We do, however, discover a technique that allows us to simplify the "Mixed" Logic Formulas in a DBNF Lattice or CBNF Lattice to arrive at the same Truth Value obtained by applying the rules of Traditional Propositional Logic.

In the end, we see that we can view Traditional Propositional Logic as a subset of a larger system of MWN Propositional Logic. Traditional Propositional Logic is a special case concerning an Order 2 Domain with a single Atom, $X = \{1\}$, and two-Element Power Set, $P(X) = (0,1)$, whereas MWN Propositional Logic goes on to examine Domains with multiple Atoms. In order to expand our system of Propositional Logic to encompass the full complexity of Ideas, we need to separate out the "Set Operations" from the "Assignment of Truth Values." The Set Operations, including the use of the Normal Form and its variations, remain intact, but in MWN Propositional Logic we propose a different methodology for assigning Truth Values.

From another perspective, we see that the Boolean Algebra "2", where the Base Set $X = \{1\}$ and the Power Set $P(X) = (0, 1)$, is perfectly adequate for switching circuits and computer logic, but not for the World of Ideas generally. A single Atom might be adequate if the only Attribute we care about is whether a Proposition is True. (We could consolidate all True Propositions into a single Atom, and ignore everything else.) Once we acknowledge that there are other Attributes, however, such as the relationships among Subjects and Predicates, then we need more than one Atom. Multiple Atoms give us the flexibility to sort Propositions based upon Attributes other than Truth Value.

In any event, the reality is that the Mathematics of Ideas is not "binary." It is still "Boolean," but we need to expand our system of mathematics and Propositional Logic to encompass more than one Atom. That is what we do in this book. We expand the simple binary Boolean Logic based upon a single Atom, to encompass a more complex Boolean Logic with many Atoms. In the course of doing so, we discover that mathematics can tell us *how* we think, and where the "gray" areas occur in our thought process, but mathematics cannot tell us *what* to think.

In the course of our studies, we learn that Traditional Propositional Logic combines two distinct tasks in the Logic Operations of OR, AND, and NOT, *i.e.*, (1) the Set Operations of Union, Intersection, and

Complementation, and (2) the Assignment of a binary Truth Value to sets of Propositions. In MWN Propositional Logic, we redefine OR, AND, and NOT to be roughly equivalent to Union, Intersection and Complementation, and propose a new approach to assigning Truth Values to Sets of Propositions. (We say "roughly" equivalent, because NOT ("¬") will have a slightly different meaning from Complementation ("_'") in that we will use NOT, in the sense of "Sign Reversal," only in the Order 3 Domain of Logic Formulas, and even then, with some restrictions to prevent us from inadvertently switching Domains. *See*, **Chapter 7**.) The MWN approach to Truth Value is designed to apply more broadly to Sets of *all* Ideas, not just Propositions. The key is to understand that "Mixed" Sets of True and False Atoms may not be True or False when taken as a whole. We can, however, develop context specific rules for assigning Truth Values to Mixed Sets. For Propositions, the rule is simple if we want the same result as in Traditional Propositional Logic: Mixed Elements in DBNF are "True"; Mixed Elements in CBNF are "False."

In other contexts (*i.e.*, not Propositions), we may elect to apply a different rule, such as:

- True, if at least one Mixed Element is True
- True, if > 50% of the Mixed Elements are True
- True, if > 66 2/3 % of the Mixed Elements are True
- True, only if 100% of the Mixed Elements are True

This result is consistent with the fundamental premise in MWN that mathematics can tell us *how* to think, but not *what* to think. There are instances where we must exercise discretion and make judgment calls.

The author's professional training is as a lawyer, not a mathematician, so we apologize in advance for any inaccuracies or errors when viewed through the eyes of a true mathematician. Still, if we are to bridge the gap between the World of Ideas and the World of Mathematics and numbers, then someone must take the first step outside his or her field of expertise and risk offending the true experts. The author welcomes any comments, from typographical errors to fundamental conceptual differences of opinion, at MWNMathWithoutNumbers@gmail.com.

1. INTRODUCTION

In this book, we explore whether Traditional Propositional Logic using the Logic Operations AND ($\wedge$), OR ($\vee$), and NOT ($\neg$) forms a Boolean Algebra when viewed in the broader context of the Mathematics of Ideas as developed in the book "Math Without Numbers – The Mathematics of Ideas – Vol.1 Foundations" ("**MWN Vol. 1**"). *See*, [Veatch 2016]. We will see that there are several Boolean Algebras relevant to the study of Propositional Logic, but that the solution is not as simple as equating OR, AND, and NOT ($\vee, \wedge, \neg$) to Union, Intersection, and Complementation ($\cup, \cap, \_'$). Rather, we need to examine the relationships among Ideas, Propositions, and Logic Formulas using principles of Set Theory and Lattice Theory. *See*, **Fig. 1-1**.

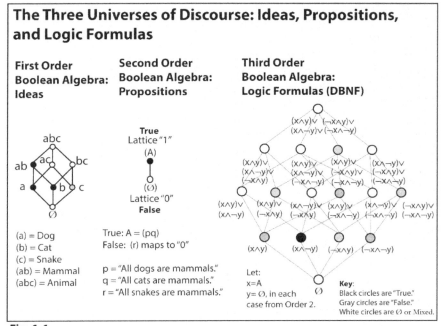

Fig. 1-1

1.1. *The Three Related Universes of Discourse: Order 1: Ideas, Order 2: Propositions, and Order 3: Logic Formulas*

We start by introducing the concept of the three Universes of Discourse and the relationships among them that we will study in detail in this book: Ideas, Propositions, and Logic Formulas. In the study of Traditional Propositional Logic, logicians often start by defining a Proposition as a Declarative Sentence that is either True or False, but that has no other properties of interest. In MWN, however, we take a different approach. We start by acknowledging that a Proposition is a statement about the relationship between two Sets of Ideas. Since our overall goal is to explore the Mathematics of Ideas, we need to understand how Propositions reflect the relationships among Ideas. In **Fig. 1-1**, we start on the left with a P_3 Lattice (*i.e.*, a Power Set Lattice with three Atoms) reflecting the relationships among the Atomic Ideas: Dog, Cat, and Snake, which give rise to the Compound Ideas: Mammal and Animal. We refer to this Universe of Discourse ("U_D") of Ideas as being of the "**First Order**" or "**Order 1**." (Note that our use of "First Order" as used to refer to the Universe of Discourse of Ideas, is not to be confused with the concept of "First Order Logic," which is often used in traditional logic books to refer to predicate logic.)

Immediately to the right is a P_1 Lattice with a single Atom "A" representing the consolidation of "True" Propositions p and q; the "False" Proposition r Maps to the Empty Set. The Propositions are formed by making a statement about the Set relationship between two Ideas in the First Order U_D of Ideas. For example, the Proposition p = "All dogs are Mammals," reflects the fact that the Idea (a) = "Dog" is a Subset of the Idea (ab) = "Mammal." Note that Lattice Elements with a Truth Value of "True" are shaded black; Lattice Elements with a Truth Value of "False" are shaded gray; and the Empty Set and the Lattice Elements with a mixture of "True" and "False" Atoms are left unshaded. We refer to this Universe of Discourse of Propositions as being of the "**Second Order**" or "**Order 2**."

To the far right is a P_4 Lattice of Logic Formula Atoms: $(x \wedge y)$, $(x \wedge \neg y)$, $(\neg x \wedge y)$, and $(\neg x \wedge \neg y)$. Logic Formulas constitute a distinct Universe of Discourse where Atoms are defined by a specified number of Propositional Variables (x and y in our example) and their negatives ($\neg$ x and $\neg$ y in our example), connected by either AND ("$\wedge$") in the case of "DBNF" Atoms, or OR ("$\vee$") in the case of "CBNF" Atoms. First, we assign Truth Values to the Order 3 Atoms by determining the Value of the Logic Formula when we assign specific Order 2 Elements to "x" and "y". Then, as in the Second Order Lattice, compound Lattice Elements consisting of "True" Atoms are shaded black; compound Lattice Elements consisting of "False" Atoms are shaded gray; and the Empty Set together with the Lattice Elements with a mixture of "True" and "False" Atoms are left unshaded. We refer to this Universe of Discourse of Logic Formulas as being of the "**Third Order**" or "**Order 3**."

The concepts of Disjunctive Boolean Normal Form ("**DBNF**") and Conjunctive Boolean Normal Form ("**CBNF**") are so important in our study of Propositional Logic, that we take a moment to explain what the DBNF and CBNF Atoms represent. *See*, **Fig. 1-2**, which uses Venn Diagrams to illustrate the meaning of the four Atoms. It also helps the reader to understand why, assuming the Domain is the Order 2 Boolean Algebra (0, 1), only one Atom in DBNF can be True; and only one Atom in CBNF can be False. For example, if each of "x" and "y" is equal to "1", then only "$(x \wedge y)$" (represented by the Intersection of the circles) can be True, *i.e.*, equal to "1". Conversely, if each of "x" and "y" is equal to "1", then only "$(\neg x \vee \neg y)$" (again, represented by the Intersection of the circles) can be False, *i.e.*, equal to "0". (We leave it to the reader to work through each possible combination of assigned Values for the Variables "x" and "y".) Of course, this rule does not hold true if the Order 2 Domain has more than one Atom.

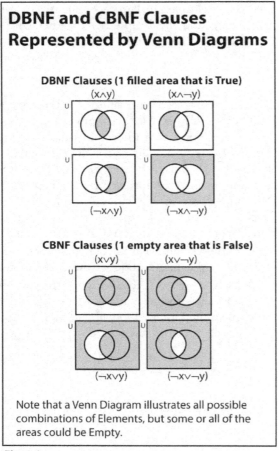

DBNF and CBNF Clauses Represented by Venn Diagrams

DBNF Clauses (1 filled area that is True)

CBNF Clauses (1 empty area that is False)

Note that a Venn Diagram illustrates all possible combinations of Elements, but some or all of the areas could be Empty.

Fig. 1-2

When we study the Truth Value of Logic Formulas, what we see is that the Truth Values in the Third Order Lattice of Logic Formulas depend upon the Truth Values of the Propositions in the Second Order Lattice of Propositions; and the Truth Values in the Second Order Lattice of Propositions depend upon the Set Relationships of the Ideas in the First Order Lattice of Ideas. The study of the Logic of Propositions is inextricably linked to the study of the Set Relationships among Ideas. By separating Ideas, Propositions, and Logic Formulas into three distinct Universes of Discourse, we can study each one separately, and then examine the relationships among the three. Each Universe of Discourse constitutes a Boolean Lattice created by the Elements of a Power Set of Atoms, so all of the rules of Boolean Algebra apply to each Universe of Discourse.

Note that the MWN approach to creating Boolean Algebras of Logic is different from the traditional approaches found in other books. We are not saying that one approach is better than another, but simply that they are different. **Sections 1.8** and **1.9** discuss the assumptions (or axioms) of MWN that make the MWN approach to Propositional Logic different from Traditional Propositional Logic as found in most books on Symbolic Logic or Mathematical Logic. **Section 1.10** lists a number of books and articles that use other techniques to establish a Boolean Algebra of Logic. In some cases, the techniques used are consistent with the MWN approach, but in other cases they are not.

1.2. Should the Boolean Algebra of Propositions (Order 2) have a Single Atom (Representing All True Propositions) or Multiple Atoms?

In this Section, we raise the question: Should the Boolean Algebra of Propositional Logic be based on a single Atom (representing all True Propositions) or Multiple Atoms? In other words: How many Atoms are in the Second Order Universe of Discourse of Propositions? This may seem like a technical point to address so early in the book, but it goes straight to the heart of the issue that we face when attempting to construct a Boolean Algebra of Propositional Logic.

Traditional Propositional Logic ("**TPL**") assumes that there is only one Atom. To achieve this result, in TPL we assume that all "True" Propositions are consolidated into a single Atom that we will label "A". All "False" Propositions are represented by the Empty Set. The primary advantage to this approach is that we have a very simple binary logic to apply to the Logic Formulas in the Order 3 Universe of Discourse. In other words, for each x, y, z, ... in an Order 3 Logic Formula, we simply assign a "0" (representing "False" Propositions) or a "1" (representing "True" Propositions) and then solve the Formula for "0" or "1". *See*, **Fig. 1-3**.

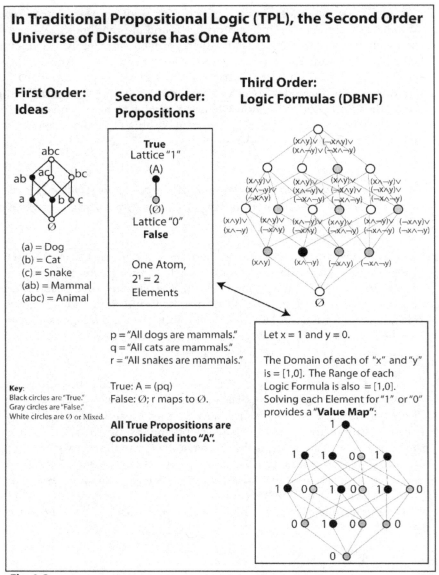

In Traditional Propositional Logic (TPL), the Second Order Universe of Discourse has One Atom

First Order: Ideas

abc
ac
ab bc
a b c
Ø

(a) = Dog
(b) = Cat
(c) = Snake
(ab) = Mammal
(abc) = Animal

Key:
Black circles are "True."
Gray circles are "False."
White circles are () or Mixed.

Second Order: Propositions

True
Lattice "1"
(A)

(Ø)
Lattice "0"
False

One Atom,
$2^1 = 2$
Elements

p = "All dogs are mammals."
q = "All cats are mammals."
r = "All snakes are mammals."

True: A = (pq)
False: Ø; r maps to Ø.

All True Propositions are consolidated into "A".

Third Order: Logic Formulas (DBNF)

Let x = 1 and y = 0.

The Domain of each of "x" and "y" is = [1,0]. The Range of each Logic Formula is also = [1,0]. Solving each Element for "1" or "0" provides a "**Value Map**":

Fig. 1-3

The Third Order Boolean Lattice is formed by mapping True or False to each Atom. Then we form a Boolean Lattice in the usual way, *i.e.*, a Compound is "True" if all Atoms are True; False if all Atoms are "False"; and otherwise has a "Mixed" Truth Value. *See,* **Section 1.4** for a detailed discussion of Truth Value.

Below the Order 3 Boolean Lattice in **Fig. 1-3** is something different called a Value Map. A Value Map shows the Order 2 value of each Element in the Order 3 Boolean Lattice, if we solve the Boolean Expressions for specified Elements taken from the Order 2 Domain, such as x = 1, and y = 0. Note that since "∨" and "∧" are closed operations on the Elements of the Order 2 Lattice, each Logic Formula (or Boolean Function) in Order 3 maps to an Order 2 value expressed in terms of Objects: "A" or "Ø"; or Attributes: "1" or "0". As we proceed, we will often compare an Order 3 Boolean Lattice of Logic Formulas to its related Value Map. It is important, however, not to confuse the two. In **Fig. 1-3**, the Lattice of Logic Formulas contains seven unshaded Elements with a "Mixed" Truth Value; whereas in the Value Map, those same seven Elements have a Value of "1".

There are some disadvantages to using a Universe of Discourse of Propositions with a single Atom, however, that lead us to explore an Order 2 Universe of Discourse with more than one Proposition Atom. The principal disadvantages are the following:

- In MWN, we do not Map Objects to the Empty Set. Rather, the Empty Set is "empty," so it cannot represent the class of False Propositions.
- In MWN, we consider Propositions to have many Attributes, such as the Subject and the Predicate taken from the Lattice of Ideas, and the relationship to other Propositions. If we consolidate all True Propositions into a single Atom, and all False Propositions into the Empty Set, then we lose the ability to draw distinctions among various Propositions, and the ability to sort them, based upon Attributes other than Truth Value.

Throughout the rest of this book, we explore what happens when we add more Atoms to the Order 2 Universe of Discourse of Propositions. We will see that for any single Attribute, no matter how many Atoms we add, the Order 2 Lattice is Isomorphic to a Lattice with two Atoms, and therefore $2^n = 2^2 = 4$ Elements.

1.3. Understanding the Boolean Algebra of Logic Formulas (Order 3) – a Free Algebra with "n" Generators

In the language of Abstract Algebra, a Boolean Algebra of Logic Formulas is a Free Boolean Algebra with "n" Generators. We will examine Free Boolean Algebras in detail in **Chapter 4**, but for now the key point to understand is that there are two different Lattices at play. One is the Lattice of Logic Formulas (expressed in terms of DBNF Clauses or CBNF Clauses) and the other is a Subalgebra generated when we solve the Boolean Expressions by assigning Values from the Order 2 Domain to the Propositional Variables to create a Value Map.

In Traditional Propositional Logic, we use the Value Map as the assignment of Truth Values to the Logic Formulas. In MWN Propositional Logic, however, we take a different approach to assigning Truth Values. Basically, we use the Values from the Value Map to assign Truth Values only to the Atoms in the Order 3 Lattice. Compounds will be "True" if all Atoms are True; "False" if all Atoms are False; and otherwise "Mixed."

Why do we not use the Value Map to assign all Truth Values in MWN Propositional Logic? The reason is that while Free Algebras are a useful tool for generating Subalgebras, the Values, which are based upon notions of Complementation, do not really reflect Truth Values as we understand them intuitively in practical applications in the social sciences and humanities. Therefore, we need to seek an alternative means of assigning Truth Value.

For example, to assign Truth Values in an Order 3 Boolean Lattice of Logic Formulas, we start by assigning a binary True or False Value to each Atom, *e.g.*, in DBNF: $(x \wedge y)$, $(x \wedge \neg y)$, $(\neg x \wedge y)$, and $(\neg x \wedge \neg y)$. For each x, y, z, ... in an Order 3 Logic Formula, we simply assign an Element from the Order 2 Domain, for example, a "(B)" (representing "False" Propositions) or an "(A)" (representing "True" Propositions), and then solve the Formula for an Element in the Order 2 Domain of $P(X) = (AB, A, B, \emptyset) = [\emptyset, 2, 1, 21] = $ (Mixed, True, False, Empty). *See,* **Fig. 1-4**.

If we want to achieve the same result with respect to the Truth Values of Atoms as with the P_1 Order 2 Domain of Traditional Propositional Logic, then we can elect to treat the value "($\emptyset$)" as being "False" rather than "Empty." (We will discuss this decision to treat "($\emptyset$)" as "False" in the DBNF Domain, in **Chapter 7**.) We then complete the Boolean Lattice in the normal way. *See,* **Fig. 1-4**.

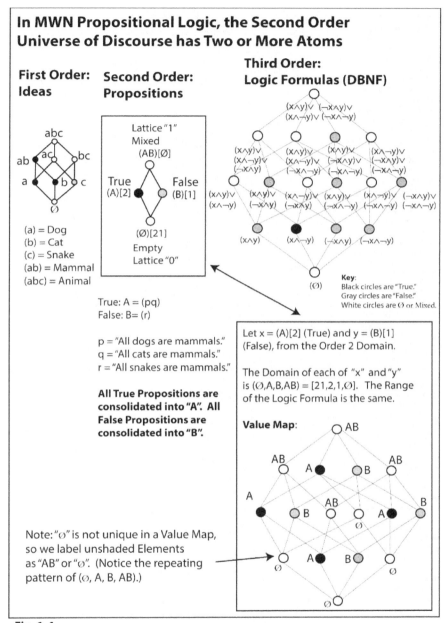

Fig. 1-4

Once again, we can create a Value Map based upon the Map of each Element to an Element of the Order 2 Boolean Lattice by solving the Boolean Function (treating $(\vee, \wedge, \neg)$ as $(\cup, \cap, \_')$). The Value Map is similar to the Boolean Lattice, except that we have elected (in DBNF) to treat the Value "(Ø)" taken from the Order 2 Domain as "False" in the Boolean Lattice.

The reader should not expect to understand every aspect of **Fig. 1-4** at this stage of the book. We will explore each component in detail as we proceed through the book.

While the math becomes more complicated with four Elements in the Range rather than two, it is not insurmountable. In fact, we develop techniques that allow us to achieve the same results as to Truth Value that we would achieve with Traditional Propositional Logic, if that is the goal. For example, one such technique is to deem:

- True = (AB, A) = [Ø, 2] = (Mixed, True)
- False = (B, Ø) = [1, 21] = (False, Empty)

By making this assumption, the Truth Values in Order 3 become identical whether using one Atom or two or more Atoms in Order 2. *See,* **Fig. 1-5**.

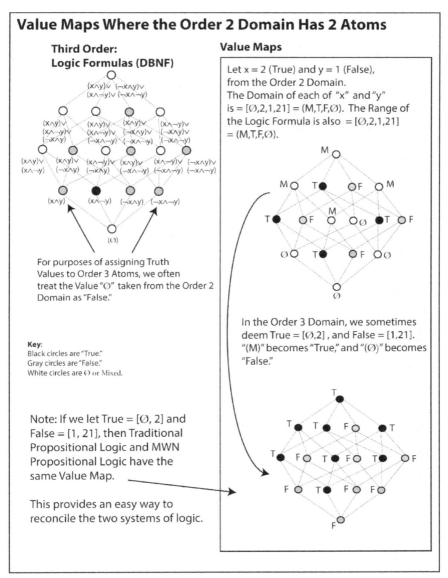

Fig. 1-5

The advantages to using multiple Atoms in the Order 2 Domain, however, are enormous. With multiple Atoms, we can analyze relationships among Propositions other than simply Truth Value. In **Chapter 13**, we will see that this opens the door to a new interpretation of the classic debate over the meaning of Material Implication.

1.4. *The Logic of Lattices*

Throughout this book we use Set Theory to explore the logic that is inherent in the structure of Lattices that have more than one Atom (the "**Logic of Lattices**"). Our end goal is to develop a system of Propositional Logic that is consistent with the Mathematics of Ideas as developed in the Math Without Numbers (MWN) series of books. **Fig. 1-6** sets forth what is perhaps the most important lesson of this book: the inherent Logic of Lattices.

Mapping the Truth Value "True"

We Map the Truth Value "True" to the Element in the Lattice (the "**Attribute Element**") consisting of all Atoms that exhibit the Attribute "True." In **Fig. 1-6**, Atoms (p) and (q) are True, so the Attribute Element is (pq).

Mapping the Truth Value "False"

Since Truth Values of Atoms are binary, *i.e.*, either True or False, the Attribute "False" will Map to the Set Complement of the Attribute Element for the Attribute "True." Therefore, in our example, "False" Maps to (r).

Inheritance of Attributes

Each Element in the Down Set of the Attribute Element (*i.e.*, each Element in a downward path towards (∅)) inherits the given Attribute. We can see this most easily by noting in our example that any Element with [3] in its Attribute Signature inherits the Attribute "True."

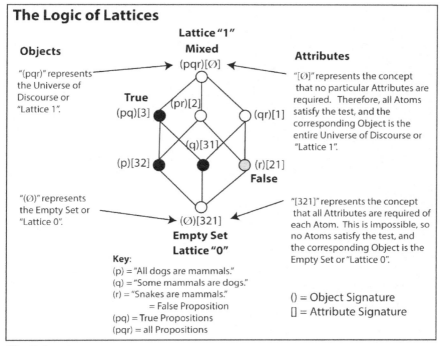

Fig. 1-6

Four Types of Elements in an Attribute Lattice of Ideas

There are four types of Ideas in an "**Attribute Lattice**," *i.e.*, a Lattice in which we have designated a particular Attribute as "Yes/True" and its Complement as "No/False":

- **True**: The Attribute Element together with its Down Set, *i.e.*, the Elements on a path down to "(∅)", are all "True." See the Elements shaded black in **Fig. 1-6**.

- **False**: The Complement of the Attribute Element together with its Down Set, *i.e.*, the Elements on a path down to "(∅)", are all "False." See the Element shaded gray in **Fig. 1-6**.

- **Empty Set**: The Empty Set is in theory made up of Elements that are both True and False at the same time. This is impossible, which explains why it is empty.

- **Mixed**: The remaining Elements are Mixed Sets of Atoms, some of which are True and some of which are False. See the unshaded Elements in **Fig. 1-6**, other than the Empty Set.

An important consequence of the foregoing properties of an Attribute Lattice is that we cannot Map Ideas to the Empty Set. For example, in MWN we cannot equate the "0" Element at the bottom of the Lattice with "False Propositions." Conversely, we cannot equate the "1" Element at the top of the Lattice with "True," unless all of the Atoms in the Base Set of Atoms are True. If there is even one False Atom, then at least half of the Elements of the Lattice will be either False or Mixed True/False Elements.

Although the example in **Fig. 1-6** relates to a Lattice of Propositions (Order 2), the same Logic of Lattices where each Element is either True, False, Empty, or Mixed, is inherent in Lattices of Ideas (Order 1) and Lattices of Logic Formulas (Order 3).

As illustrated in **Fig. 1-7**, we can represent every Attribute Lattice as a "**Nested P$_2$ Attribute Lattice**." The total number of Elements in the Attribute Lattice remains constant.

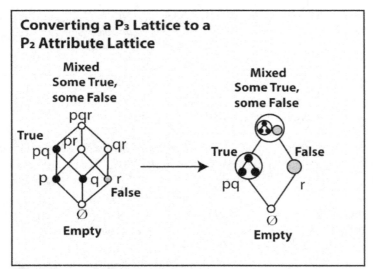

Fig. 1-7

We use the Nested P$_2$ Attribute Lattice to highlight the fact that *every* Attribute has the effect of dividing the Universe of Ideas into the same four-Element Power Set structure where each Element in the Power Set of Atoms is either Mixed, True, False, or Empty. We will discuss this important point further in **Section 6.8**.

1.5. *Propositional Logic as a Boolean Algebra*

By Propositional Logic, we mean a logic of "Propositions" as opposed to a logic of individual "Ideas." A Proposition is defined as a sentence consisting of a Subject and a Predicate connected by a Copula (*i.e.*, a form of the verb "to be"), that is either True or False. (Since a Proposition is itself an Idea, the Logic of Propositions is a subset of the overall Logic of Ideas.) Many scholars have written about this topic, and have developed a number of arguments and proofs showing how a Propositional Logic can constitute a Boolean Algebra, yet there are still many unanswered questions when it comes to developing a system of Propositional Logic for application in the social sciences and humanities. We submit that using Lattices along with other techniques developed in MWN Vol. 1, results in a Boolean Algebra of Propositional Logic that more accurately reflects how we apply Logic in the social sciences and humanities. The Math Without Numbers (MWN) approach to Propositional Logic is easy to apply and is consistent with a more general theory of the Mathematics of Ideas.

Many readers may be familiar with the definition of a Boolean Algebra, but for those who are not, we take a moment to review the definition of an "Algebra" generally, and what makes an Algebra a "Boolean Algebra." (We will provide a more formal definition in **Chapter 3**.) "Algebra" refers to an abstract algebraic structure consisting of a Domain and one or more Operations on the Elements of the Domain. What makes an Algebra "Boolean" are the following properties:

- Both Addition and Multiplication are Idempotent, meaning that $a + a = a$; and $a \times a = a$. This is obviously true for the Operations of Set Union and Intersection on the Elements of a Power Set, where "Union" is Addition and "Intersection" is Multiplication.
- Every Element "a" in the Domain has a unique Complement denoted "a'".
- There is a unique "zero" Element (at the bottom of a Boolean Lattice) and a unique "1" Element (at the top of a Boolean Lattice), such that for any Element "a":
  - $a + 0 = a$
  - $a \times 1 = a$
  - $1' = 0$
  - $0' = 1$
- Every Boolean Algebra is Isomorphic (*i.e.*, has the same shape and structure) to a Boolean Algebra of Sets. The classic example is the

Power Set Boolean Algebra, where the Domain consists of the Base Set X and all subsets of X, including the Empty Set; and the Operations are Set Union, Intersection, and Complementation.

This last point is particularly important, because it means that we are justified in viewing Propositional Logic from a Set Theoretic perspective, if our goal is to establish a Boolean Algebra.

In **Section 1.6** below, "Historical Context," we reference a number of different writings on this topic. We do not, however, attempt to reconcile all of the different views. Rather, informed by the various writings, we look at a number of different approaches to establishing a Propositional Logic that constitutes a Boolean Algebra, starting with the P_1 Power Set Lattice with a single Atom, then moving on to the P_2, P_3, and P_4 Lattices to see how each of these Boolean Lattices is relevant to the study of Propositional Logic.

Our goal is to meet the following requirements:

- **Easy to apply:** The Boolean Algebra of Propositional Logic must be easy to understand and easy to apply in the real world, particularly in analyzing subjects in the social sciences and humanities.

- **Consistent with MWN**: The Boolean Algebra of Propositional Logic must be consistent with the Mathematics of Ideas that we created previously, including dual Boolean Algebras of Objects and Attributes, which is based on Set Theory. *See*, [Veatch 2016]. After all, Propositions are a Subset of the World of Ideas, so in theory the Boolean Algebra of Propositional Logic should be a Subset or Universe of Discourse within the broader Universe of Ideas.

- **Treat "Truth" and "Falsity" in the same manner as any other Attribute**: While there are many possible theories of Truth and Falsity of Propositions, our goal is to explore Truth and Falsity as Attributes of an Idea, *i.e.*, the "Idea" is a Proposition in this case. Therefore, our treatment of "True" and "False" must follow all of the rules applicable to other Attributes. Similarly, any rules that we develop for the treatment of "True" and "False" as Attributes of the "Proposition Idea," should be equally applicable to any Attribute of any other Idea.

- **Interpret "0" and "1" in a Boolean Lattice as the Empty Set and the Universe of Discourse, respectively**: Over the years, scholars have struggled with how to interpret the Elements "0" and

"1" at the bottom and top of the Boolean Lattice in the context of Propositional Logic. One approach is to view "1" as representing "True" and "0" as representing "False." In our MWN approach, however, the Elements 0 and 1 in a Lattice of Ideas represent the Empty Set and the Universe of Discourse, respectively. The "1" Element may represent one or more Atoms, but the "0" Element represents the Empty Set and cannot represent a Set of Objects such as the "Set of all False Propositions." We will explore this concept in detail in this book.

We will develop a simple Boolean Algebra of Propositions that works for our purposes. This does not mean that it is the only possible Boolean Algebra of Propositional Logic, or that it is the best one for all purposes. It will, however, meet our requirements as set forth above, and will prove to be useful as a practical tool in the study of mathematics (without numbers) as applied to the social sciences and humanities.

(Unless otherwise defined herein, capitalized terms have the meanings given to them in MWN Vol. 1. Please use the Index at the back of this book to locate particular definitions. Please note that the notation used in MWN was developed specifically for the Mathematics of Ideas, and is different in some cases from the notation used in other areas of mathematics. The reader is urged to read MWN Vol. 1 for a detailed description of the notation used, and why it is the way it is.)

1.6. Historical Context

There have been many contributions over the years to the study of the Algebra of Propositional Logic. There are too many works to list them all, but the following list provides some of the highlights:

- **1846-1900**:
    - **De Morgan**: In 1847, Augustus De Morgan wrote *Formal Logic: or, The Calculus of Inference, Necessary and Probable. See,* [De Morgan 1847].
    - **Boole**: In 1854, George Boole wrote *An Investigation of The Laws of Thought, On Which are Founded The Mathematical Theories of Logic and Probabilities. See,* [Boole 1854].
    - **Jevons**: In 1877, William Stanley Jevons wrote *Elementary Lessons in Logic. See,* [Jevons 1877].
    - **Frege**: In 1879, Gottlob Frege wrote "Begriffsschrift, a formula language, modeled upon that of arithmetic, for pure thought." *See,* [Frege 1879].

- o **Venn**: In 1894, John Venn wrote *Symbolic Logic*, which remains an important work to read. *See*, [Venn 1894].
- **1900-1950**:
  - o **Russell and Whitehead**: In 1910, Bertrand Russell and Alfred North Whitehead wrote *Principia Mathematica*. See, [Russell and Whitehead 1910].
  - o **C.I. Lewis**: In 1918, Clarence Irving Lewis wrote *A Survey of Symbolic Logic*. *See*, [Lewis 1918].
  - o **Huntington**: In 1933, Edward V. Huntington wrote "New Sets of Independent Postulates for the Algebra of Logic, With Special Reference to Whitehead and Russell's Principia Mathematica." *See*, [Huntington 1933].
  - o **Stone**: In 1936, M. H. Stone wrote "The Theory of Representation for Boolean Algebras." *See*, [Stone 1936].
  - o **Hilbert and Ackermann**: In 1938, D. Hilbert and W. Ackermann wrote *Principles of Mathematical Logic*. *See*, [Hilbert and Ackermann 1938].
- **1950-2000**:
  - o **Quine**: From 1950 to 1982, Willard Van Orman Quine wrote *Methods of Logic*. *See*, [Quine 1982].
  - o **Whitesitt**: In 1960, J. Eldon Whitesitt wrote *Boolean Algebra and Its Applications*. *See*, [Whitesitt 1960].
  - o **Evenden**: In 1962, John Evenden wrote: "A Lattice-Diagram for the Propositional Calculus." *See*, [Evenden 1962].
  - o **Langer**: In 1967, Susanne K. Langer wrote *An Introduction to Symbolic Logic*, 3d. *See*, [Langer 1967].
  - o **Abbott**: In 1969, James C. Abbott wrote *Sets, Lattices, and Boolean Algebras*. [Abbott 1969].
  - o **Curry**: In 1976, Haskell B. Curry wrote *Foundations of Mathematical Logic*. *See*, [Curry 1976].
  - o **Burris and Sankappanavar**: In 1981, Stanley Burris and H.P. Sankappanavar, wrote *A Course in Universal Algebra*. *See*, [Burris and Sankappanavar 1981]. In his writings, Stanley Burris analyzes Boolean Logic in great detail, and provides extensive historical context for the development of Boolean logic.
  - o **Burris**: In 1998, Stanley Burris wrote *Logic for Mathematics and Computer Science*. *See*, [Burris 1998].
  - o **Givant and Halmos**: In 1998, Paul Halmos and Steven Givant wrote *Logic as Algebra*. *See*, [Givant and Halmos 1998].

- **2000-2017**:
  - **Davey and Priestley**: From 1990 - 2001, B.A. Davey and H.A. Priestley wrote *Introduction to Lattices and Order (2d Ed.)*. *See*, [Davey and Priestley 2001]. This book further develops the lattice theory necessary to develop the theory of the Logic of Lattices.
  - **Grätzer**: In 2003, George Grätzer wrote *General Lattice Theory, 2d*. See, [Grätzer 2003]. While not a book on logic, advances in the study of Lattice Theory have made it possible to develop a robust theory of the "Logic of Lattices" that we explore in this book.
  - **Givant and Halmos**: In 2009, Paul Halmos and Steven Givant wrote *Introduction to Boolean Algebras*. *See*, [Givant and Halmos 2009]. While not focused on Propositional Logic, this book is essential to the understanding of Boolean Algebras, which is the foundation of the Logic of Lattices.
  - **Smullyan**: In 2014, Raymond M. Smullyan wrote *A Beginner's Guide to Mathematical Logic*. *See*, [Smullyan 2014].

For the reader who wants to understand the premises underlying MWN, it is absolutely critical to understand that historical context. For the learner who has the time and interest, the above list is a good place to start.

In particular, if the reader has not yet read *Principia Mathematica* [Russell and Whitehead 1910], it is well worth the effort to do so. To make the work more accessible, however, we recommend that the reader read [Langer 1967] first, particularly Chapter XII, and then read portions of Principia Mathematica as they are discussed by Langer. Langer does an excellent job of setting the stage for Principia Mathematica by explaining the issues that mathematicians were struggling with in connection with developing a Boolean Algebra of Propositional Logic. Willard Van Orman Quine in [Quine 1969] at 251 *et seq.* also provides helpful background and analysis regarding Principia Mathematica. *See also*, [Eves 1990] at 267.

1.7. The Attributes of Traditional Propositional Logic

In this Section, we examine the Attributes of Traditional Propositional Logic. Then, in **Section 1.8** we will examine the Attributes of MWN Propositional Logic, and compare and contrast the two systems.

1.7.1.Scope: *Propositions and Logic Formulas*

Traditional Propositional Logic, as taught in most books on Symbolic Logic or Mathematical Logic, focuses exclusively on "Propositions," which are by definition Declarative Sentences that are either "True" or "False." Declarative Sentences that do not have a fixed and determinable Truth Value are not within the scope of Traditional Propositional Logic.

Propositional Variables ("x_1, x_2, x_3, …") representing Propositions, together with their negatives ("$\neg\ x_1$, $\neg\ x_2$, $\neg\ x_3$, …"), are then combined using OR and AND, and using parentheses where needed to group Propositional Variables, in order to form Well Formed Formulas ("**WFF's**").

1.7.2. *Number of Proposition Atoms? - One*

In Traditional Propositional Logic, there is only one Proposition Atom, which represents the consolidation of all True Propositions into a single Atom. The justification for this approach is that if the only Attribute we are interested in is Truth Value, then all True Propositions are the same as each other; and all False Propositions are the same as each other. With no other Attributes to distinguish one Proposition from another, only one Atom is required.

To achieve the benefits of a truly binary Logic, we Map False Propositions to the Empty Set. In a sense, this may not seem satisfactory, since the Empty Set is in fact "empty." As a result, in MWN we explore a Propositional Logic with two or more Atoms as well.

1.7.3.Examine *How the Subjects and Predicates Affect the Relationships Among Propositions? – No*

In Traditional Propositional Logic, we do not look at the Subject and Predicate of any individual Proposition.

1.7.4.Apply *Boolean Algebra Concept of Normal Form? – Yes*

We do apply the Set Theory concept of Normal Form (including DNF, CNF, DBNF, and CBNF) to Logic Formulas in Traditional Propositional Logic. Normal Form is not always described in Traditional Propositional Logic as an Attribute of Set Theory and Boolean Algebra generally, but, as described in **Chapter 3**, Normal Form is in fact a feature of Set Theory and the Operations of Union, Intersection, and Complementation as found in the classic Boolean Algebra of Sets.

1.7.5. Binary Truth Value? – Yes, the Order 2 Universe of Discourse has One Atom, and therefore Two Elements Representing "True" and "False"

In Traditional Propositional Logic, the Logic Operations $(\vee, \wedge, \neg)$ perform two distinct functions: Set Operations and Assignment of Truth Values.

First, Propositions are combined in much the same way that we combine Atoms to make Sets using the Set Operations of Union, Intersection, and Complementation. In particular, the concept of "Normal Form" (and its four variations: DNF, CNF, DBNF, and CBNF) is taken from Set Theory as is applied to Propositions using the three Logic Operations of OR, AND, and NOT, and treating them, in essence, as if they were the same as Union, Intersection, and Complementation.

Second, the Logic Operations also operate to assign a binary Truth Value, i.e., either True or False, to any Well-Formed Formula consisting of Propositional Variables $(x_1, x_2, x_3, \ldots)$ and their Negatives $(\neg x_1, \neg x_2, \neg x_3, \ldots)$ connected by any combination of the three Logic Operations. As we proceed, we will see that this is where Traditional Propositional Logic and MWN Propositional Logic differ. MWN applies the same Set Operations (including the rules applicable to Normal Form), but uses a different approach to determining Truth Values. Traditional Propositional Logic uses the Value Map of Values from Order 2 to determine the Truth Values of Logic Formulas in Order 3, but MWN Propositional Logic does not take this approach.

1.7.6. Four-Valued Truth Value? – No

Traditional Propositional Logic assigns a binary True/False "Truth Value" both to Atoms and Sets of Atoms, so there is no need to use a four-valued Truth Value.

In Traditional Propositional Logic, we are working in an Order 2 Domain with one Atom representing "True" Propositions. Therefore, the Order 2 Domain has only two Elements: True and $\varnothing$, which in Traditional Propositional Logic represents "False." Each Element of the Order 3 Domain will therefore Map to either "True" or "False."

1.7.7. Use an Order 2 "Value Map" to Determine Truth Values in Order 3? - Yes

In Traditional Propositional Logic, we assign the Values from the Value Map (Order 2) to the Logic Formulas (Order 3). This is contrary to how we assign Truth Values in MWN Propositional Logic.

1.8. How the Math Without Numbers (MWN) Approach to Propositional Logic is Similar, But Different

In MWN, we take a different approach to addressing some of these same issues that logicians have struggled with for many years. We start with the assumption that every Idea in the World of Ideas is either an Atom or a Compound made up of Atoms, and that only Atoms have a fixed and determinable, binary Truth Value.

1.8.1. Scope: Ideas, Propositions, and Logic Formulas

In MWN, we look at three "Orders" consisting of Order 1 "Ideas," Order 2 "Propositions," and Order 3 "Logic Formulas." What we see is that the three Orders are inextricably linked. We can Map values from one Order to another, but we must exercise care not to mix calculations across Orders.

1.8.2. Number of Proposition Atoms? - Two or More

As mentioned above, in MWN we view the Lattice "0" as the Empty Set, so it is not appropriate to Map False Propositions to "0'". Instead, we create a second Atom to represent False Propositions. If we are not concerned with any Attributes other "True" and "False," then we can work with only two Atoms. If, however, we want to work with other Attributes of Propositions, then we can add additional Proposition Atoms to our Domain.

1.8.3. Examine How the Subjects and Predicates Affect the Relationships Among Propositions? – Yes

In MWN Propositional Logic, we look at the relationships among the Ideas that form the Subjects and Predicates of the Propositions. The "Attribute Value" of an Atomic Idea, i.e., the Yes/No or True/False answer to whether an Idea exhibits a particular Attribute, depends upon these relationships. The

Attribute Value of a Subject determines the Truth Value of the related Proposition. The Truth Values of a number of Propositions in turn determine the Truth Value of a Logic Formula.

1.8.4. Apply Boolean Algebra Concept of Normal Form? – Yes

In MWN Propositional Logic, we equate (roughly speaking) $(\lor,\land,\neg)$ to $(\cup,\cap,\_')$, so the concept of Normal Form (including the four variations DNF, CNF, DBNF, and CBNF) applies to MWN Propositional Logic. The other advantage to equating Logic Operations to Set Operations, is that the MWN Propositional Logic is clearly a Boolean Algebra, since it is a variation of the classic Boolean Algebra of Sets. The challenge, then, is how to treat Truth Values.

1.8.5. Binary Truth Value? - Only for Atomic Ideas, Not Compounds

In MWN Propositional Logic, only Atomic Ideas necessarily have a fixed and determinable Truth Value. Compound Ideas, *i.e.*, Sets of Atomic Ideas, may have a fixed and determinable Truth Value if they are Homogeneous as to the Attribute in question. In other words, if all Atoms in a Set comprising a Compound Idea share the same Attribute Value as to a given Attribute, then we can say that the Compound Idea has that Attribute.

1.8.6. Four-Valued Truth Value? – Yes, the Order 2 Universe of Discourse has at least Two Atoms, and therefore at least Four Elements: P(Y) = [Ø, 2, 1, 21] = (Mixed, True, False, Empty)

In MWN, we assign a binary True/False "Truth Value" to Atoms, but not to Sets of Atoms. The reason for this is that we view a Set containing some "True" Atoms and some "False" Atoms as having a "Mixed" Truth Value. A helpful way to visualize the four-valued Truth Value is to note that the range of Truth Values of an Atom is represented by the Set $Y = [2, 1] =$ [True, False]; and the range of Truth Values of a Set of Atoms is represented by the Set $P(Y) = [Ø, 2, 1, 21] =$ (Mixed, True, False, Empty), *i.e.*, when we are looking at Sets, we are in a Power Set Domain, so logically speaking the range of Truth Values of "Sets" should be the Power Set of the range of Truth Values of "Atoms." To better understand the MWN approach to Domains of Atoms (Dimension 1) and Domains of Sets (Dimension 2), *see* MWN Vol. 1 [Veatch 2016].

Depending upon the context we may be able to create a rule for assigning a definite Truth Value to a Set of Mixed True/False Atoms, but the approach taken will vary depending upon the circumstances. MWN Propositional Logic does not simply use the Value Map of values from Order 2 to determine the Truth Values of Logic Formulas in Order 3.

(Note that if we are examining a single Attribute such as Truth Value, then we can demonstrate that any Order 2 U_D with more than two Atoms is Isomorphic to a P_2 Attribute Lattice with two Deemed Atoms. For that reason, we focus our attention on Order 2 Domains that have two Atoms.)

1.8.7. Use an Order 2 "Value Map" to Determine Truth Values in Order 3? – No, only for Atoms

In MWN Propositional Logic, we do not use the Value Map (Order 2) to determine the Truth Values of the Compound Elements in the Lattice of Logic Formulas. Rather, we use the Order 2 Values to determine the Truth Values of only the Order 3 Atoms. Then, we use the normal approach to assigning Truth Values in a Lattice, *i.e.*, Homogeneous Compounds are either True or False, but Heterogeneous Compounds are assigned a "Mixed" Truth Value.

1.8.8. Techniques for Assigning True/False Truth Values to "Mixed" Elements

In this Section, we review some of the techniques for assigning Truth Values to Mixed Elements. One of the distinguishing features of MWN Propositional Logic is that only Atoms necessarily have fixed and determinable Truth Values; Compounds made up of a mixture of True and False Atoms may not have a clear Truth Value. Even though the Order 2 Domain has more than one Atom, there are several easy ways to determine the Truth Value of a Mixed Element in the Order 3 Domain. In this Section, we touch on two techniques: the "**Deemed Binary Truth Value**" approach and the "**Simplification by Elimination**" approach.

In the Deemed Binary Truth Value approach, we create an Order 3 "**Value Map**" with the solutions to the Logic Formulas, and then, in DBNF, deem Mixed Elements to be "True," and Empty Elements to be "False." To create the Value Map, we treat the Logic Operations $(\vee, \wedge, \neg)$ as if they are the same as the Boolean Set Operations $(\cup, \cap, {\_}')$. For example, to solve $(x \wedge y)$ where $X = A$ and $y = B$, we take the Intersection of A and B, which is the empty Set. *See*, **Fig. 1-8**.

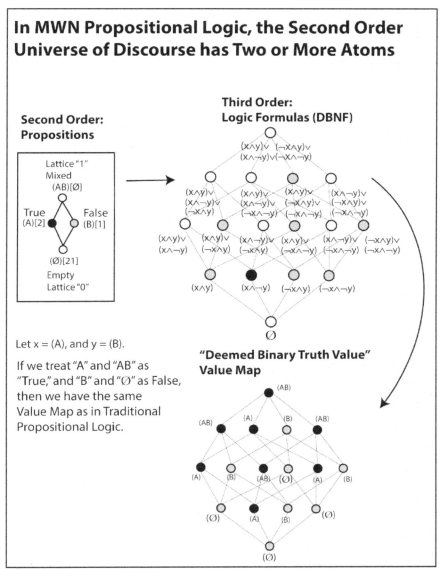

In MWN Propositional Logic, the Second Order Universe of Discourse has Two or More Atoms

Second Order: Propositions

Third Order: Logic Formulas (DBNF)

"Deemed Binary Truth Value" Value Map

Let x = (A), and y = (B).

If we treat "A" and "AB" as "True," and "B" and "Ø" as False, then we have the same Value Map as in Traditional Propositional Logic.

Fig. 1-8

If we deem (A) and (AB) to be "True," and (B) and (Ø) to be "False," then we end up with the same result that we have with an Order 2 Domain that has only one Atom. For example, compare the Value map in **Fig. 1-8** with the Value Map in **Fig. 1-3**, where shaded black indicates "True," and shaded gray indicates "False." Arguably, it makes sense in this context to treat the "Mixed" (AB) Elements as True, because we view a "True Proposition OR False Proposition" to be True. (We can state an Inverse, Dual rule for a CBNF Lattice, where we treat the "Mixed" (AB) Elements as False, because we view a "False Proposition AND True Proposition" to be False.)

Alternatively, we can use the **"Simplification by Elimination"** approach to simplify complex Logic Formula Polynomials: in DBNF the Mixed Elements in the Order 3 Domain are deemed to be "True" and we drop any "OR False" Clauses; and in CBNF the Mixed Elements are deemed to be "False" and we drop any "AND True" Clauses. We are able to achieve this result by simplifying the Mixed Element using the following principles:

(1) It adds nothing to a "True" Proposition in DBNF to connect a string of "False" Propositions by OR. Therefore, a WFF with the Truth Values "$T \vee F \vee F \vee F$" can be simplified to simply "T".

(2) Similarly, it adds nothing to a "False" Proposition in CBNF to connect a string of "True" Propositions by AND. Therefore, a WFF with the Truth Values "$F \wedge T \wedge T \wedge T$" can be simplified to simply "F".

For Domains other than Propositions, we may need to develop a different rule for assigning Truth Values to Mixed Elements, but this is the nature of complex Ideas. The reality is that most complex thinking is not simply the application of simple rules to make True/False decisions. Rather, we must exercise discretion and make judgment calls about what is right and what is wrong. This is another example of one of our themes in MWN: mathematics can tell us *how* to think, but not *what* to think.

1.8.9. Brief Summary of the Principles of MWN Propositional Logic

In this Section, we provide a brief summary of MWN Propositional Logic. We start with the assumption that every Idea in the World of Ideas is either an Atom or a Compound made up of Atoms. Then, we create a Map from the World of Ideas to the World of Abstract Sets. In essence, we assume that mathematical "Objects" do not have any properties. Rather, properties are defined as a Mapping from the World of Ideas to an Element of a Lattice in the World of Abstract Sets. For example, we start by identifying the number of Atoms in our Universe of Discourse. Then, a property such as the color "Red" is mapped to the Element of the Lattice of the Power Set of Atoms that corresponds to those Atoms that map to Objects that are Red in the World of Ideas. An Attribute is defined, therefore, by the Lattice Position of the Element comprised of all Atoms exhibiting that particular Attribute. We use the Power Set Lattice of Atoms to represent Objects from the World of Ideas; and the dual Power Set Lattice of Coatoms to represent Attributes.

Once we have a Mapping of Ideas to a Lattice, we demonstrate that there is a system of Logic inherent in the Lattice structure. In fact, we will demonstrate that there are three related Boolean Algebras:

- **First Order**: The Boolean Algebra of the underlying Ideas referenced in the Subject and Predicate of each Proposition,
- **Second Order**: The Boolean Algebra of True/False Propositions related to the Ideas in the First Order Boolean Algebra, and
- **Third Order**: The Boolean Algebra of Logic Formulas related to the Propositions in the Second Order Boolean Algebra.

(Note that we use the term "Order" in a different way from traditional Propositional Logic. In MWN, we use three "Orders" to distinguish among U_D's of Ideas, Propositions, and Logic Formulas. In traditional Propositional Logic, "1st Order Logic" refers to Predicate Logic. *See, for example*, [Smullyan 2014] at 133 *et seq*.)

Whether the Boolean Algebra is of the First, Second, or Third Order, there are three fundamental principles that are always true in the MWN system:

- The meaning of "Lattice 0", *i.e.*, the bottom of a Lattice of Objects:
  - In a Lattice of Objects, "(Ø)" at the bottom of the Lattice represents the Empty Set.
  - In a two-Atom Lattice of Attributes, "[21]" at the bottom of the Lattice represents those Objects that exhibit all possible Attributes, including for any Attribute "a", the Attribute "not-a". Since this is impossible, "[21]" represents the Empty Set.
- The meaning of "Lattice 1", *i.e.*, the top of a Lattice of Objects:
  - In a two-Atom Lattice of Objects, "(ab)" at the top of the Lattice represents the entire Universe of Discourse.
  - In a Lattice of Attributes, "[Ø]" at the top of the Lattice means that no Attribute is required of Atoms in that Element, so all Atoms qualify and are present. Therefore,

"[Ø]" represents the complete Universe of Discourse.

- Attributes of any Element in a Lattice are inherited through the Down Set of that Element.

See, **Fig. 1-9**.

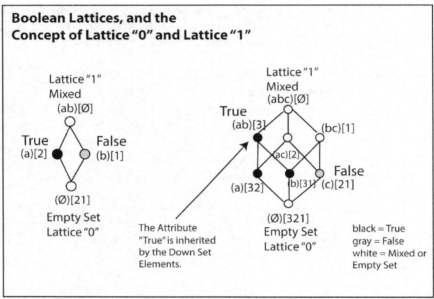

Boolean Lattices, and the Concept of Lattice "0" and Lattice "1"

Fig. 1-9

Table 1-1 summarizes the similarities and differences between the traditional approach to Propositional Logic as found in most books on Symbolic Logic or Mathematical Logic, and the approach taken in MWN.

Table 1-1

Attribute	Traditional Propositional Logic (TPL)	MWN Propositional Logic
Use Set Theory concept of Normal Form (DNF, CNF, DBNF, and CBNF)?	Yes	Yes
No. of Order 2 Atoms	1 Atom	2 Atoms (or more than 2, but the result is always Isomorphic to a P_2 Lattice for any given Attribute)
Apply binary Truth Values $Y = [T, F] = [2, 1]$?	Yes	No; only Atomic Ideas necessarily have a binary Truth Value.
Apply four-valued Truth Values $P(Y) = $ (Mixed, True, False, Empty) $= [\emptyset, 2, 1, 21]$?	No	Yes
Scope of the Domain	True/False Propositions combined to form Logic Formulas	**Three Domains:** **Order 1**: Ideas, **Order 2**: True/False Propositions, **Order 3**: Logic Formulas
Examine how the Ideas comprising the Subject and Predicate of each Proposition affect the relationships among the Propositions?	No	Yes
Meaning of $(p \vee q)$?	Clause is "True" if one or the other or both of p and q is True.	Meaning is "p Union q". Truth Value is determined separately.
Meaning of $(p \wedge q)$?	Clause is "True" if both p and q are True.	Meaning is "p Intersection q". Truth Value is determined separately.
" $\neg$ " is used to mean Sign Reversal?	Yes	No, " $\neg$ " is used to mean Complementation. In many circumstances, the result is the same as Sign Reversal, but we must restrict the use of " $\neg$ " to Order 3.

As we can see from **Table 1-1**, Traditional Propositional Logic and MWN Propositional Logic share some Attributes relating to the use of concepts from Set Theory such as Normal Form, but differ when it comes to the assignment of Truth Values. Also, MWN Propositional Logic examines the Ideas that comprise the Subject and Predicate of each Proposition, whereas Traditional Propositional Logic does not.

The key to understanding MWN Propositional Logic is to note that only Atomic Ideas have a binary Truth Value Domain, *i.e.*, $Y = [2,1]$; Compound Ideas have a four-valued Truth Value Domain, *i.e.*, $P(Y) = [\varnothing, 2, 1, 21]$. This is consistent with the MWN approach to Atoms being in Dimension 1 and Sets being in Dimension 2, which is the Power Set of Atoms. *See generally,* MWN Vol. 1. It makes sense that Attributes such as Truth Values would follow the same structure.

1.9. What is it Precisely that Makes MWN Propositional Logic Different from Traditional Propositional Logic?

The precise moment when Traditional Propositional Logic and MWN Propositional take different paths leading to different conclusions, is when Truth Values are assigned to the Propositional Variables x_1, x_2, x_3, ... In Traditional Propositional Logic, this step where Truth Values are assigned passes without notice (*see* Step 4 in **Example 1** below), but in in MWN Propositional Logic we have a problem, as illustrated in **Example 2**.

Example 1: In Traditional Propositional Logic, we follow the steps below to create a Well-Formed Formula ("**WFF**") that has a defined Truth Value:

- **Step 1**: Any Propositional Variable x_1, x_2, x_3, ... is a WFF.
- **Step 2**: If φ and ψ are WWF's, then so are $(\varphi \vee \psi)$, $(\varphi \wedge \psi)$ and $(\neg \varphi)$.
- **Step 3**: Any finite application of Steps 1 and 2 gives rise to a WFF.
- **Step 4**: To obtain the Truth Value of a WFF, simply assign a Truth Value in {T,F} to each Propositional Variable, substitute the Truth Values into the WFF, and compute the resulting Truth Value for the WFF. Typically, we use a Truth Table.

Example 2: Suppose we have two Propositions "p" and "q" in an Order 2 Domain, each of which we deem to be True. If we start with a Propositional Variable x = "p" in an Order 3 Domain and add a second Propositional Variable y = "q", the effect is to subdivide p into $(p \wedge q)$ and $(p \wedge \neg q)$, since $p = (p \wedge q) \vee (p \wedge \neg q)$. It is well-established in

Traditional Propositional Logic (where the Order 2 Domain has one Atom), however, that only one or the other of these two Clauses can be True; the other must necessarily be False. *See,* **Fig. 1-10**.

Venn Diagram Ilustrating the Effect of Subdivision on Truth Values

Universe - Object Venn Diagram

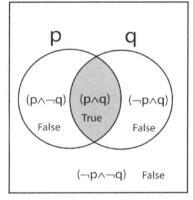

Each of the four regions could be shaded or unshaded, true or false.

We can use the four regions as Atoms in a Boolean Algebra.

Fig. 1-10

    This would seem at first to be a contradiction: we started out saying that "p" is True, but now we are saying that half of "p" is True and half is False. The solution is to recognize that initially we were in an Order 2 Domain where the Atoms are Propositions: p and q; but the Logic Formulas are in an Order 3 Domain where the Atoms are DBNF Logic Formulas: $(p \wedge q)$, $(p \wedge \neg q)$, $(\neg p \wedge q)$, and $(\neg p \wedge \neg q)$. The two rules of MWN Propositional Logic that are violated by Traditional Propositional Logic are the following:

- Only Atoms (and Homogeneous Sets of Atoms) necessarily have a fixed and determinable Truth Value.
- We cannot mix calculations across two different Domains.

From a MWN perspective, Traditional Propositional Logic violates these two rules:

- by assuming that we can assign a Truth Value to "p" and "q" in

Order 3 when these two Variables are no longer Atoms in the Order 3 Domain of Logic Formulas; and

- in effect, by mixing Order 2 calculations with Order 3 calculations.

In the end, we will come up with a means of assigning Truth Values to the "Mixed" Elements consisting of a mixture of True and False Atoms. In the case of Propositional Logic, the rule is easy:

- Mixed Elements in a DBNF Lattice are deemed to be True, and can be simplified by eliminating the extraneous False Clauses connected by OR ($\vee$).
- Mixed Elements in a CBNF Lattice are deemed to be False, and can be simplified by eliminating the extraneous True Clauses connected by AND ($\wedge$).

The reasoning here is that it adds nothing to a "True" Proposition in DBNF to connect a string of "False" Propositions by OR. Therefore, a WFF with the Truth Values "$T \vee F \vee F \vee F$" can be simplified to simply "T".

Similarly, it adds nothing to a "False" Proposition in CBNF to connect a string of "True" Propositions by AND. Therefore, a WFF with the Truth Values "$F \wedge T \wedge T \wedge T$" can be simplified to simply "F".

We will see that the Truth Values of a WFF are the same in both Traditional Propositional Logic and MWN Propositional Logic, provided that we deem True = (A, AB) and False = ($\emptyset$, B) in the standard MWN four-Atom Lattice $P(X) = (\emptyset, A, B, AB)$, although we are able to simplify the WFF somewhat in MWN Propositional Logic by eliminating extraneous Clauses in the Mixed Elements.

We will discuss all of these concepts in more detail as we proceed through the book.

1.10. References, Historical Notes, and Further Reading

Historical Background

For a more detailed discussion of historical development of Boolean logic and Propositional Logic, see generally the writings of Stanley Burris listed in the Bibliography, including materials available on his website at the University of Waterloo.

Discussion of how Traditional Propositional Logic Uses a Single Atom Representing All True Propositions Consolidated into One Atom

[Davey and Priestley 2001] at 95-97, 252-255.

[Langer 1966] at 260 and 283.

Other Works Establishing a Boolean Algebra of Propositional Logic

Below are works that discuss how to create a Boolean Algebra of Propositional Logic, listed in reverse chronological order:

[Davey and Priestley 2001] at 94 *et seq.* and 252 *et seq.*, discussing the Boolean Algebra commonly referred to as LINDA.

[Cori and Lascar 1993] at 106 and 270. The authors demonstrate that the Operations ⟷ and ∧ form a Boolean Algebra on the Set of Equivalence Classes of Logic Formulas. (Note the similarity of ⟷ to Symmetric Difference used in a Boolean Ring.)

[Eves 1990] at 256. The calculus of Propositions is an example of a Boolean Algebra.

[Abbott 1969] at 212-213. The Set "P_n" of Equivalence Classes of Boolean Functions related to "E_n", the Set of all Boolean expressions in "n" Variables, is itself a Boolean Algebra. The Elements of P_n are Boolean Polynomials.

[Langer 1966] at 260 and 283, discusses the two-valued calculus of Propositions where every true Proposition = 1, and every False Proposition = 0. Langer also discusses the difficulties in the two-valued calculus that led to the development of Principia Mathematica by Russell and Whitehead.

[Curry 1963] at 300, discussing "L", a free extension of a Boolean Algebra K with respect to indeterminates $E_1, \ldots E_m$, as constituting a Boolean Algebra.

[Arnold 1962] at 66, 72, and 81. The set B_n of all Boolean functions of n independent variables is a Boolean Algebra.

[Whitesitt 1960] at 49-50. The algebra of propositions is a Boolean algebra.

[Rosenbloom 1950] at 29, asserting that True and False form a two-Element Boolean Algebra with respect to the operations " ∧ " and " ¬ ".

[Stone 1936].

Descriptions of WFF's and how Truth Values are assigned to Variables, leading to definite Truth Values in a Truth Table

[Davey and Priestley 2001] at Chapter 4.19.

Free Algebras with "n" Generators

[Givant and Halmos 2009] at 256-266.

[Birkhoff and Mac Lane 1999] at 491-493.

[Vladimirov 1994] at 68-69.

2. FUNDAMENTAL PREMISES

Before we create Universes of Discourse consisting of Propositions, we need to have a basic understanding of the MWN approach to the Mathematics of Ideas. In this Chapter, we will explore the following fundamental premises of the MWN System:

- **Three Worlds**: There are three Worlds: Physical, Ideas, and Abstract Sets. Within the World of Abstract Sets there are six principal Domains that are relevant to the Mathematics of Ideas:

  o Atoms,
  o Coatoms,
  o Power Set of Atoms,
  o Power Set of Coatoms,
  o Power Set of Power Sets of Atoms, and
  o Power Set of Power Sets of Coatoms.

- **Ideas as Sets - Atoms and Compounds**: Every Idea is a Set consisting of either a single Atom or a Compound made up of multiple Atoms. Every Idea expressed as a Set of Atoms has associated with it an Inverse, Dual Set of Coatoms.
- **Attribute Values**: Every Atomic Idea in the World of Ideas either has or does not have any given Attribute. Therefore, there must be an Element of the Power Set in the World of Abstracts Sets that reflects the Set of Atoms exhibiting any given Attribute, since the Power Set by definition includes all possible Subsets.
- **Assertion of Attributes**: When we create a Map from the World of Ideas to the World of Abstract Sets, we are making an Assertion of something we believe to be true (in the World of Ideas) about the

Ideas we are Mapping, including the following statements:

- o   If the Idea is an Atom, it is not divisible any further,
- o   If the Idea is a Compound, we are mapping to an Element that includes all Atoms that exhibit the Attributes that we associate with the label used. *E.g.*, "Mammal" is defined by the Set of all Atoms that we consider to be Mammals.

- **The Power Set Lattice creates a Boolean Algebra**: A Power Set Lattice, together with the operations of Union, Intersection, and Complementation forms a Boolean Algebra.

- **Logic Formulas**: We can reduce any WFF, Boolean Expression, or Logic Formula using OR, AND, and NOT to either the Disjunctive Boolean Normal Form ("**DBNF**") or the Conjunctive Boolean Normal Form ("**CBNF**"). We can use the clauses of the Logic Formula in CBNF or DBNF as Atoms to form a Boolean Lattice.

2.1. *Three Worlds; Six Principal Domains*

In the MWN system, we assume that there are three Worlds: the Physical World, the World of Ideas, and the World of Abstract Sets. In the Physical World, we are restricted by the laws of physics and chemistry. In the World of Ideas, however, we are not limited by laws that restrict us in the Physical World. In a sense, the entire Physical World is encompassed by the World of Ideas, since everything in the Physical World may also be an Idea; but the World of Ideas goes much further and encompasses every thought that we are capable of thinking. Purple cows and unicorns can exist in the World of Ideas.

The World of Abstract Sets is much less glamorous, as it is made up of Atoms and Sets of Atoms, where each Atom has only two Attributes: it exists and it is unique, making it differentiable. The World of Abstract Sets, however, is extremely powerful in that it reveals the structure inherent in Objects of both the Physical World and the World of Ideas. The challenge is to create a Map from an Idea in the World of Ideas to an Element of a Lattice the World of Abstract Sets. It is the relative position of the Ideas in the Lattice that gives rise to the Set Relationships that in turn give rise to Propositions that we use in Logic. We refer to this as the Logic of Lattices.

To create a Mapping from the World of Ideas to the World of

Abstract Sets, we use the following methodology:

- Does the Idea Attribute in question relate to a single Atom or to a Compound (as it must be one or the other)? Idea $_{PE}$ = (Atom + Compound).
- If the Idea is a Compound, we find all of the Atoms that exhibit that Attribute and Map to the corresponding Element in the Power Set Lattice (the "**Attribute Element**").

As always, we need to specify our Domain. As discussed in MWN Vol. 1, there are six principal Domains:

Domain $_{PE}$ =

Two Types:
(Objects (X) +
Attributes (Y))

×

Three Dimensions:
(Set +
Power Set +
Power Set of Power Sets)

=

Six Domains:
(Objects: X +
Attributes: Y +
Power Set of Objects: $P(X)$ +
Power Set of Attributes: $P(Y)$ +
Power Set of Power Sets of Objects: $P(P(X))$ +
Power Set of Power Sets of Attributes: $P(P(Y))$)

Fig. 2-1 illustrates the relationships among the six principal Domains.

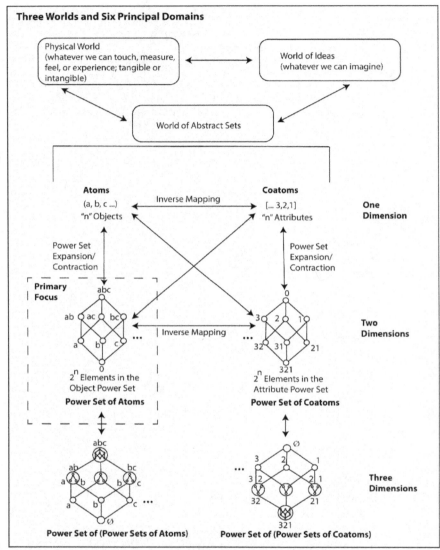

Fig. 2-1

In this book, our primary focus is on the Domain consisting of the Power Set of Objects. Within that Domain, we hone in on specific subsets of Objects, or "Universes of Discourse," that are relevant to the study of Propositional Logic. One possible such Subset is the Set of "Propositions" as that term is used in Classical Logic. As a reminder, a Proposition in

Classical Logic consists of a Subject and a Predicate connected by a Copula, *i.e.*, a form of the verb "to be," and is characterized by the fact that it must be either True or False:

- A: All S are P.
- E: No S are P.
- I: Some S are P.
- O: Some S are not P.

In fact, the Propositions of Classical Logic form two distinct Partitions of the Set of all Propositions, *i.e.*, every Proposition is either an A or an O Proposition; and every Proposition is either an E or an I Propostion:

- Proposition $_{PE}$ = (A+O)×(E+I)

The problem we face is that the A, E, I, and O forms of Propositions, taken as a whole, are not Mutually Exclusive, and therefore cannot constitute Atoms. *E.g.*, every "A" Proposition is also true when stated as an "I" Proposition. Every "E" Proposition is also true when stated as an "O" Proposition. Every "I" Proposition is also true when stated as one or the other of either an "A" Proposition or an "O" Proposition. Every "O" Proposition is also true when stated as one or the other of either an "I" Proposition or an "E" Proposition. We will see, however that each of (A+O) and (E+I) constitutes a Partition of the Set of all Propositions, and each of these pairs can form the base of a Universe of Discourse. We discuss this topic further in **Section 6.4** of this book.

Another possible Universe of Discourse is the Set of Propositions corresponding to the five Two-Set Relationships formed by starting with the A, E, I, and O Propositions and Quantifying the Predicate in a manner suggested by John Venn in 1898:

- A_{V1}: All S are all P (S=P).
- A_{V2}: All S are some P (S $\subset$ P).
- I_{V1}: Some S are all P (S $\supset$ P).
- I_{V2}: Some S are some P (S Π P).
- E_V: No S are any P (S Ω P).

See, [Venn 1894] at 6-7. The symbols used above are defined as follows:

- "=" means that the two Sets are Identical.
- "⊂" means that the two Sets are in a Subset-Superset Relationship.
- "⊃" means that the two Sets are in a Superset-Subset Relationship.
- "∏" means that the two Sets are Partially-Overlapping.
- "Ω" means that the two Sets are Disjoint.

Yet another possible Universe of Discourse is the Set of "Well Formed Formulas" or "WFF's" from Symbolic Logic. We define a Set of symbols that we can string together to form sentences in accordance with certain specified rules. As with Propositions, a WFF is characterized by the fact that it has a Truth Value, *i.e.*, it must be either True or False.

The reason that it is so important to understand Domains, is that it is critical that we not mix calculations across Domains. We can convert all Elements to the same Domain and then perform calculations, but we cannot perform calculations on Elements taken from different Domains. *See*, [Veatch 2016].

Within a Domain, we may have many U_D's. *See*, **Fig. 2-2**. For purposes of Propositional Logic we focus on the following U_D's:

- The First Order U_D of "Ideas" that is the source of the Subject and Predicate of Propositions.
- The Second Order U_D of "Propositions" describing the relationship between two Ideas in terms of their Set Relationship.
- The Third Order U_D of "Logic Formulas," and in particular the 16 Element Power Sets based on the four Logic Formulas in two Variables that constitute Clauses in either DBNF or CBNF of a Boolean Function.

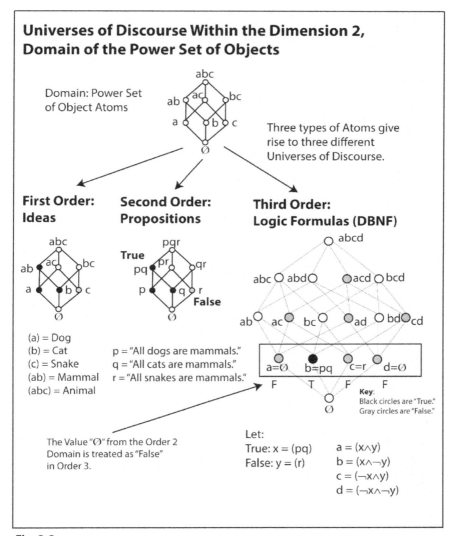

Fig. 2-2

The three Universes of Discourse: Ideas, Propositions, and Logic Formulas, are inextricably linked. The Set Relationship of any two Ideas in Order 1 determines the related Truth Values in Order 2 or 3.

We will see that when we have related First, Second, and Third Order U_D's as we do here, it is equally important not to mix calculations across U_D's, as it is not to mix calculations across Domains.

2.2. Assertion of Attributes: Attributes are Represented by Mappings from the World of Ideas to a Lattice in the World of Abstract Sets

In MWN, when we create a Map from an Idea in the World of Ideas to an *"Atom"* in a Lattice in the World of Abstract Sets, we are making certain statements about the Idea and the related Atom:

- With respect to **Atoms** in the World of Ideas:

    o The Idea is Atomic in nature, *i.e.*, either it is not capable of Subdivision in such a way that each subpart retains its essential Attributes, or it is a "Deemed Atom." A Deemed Atom is a Compound Idea that we believe to be Homogeneous as to the Attribute in question.

- With respect to **Atoms** in the World of Abstract Sets:

    o The Atom exists and is unique, meaning that it is distinguishable from any other Atoms.
    o Atoms do not have any other Attributes, in the World of Abstract Sets.

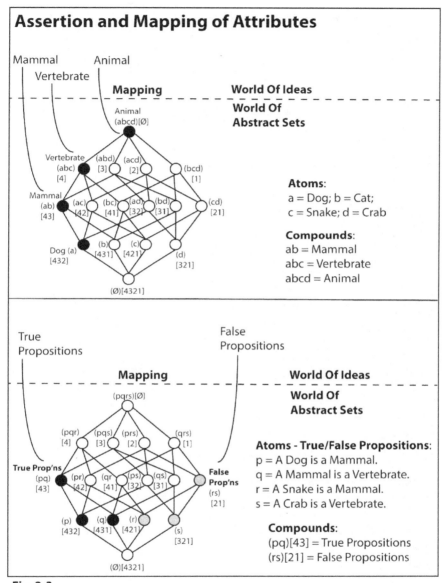

Assertion and Mapping of Attributes

Mapping   World Of Ideas

World Of
Abstract Sets

Atoms:
a = Dog; b = Cat;
c = Snake; d = Crab

Compounds:
ab = Mammal
abc = Vertebrate
abcd = Animal

Mapping   World Of Ideas

World Of
Abstract Sets

Atoms - True/False Propositions:
p = A Dog is a Mammal.
q = A Mammal is a Vertebrate.
r = A Snake is a Mammal.
s = A Crab is a Vertebrate.

Compounds:
(pq)[43] = True Propositions
(rs)[21] = False Propositions

Fig. 2-3

In MWN, when we create a Map from an Idea in the World of Ideas to a *"Compound"* in a Lattice in the World of Abstract Sets, we are making certain statements about the Idea and the related Compound:

- With respect to **Compounds** in the World of Ideas:

    o If not an Atom, then the Idea is a Compound made up of multiple Atoms (or Deemed Atoms).

    o The word or label that we attach to the Compound represents an Attribute of each Atom in the Compound. For example, if we say that a Set is "Red", then each Atom in the Set is "Red".

- With respect to **Compounds** in the World of Abstract Sets:

    o Once we Map a Compound Idea in the World of Ideas to a Compound Element in a Lattice in the World of Abstract Sets, we have asserted the "Attribute Value" of that Attribute, *i.e.*, either "Yes" or "No," as to each Atom in the Compound. We refer to the Element as the "**Attribute Element**."

    o The Attribute Element is, therefore, Homogeneous as to the Attribute Value in question. (*See*, **Chapter 6**, pages 162-164 for a discussion of Homogeneous and Heterogeneous Sets.)

    o Every Element in the Down Set of the Attribute Element has the same Attribute Value with respect to the Attribute in question, and is also Homogeneous.

    o We can see the Inheritance of the Attribute most easily in the Attribute Signature of the Idea in the Lattice of Attributes/Coatoms.

A key point here is that in the World of Ideas, Attributes "belong to" or "are characteristics of" Ideas, but in the World of Abstract Sets an Attribute is simply a Mapping to Dual Sets of Objects and Attributes.

While in the MWN system there is only a single Lattice with two different labeling conventions, we choose to Map Objects to the Power Set of Atoms, and Attributes to the Inverse Dual Power Set of Coatoms. The reason for this is that we can easily see, and calculate, the Inheritance of Attributes in the Power Set of Attributes.

In **Fig. 2-3**, in effect, when we Map the Attribute "True" to [43], we are asserting that the Element (pq) represents the Attribute "True." In addition, every Element in the Down Set of (pq) also inherits the Attribute "True."

Similarly, when we Map the Attribute "False" to [21], we are asserting that the Element (rs) represents the Attribute "False." In addition, every Element in the Down Set of (rs) also inherits the Attribute "False."

For example, we could be considering two possible Propositions: p = "February 14 is Valentine's Day" and q = "It is not the case that: February 14 is Valentine's Day." Both sentences are valid True/False Propositions, although "p" has the Truth Value "True," so it will appear in the Down Set of the Element to which we Map the Attribute "True"; and "q" has the Truth Value "False," so it will appear in the Down Set of the Element to which we Map the Attribute "False."

The impact of the Assertion of Attribute Values when we create a Map to a Lattice in the World of Abstract Sets is quite profound, because it means that we do not need to consider all of the possible combinations of Attribute Values that Elements might have in theory. For example, once we assign Truth Values of "True" to Propositions "p" and "q", we no longer have to consider what happens if they are "False," so we no longer need to consider all possible combinations of values in a Truth Table. If we determine that the Proposition "All dogs are mammals" is True, then we do not need to spend much time considering the Proposition "It is not the case that: All dogs are mammals."

Of course, if we change our designated Truth Values, then there will be a ripple effect throughout our Lattice structure, including in both the Second and Third Order Lattices.

2.3. Using Power Set Lattices and Set Union, Intersection, and Complementation to Create a Boolean Algebra

In MWN, we use Set Union, Intersection, and Complementation to create a Boolean Algebra. In the history of Propositional Logic, however, there have been many attempts to create a Boolean Algebra using the Logic Operations OR, AND, and NOT. As noted in **Section 1.8.9**, however, the Operations of Union, Intersection, and Complementation function in a different way from OR, AND, and NOT, so the analogy is not a perfect one. In Traditional Propositional Logic, the Logic Operations create an "Algebra," but it is not truly "Boolean" in nature in an Order 2 Domain. *See*, **Table 2-1**.

Table 2-1

	Boolean Operations			Logic Operations on Propositions in Traditional Propositional Logic (TPL)		
	Union	Inter-section	Complementation	OR	AND	NOT
Associative	Yes	Yes	-	Yes	Yes	-
Commutative	Yes	Yes	-	Yes	Yes	-
Unique "1" Element	-	-	Yes. $1 = X$, where X is the Base Set of Atoms for the Power Set $U_D = P(X)$	-	-	Yes. $1 = $ True
Unique "0" Element	-	-	Yes. $0 = \emptyset$	-	-	Yes. $0 = $ False
Unique Complement	-	-	Yes, for example: $(x \cup x') = 1$ $(x \cap x') = 0$	-	-	Not unique. If p is True, then $(p \vee q) = 1$ and $(p \vee r) = 1$ are both True, so the Complement of p is not unique.
Distributive	Yes, over Intersection	Yes, over Union	-	Yes	Yes	-

In particular, if, as is often the case in Traditional Propositional Logic, we elect to treat "True" as the "1" Element at the top of the Lattice, and "False" as the "0" Element at the bottom of the Lattice (which we reject in MWN), then the Complements of an Element are not unique as is required in a Boolean Algebra. To better illustrate the differences relating to "Complementation" and "NOT", in **Table 2-1** we set forth the unique Complements in a Boolean Logic and then show how multiple combinations of Elements can result in a "1" or "0" in Traditional Propositional Logic, such that there is no unique Complement.

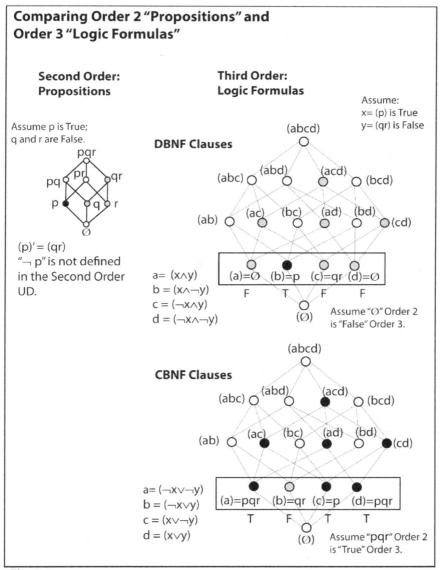

Fig. 2-4

Some scholars have advocated the position that we can create a Boolean Algebra of Propositional Logic by applying a principle of "equality," stating that all True Propositions are equal, and all False Propositions are equal, such that there are only two Propositions. *See*, [Whitesitt 1960] at 47. If we let True Propositions = 1, and False Propositions = 0, then we have created a Boolean Algebra. We reject this approach, however, in MWN. The primary issue under MWN is that the Lattice "0" represents the Empty Set, so in MWN we do not Map Atoms, such as False Propositions, to the Empty Set. Conversely, the Lattice "1" has Attribute [Ø], which we interpret to mean that Lattice "1" has no required Attributes; *i.e.*, an Atom in Lattice "1" may have a Truth Value of either True or False. Therefore, generally speaking, it would be a contradiction to state that Lattice "1" has a Truth Value of True (unless Lattice "1" consists of only True Atoms).

We can, however, create a new Third Order Universe of Discourse made up of Logic Formulas that use the Algebra of Logic Operations. We can use the Clauses of the Logic Formulas in DBNF or CBNF as Atoms to create a new Universe of Discourse and related Boolean Lattice. Note, however, that the Operations that we use within the Boolean Lattice are Union, Intersection, and Complementation, not OR, AND, and NOT as used in Traditional Propositional Logic.

2.4. Logic Formulas: Using the Three Primary Logic Operations (OR, AND, and NOT, i.e., Negation in the Sense of Sign Reversal) as a Tool for Creating a New Universe of Discourse

Although the Logic Operations OR, AND, and NOT as used in Traditional Propositional Logic are not equivalent to Union, Intersection, and Complement in terms of creating a Boolean Algebra, we can use the Logic Operations to create Atoms in the form of Logic Formulas that *do* in fact form a Boolean Algebra using our standard Union, Intersection, and Complementation Operations. *See,* **Fig. 2-4**. In **Chapter 7** we will discuss in detail how we can form compound formulas from simple Propositional Variables, *i.e.*, Atomic Formulas. Then, in **Chapter 12**, where we discuss the P_4 Lattice, we will demonstrate how compound formulas, together with the Operations of Union, Intersection, and Complementation form a Boolean Algebra and a related Boolean Lattice. Here, we just provide a brief overview to introduce the concept.

Suppose that we have identified two Propositions p and q. Treating p and q as Atoms, we can create a P_2 Boolean Lattice which, together with the operations of addition (based on Set Union), multiplication (based on Set Intersection), and Complementation, forms a Boolean Algebra. Using those two Atoms, we can create additional Atoms in the form of formulas created using the standard Logic Operations: $\vee$, $\wedge$, and $\neg$, where the formula will have a fixed Truth Value determined in accordance with the rules governing the Logic Operations, the rules governing Free Boolean Algebras, and the MWN rules for assigning Truth Values (discussed in **Chapter 4**). The Truth

Value of the formula is a function of the Truth Values of the Atoms p and q as set forth in a Truth Table.

Interestingly, the number of possible formulas with different Truth Table values is equal to 2 to the power of "m", where "m" is equal to 2^n and "n" is the number of Variables in the Logic Formula, but is not limited in any way by the number of Propositions in the Order 2 Domain. For example, given two Variables, we have four Logic Formula Atoms and the following number of Logic Formulas: $2^m = 2^4 = 16$. Also, the 16 Elements form a P_4 Boolean Algebra and Boolean Lattice where the four Atoms are: DBNF: $(x \wedge y)$, $(x \wedge \neg y)$, $(\neg x \wedge y)$, and $(\neg x \wedge \neg y)$, or alternatively, CBNF: $(x \vee y)$, $(x \vee \neg y)$, $(\neg x \vee y)$, and $(\neg x \vee \neg y)$.

Similarly, we can create an Order 2 Domain with three Propositions: p, q, and r, or four Propositions: p, q, r, and s. The number of Variables in the Logic Formula, however, can be 1, 2, 3, or more, regardless of the number of Propositions in the Order 2 Domain. The number of new Logic Formula Atoms and Power Set Elements is set forth in **Table 2-2** and in **Table 2-3**. **Table 2-2** covers DBNF Clauses, and **Table 2-3** covers CBNF Clauses.

Table 2-2 – DBNF Clauses

No. of Propositional Variables	No. of Possible Truth Tables = No. Possible Non-Isomorphic Logic Formulas: 2^m, where $m=2^n$	New Atoms Consisting of DBNF Clauses
2: x and y	$2^4 = 16$	4 Atoms: $(x \wedge y), (x \wedge \neg y),$ $(\neg x \wedge y), (\neg x \wedge \neg y)$
3: x, y, and z	$2^8 = 256$	Eight Atoms: $(x \wedge y \wedge z), (x \wedge y \wedge \neg z),$ $(x \wedge \neg y \wedge z), (\neg x \wedge y \wedge z),$ $(\neg x \wedge \neg y \wedge z),$ $(\neg x \wedge y \wedge \neg z),$ $(x \wedge \neg y \wedge \neg z),$ $(\neg x \wedge \neg y \wedge \neg z)$
4: w, x, y, and z	2^{16} $= 65,536$	Sixteen Atoms: $(w \wedge x \wedge y \wedge z),$ $(w \wedge x \wedge y \wedge \neg z),$ $(w \wedge x \wedge \neg y \wedge z),$ $(w \wedge \neg x \wedge y \wedge z),$ $(\neg w \wedge x \wedge y \wedge z),$ $(\neg w \wedge \neg x \wedge y \wedge z),$ $(\neg w \wedge x \wedge \neg y \wedge z),$ $(\neg w \wedge x \wedge y \wedge \neg z),$ $(w \wedge \neg x \wedge \neg y \wedge z),$ $(w \wedge \neg x \wedge y \wedge \neg z),$ $(w \wedge x \wedge \neg y \wedge \neg z),$ $(\neg w \wedge \neg x \wedge \neg y \wedge z),$ $(w \wedge \neg x \wedge \neg y \wedge \neg z),$ $(\neg w \wedge x \wedge \neg y \wedge \neg z),$ $(\neg w \wedge \neg x \wedge y \wedge \neg z),$ $(\neg w \wedge \neg x \wedge \neg y \wedge \neg z)$

Table 2-3 – CBNF Clauses

No. of Propositions	No. of Possible Truth Tables = No. Possible Non-Isomorphic Logic Formulas: 2^m, where $m=2^n$	New Atoms Consisting of CBNF Clauses
2: x and y	$2^4 = 16$	4 Atoms: $(x \vee y), (x \vee \neg y),$ $(\neg x \vee y), (\neg x \vee \neg y)$
3: x, y, and z	$2^8 = 256$	Eight Atoms: $(x \vee y \vee z), (x \vee y \vee \neg z),$ $(x \vee \neg y \vee z), (\neg x \vee y \vee z),$ $(\neg x \vee \neg y \vee z),$ $(\neg x \vee y \vee \neg z),$ $(x \vee \neg y \vee \neg z),$ $(\neg x \vee \neg y \vee \neg z)$
4: w, x, y, and z	2^{16} $= 65,536$	Sixteen Atoms: $(w \vee x \vee y \vee z),$ $(w \vee x \vee y \vee \neg z),$ $(w \vee x \vee \neg y \vee z),$ $(w \vee \neg x \vee y \vee z),$ $(\neg w \vee x \vee y \vee z),$ $(\neg w \vee \neg x \vee y \vee z),$ $(\neg w \vee x \vee \neg y \vee z),$ $(\neg w \vee x \vee y \vee \neg z),$ $(w \vee \neg x \vee \neg y \vee z),$ $(w \vee \neg x \vee y \vee \neg z),$ $(w \vee x \vee \neg y \vee \neg z),$ $(\neg w \vee \neg x \vee \neg y \vee z),$ $(w \vee \neg x \vee \neg y \vee \neg z),$ $(\neg w \vee x \vee \neg y \vee \neg z),$ $(\neg w \vee \neg x \vee y \vee \neg z),$ $(\neg w \vee \neg x \vee \neg y \vee \neg z)$

Note that in Traditional Propositional Logic, "¬" means that we are to reverse the Truth Value of a Proposition, which is not the same thing as Complementation. For example, we could be considering two possible Propositions: p = "February 14 is Valentine's Day" and ¬ p = "It is not the case that: February 14 is Valentine's Day." In Traditional Propositional Logic, we use the symbol "¬" to indicate "**Sign Reversal**", *i.e.*, the reversal of the Truth Value of the Proposition from True to False, or *vice versa*. Sign Reversal ("¬") is different from Complementation ("~" or "_'"), so it is important not to confuse the two concepts. If, however, we put some restrictions on how and when we use Negation ("¬"), then it will behave in the same way as Complementation. *See*, **Section 7.10**.

The real issue is that we cannot mix Elements across U_D's. The Operation "¬" exists only in the U_D of Logic Formulas. **Fig. 2-5** compares and contrasts the Order 2 and Order 3 U_D's of Propositions and Logic Formulas, respectively.

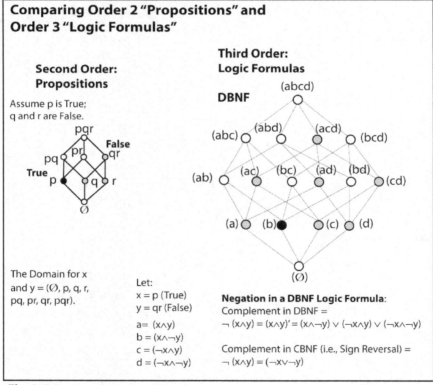

Comparing Order 2 "Propositions" and Order 3 "Logic Formulas"

Second Order: Propositions

Assume p is True; q and r are False.

The Domain for x and y = (∅, p, q, r, pq, pr, qr, pqr).

Let:
x = p (True)
y = qr (False)

a= (x∧y)
b = (x∧¬y)
c = (¬x∧y)
d = (¬x∧¬y)

Third Order: Logic Formulas

DBNF

Negation in a DBNF Logic Formula:
Complement in DBNF =
¬ (x∧y) = (x∧y)' = (x∧¬y) ∨ (¬x∧y) ∨ (¬x∧¬y)

Complement in CBNF (i.e., Sign Reversal) =
¬ (x∧y) = (¬x∨¬y)

Fig. 2-5

2.5. *References, Historical Notes, and Further Reading*

[Veatch 2016]: MWN Vol. 1 creates a detailed foundation for the Mathematics of Ideas, based upon Set Theory and Boolean Algebra.

3.   WHAT IS A BOOLEAN ALGEBRA?

The easiest Boolean Algebra to understand is the Boolean Algebra formed from the Power Set of a Base Set of Atoms. A Power Set is the Set of all possible Subsets that we can form from the Atoms in the Base Set "X", including the Empty Set "Ø" and "X" itself. For example, if we start with the Base Set X = { a, b, c }, then the Power Set $P(X)$ = (Ø, a, b, c, ab, ac, bc, abc). The Power Set is Closed with respect to the Operations of Union and Intersection, meaning that we can take the Union (or Intersection) of any two Elements in the Power Set, and the result also will be an Element of the Power Set.   Similarly, each Element in the Power Set has a unique Complement that is also in the Power Set. It is well-established that every Boolean Algebra is Isomorphic to such a Boolean Algebra of Sets. The fundamental question that we are examining is whether the logic of Propositions using "OR", "AND", and "NOT" forms a Boolean Algebra.

3.1. The P_1, P_2, P_3, and P_4 Boolean Algebras

In this book, we examine Boolean Algebras with one, two, three, and four (and sometimes five) Atoms, to see if one or more of these Boolean Algebras could form a model for a Boolean Algebra of Propositional Logic. In Traditional Propositional Logic, the Boolean Algebra with one Atom is used where the Base Set X = 1, resulting in a Power Set $P(X)$ = (Ø, 1). For reasons discussed in **Chapter 9**, in MWN we reject this approach in favor of Boolean Algebras with two, three, four, or more Atoms.

The number of Elements in a Power Set is always equal to 2^n, where "n" equals the number of Atoms in the Base Set. Each Boolean Algebra also forms a Boolean Lattice. *See*, **Fig. 3-1**.

Four Basic Boolean Lattices

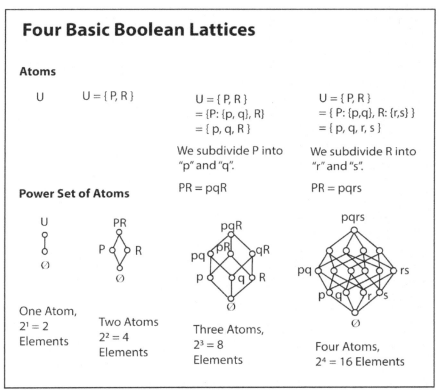

Atoms

U   U = { P, R }

U = { P, R }
= {P: {p, q}, R}
= { p, q, R }

U = { P, R }
= { P: {p,q}, R: {r,s} }
= { p, q, r, s }

We subdivide P into "p" and "q".

We subdivide R into "r" and "s".

PR = pqR

PR = pqrs

Power Set of Atoms

One Atom,
$2^1 = 2$
Elements

Two Atoms
$2^2 = 4$
Elements

Three Atoms,
$2^3 = 8$
Elements

Four Atoms,
$2^4 = 16$ Elements

Fig. 3-1

    The simplest non-trivial Boolean Algebra is created from a Base Set that has one Atom: X = {U}. When we create a Power Set based upon this single Atom, we obtain a two-Element Universe: $P(X)$ = (Ø, U). One interpretation of this Boolean Algebra, that we label P_1, is that the single Atom "U" represents the entire universe of Ideas consolidated into a single Deemed Atom. (We discuss principles of Consolidation and Subdivision of Ideas in MWN Vol. 1 at 261, 267, and 272.) If we Subdivide U into two Atoms, P and R, we obtain a two-Atom, four-Element Universe P_2: $P(X)$ = (Ø, P, R, PR). In this fashion, we can use the Subdivision of Ideas to create larger Power Sets and Universes of Discourse. As a practical matter, however, the P_1, P_2, P_3, and P_4 Power Sets are sufficient for most of our needs, particularly since larger Power Sets follow the same rules and can be formed by combining smaller Power Sets.

Now, we look at a more formal definition of a Boolean Algebra based upon a Domain equal to a Power Set of Atoms in a Base Set "X".

Definition: "**Power Set Boolean Algebra**":

The Boolean Algebra of all Subsets of X is defined as
$\langle P(X); \cup, \cap, 0, 1, \_' \rangle$ where:
○ **Domain**: P(X), where Base Set X $_{Atoms}$ = { p, q, r, s,...}.
○ **Addition**: "$\cup$" is Union, and is associative and commutative (Abelian).
○ **Additive Identity**: "0" is the Empty Set = $\emptyset$:
○ **Multiplication**: "$\cap$" is Intersection, and is associative and commutative (Abelian).
○ **Multiplicative Identity**: "1" is the Base Set of Atoms = X.
○ **Complementation**: "$\_'$" is the Complementation Unary Operation.
○ **Distributive**: Multiplication is Distributive over Addition, and *vice versa*.

The Boolean Algebra of Sets uses Set Union for addition, and Set Intersection for multiplication. The other critical operation is Complementation. **Fig. 3-2** illustrates the Complements for each element in the P_1 to P_4 Lattices. Notice how the Complement of the Atom "p" changes as we add more Atoms to the Universe of Discourse. This will be an important observation to remember later when we discuss "Negation" *versus* "Complementation". (Negation in the sense of True/False "Sign Reversal" of the Truth Value of a Proposition is not the same as Complementation.)

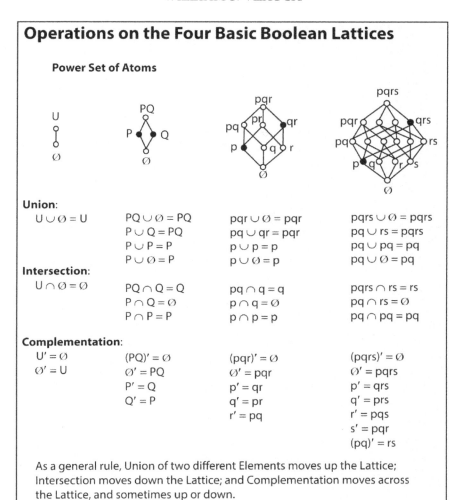

Operations on the Four Basic Boolean Lattices

Power Set of Atoms

Union:

$U \cup \emptyset = U$	$PQ \cup \emptyset = PQ$	$pqr \cup \emptyset = pqr$	$pqrs \cup \emptyset = pqrs$
	$P \cup Q = PQ$	$pq \cup qr = pqr$	$pq \cup rs = pqrs$
	$P \cup P = P$	$p \cup p = p$	$pq \cup pq = pq$
	$P \cup \emptyset = P$	$p \cup \emptyset = p$	$pq \cup \emptyset = pq$

Intersection:

$U \cap \emptyset = \emptyset$	$PQ \cap Q = Q$	$pqr \cap q = q$	$pqrs \cap rs = rs$
	$P \cap Q = \emptyset$	$p \cap q = \emptyset$	$pq \cap rs = \emptyset$
	$P \cap P = P$	$p \cap p = p$	$pq \cap pq = pq$

Complementation:

$U' = \emptyset$	$(PQ)' = \emptyset$	$(pqr)' = \emptyset$	$(pqrs)' = \emptyset$
$\emptyset' = U$	$\emptyset' = PQ$	$\emptyset' = pqr$	$\emptyset' = pqrs$
	$P' = Q$	$p' = qr$	$p' = qrs$
	$Q' = P$	$q' = pr$	$q' = prs$
		$r' = pq$	$r' = pqs$
			$s' = pqr$
			$(pq)' = rs$

As a general rule, Union of two different Elements moves up the Lattice; Intersection moves down the Lattice; and Complementation moves across the Lattice, and sometimes up or down.

Fig. 3-2

Not only is the Boolean Algebra of Sets easy to understand at an intuitive level, but in 1936 M. H. Stone proved that every Boolean Algebra is Isomorphic to (*i.e.*, has the same shape and structure as) a Boolean Algebra of Sets. *See*, [Stone 1936]. This is important, because it means that as we work to create a Boolean Algebra of Propositional Logic, we are justified in comparing the structure to a Boolean Algebra of Sets at an intuitive level.

3.2. *Fundamental Laws Applicable to All Boolean Algebras*

There are a number of fundamental laws that apply to all Boolean Algebras. *See,* **Table 3-1**.

Table 3-1

Name	Complement	Additive (Union)	Multiplicative (Intersection)
Complement of the Empty Set	$\emptyset' = 1$		
Complement of the Universal Set	$\emptyset = 1'$		
Operations with X=Lattice "1", the Universe Class		$x \cup 1 = 1$	$x \cap 1 = x$
Operations with Lattice "0", the Null Class		$x \cup \emptyset = x$	$x \cap \emptyset = \emptyset$
Laws of Complementation		$x \cup x' = 1$	$x \cap x' = \emptyset$
Commutative Laws		$x \cup y = y \cup x$	$x \cap y = y \cap x$
Associative Laws		$(x \cup y) \cup z = x \cup (y \cup z)$	$(x \cap y) \cap z = x \cap (y \cap z)$
Distributive Laws		$x \cup (y \cap z) = (x \cup y) \cap (x \cup z)$	$x \cap (y \cup z) = (x \cap y) \cup (x \cap z)$
Laws of Tautology		$x \cup x = x$	$x \cap x = x$
Laws of Absorption		$x \cap (x \cup y) = x$	$x \cup (x \cap y) = x$
Law of Double Complementation	$(x')' = x$		
Laws of De Morgan; Laws of Duality; Laws of Negation		$(x \cup y)' = x' \cap y'$	$(x \cap y)' = x' \cup y'$
Laws of Expansion		$(x \cap y) \cup (x \cap y') = x$	$(x \cup y) \cap (x \cup y') = x$

For a discussion of the fundamental laws applicable to all Boolean Algebras, *see,* [Givant and Halmos 2009] at 8-9, [Langer 1967] at 233-234, and [Whitesitt 1960] at 7-8.

3.3. Boolean Expressions, Boolean Functions, Boolean Polynomials, and Boolean Equations

In the study of Propositional Logic, we create long strings of Variables (x_1, x_2, x_3, ...) and their Negatives using NOT ($\neg\, x_1$, $\neg\, x_2$, $\neg\, x_3$, ...), connected by AND ("$\wedge$") and OR ("$\vee$"). Therefore, if our goal is to demonstrate that Propositional Logic is a Boolean Algebra, then we had better first understand the behavior of long strings of Variables connected by Boolean Operations, so that we will recognize the extent to which a system of Propositional Logic behaves, or fails to behave, like a Boolean Algebra.

First, we define "**Constant**" or "**Boolean Constant**" to mean a specific Element of a Boolean Algebra and a "**Variable**" or "**Boolean Variable**" to mean a symbol used to represent an arbitrary or unspecified Element of a Boolean Algebra. Then, we define Boolean Expression, Boolean Function, Boolean Polynomial, and Boolean Equation. The distinctions may seem subtle at first, but they are important when we start to look at transformations from one form to another. (Different authors use slightly different definitions, so it is important to read the definitions carefully.) *See*, **Fig. 3-3**.

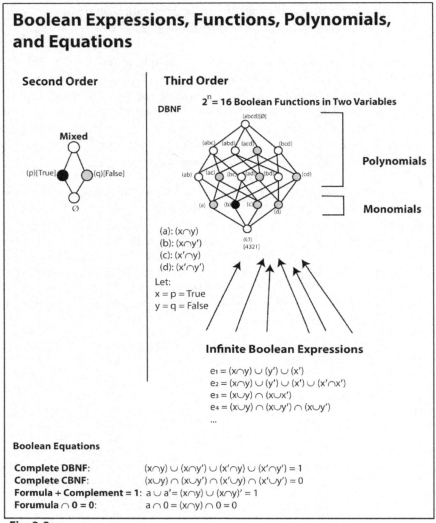

Fig. 3-3

Definition: "**Boolean Expression**": We use the term "Boolean Expression" or "Boolean Formula" to refer to an expression "$e(x_1, x_2, \ldots x_n)$" representing the combination of a finite Set of symbols, including one or more of the following:

- Each of x_1, x_2, $\ldots x_n$, each representing a Boolean Variable, is Boolean Expression.

- If (e) is a Boolean Expression, then $(e)'$ is a Boolean Expression.
- If (e_1) and (e_2) are Boolean Expressions, then $(e_1) \cup (e_2)$ and $(e_1) \cap (e_2)$ are Boolean Expressions.

Other terms that mean the same thing as "Boolean Expression" in MWN Propositional Logic are Well Formed Formula ("**WFF**") and "**Boolean Formula**." Note that some authors include Boolean Constants, or sometimes just the Lattice "1" and Lattice "0", as Boolean Expressions. For purposes of MWN Propositional Logic, however, we include only Boolean Variables in a Boolean Expression, not Boolean Constants. *Cf*, [Abbott 1969] at 212-213.

We let "E_n" represent the Set of all Boolean Expressions in "n" Variables. There can be an infinite number of Boolean Expressions. This is easy to see, because we can keep appending clauses *ad infinitum*:

- x
- $x \cup x$
- $x \cup x \cup x$
- $x \cup x \cup x \ldots$

Clearly, however, the Boolean Expressions are not necessarily different in terms of Truth Values and Truth Tables.

The most important point to remember about any Boolean Expression is that, as discussed below, assuming we exclude any Constants (*e.g.*, Lattice "0" and Lattice "1"), we can manipulate the formula to convert it into Normal Form, including any of the following: DNF, CNF, DBNF, or CBNF.

Once any two Boolean Expressions are in the form referred to as DBNF or CBNF, we can easily determine whether they are equivalent in terms of Truth Values and Mappings to Truth Tables.

"**DBNF**" means Disjunctive Boolean Normal Form, where the Boolean Expression is written as a Disjunction of Clauses, and each Clause is a Conjunction of Atomic Formulas that includes each Variable or its Negation.

"**CBNF**" means Conjunctive Boolean Normal Form, where the Boolean Expression is written as a Conjunction of Clauses, and each Clause is a Disjunction of Atomic Formulas that includes each Variable or its Negation. For example:

- **Two Variable DBNF**:

  $(x \cap y)$

  $(x \cap y) \cup (x \cap y')$

  $(x \cap y) \cup (x \cap y') \cup (x' \cap y) \cup (x' \cap y')$

- **Two Variable CBNF**:

  $(x \cup y)$

  $(x \cup y) \cap (x \cup y')$

  $(x \cup y) \cap (x \cup y') \cap (x' \cup y) \cap (x' \cup y')$

See, **Section 3.4** for a detailed discussion of DBNF and CBNF.

Definition: "**Boolean Function**": A "**Boolean Function**" $f(x_1, x_2, \ldots x_n)$ stands for the Boolean Expression $e(x_1, x_2, \ldots x_n)$, or any equivalent Boolean Expression when set forth as a formula in DBNF or CBNF. In essence, a Boolean Function Maps a Boolean Expression to a unique formula in DBNF (or CBNF).

We can write every Boolean Expression as a Boolean Function, $e(x_1, x_2, \ldots x_n) = f(x_1, x_2, \ldots x_n)$, where $x_1, x_2, \ldots x_n$ are Boolean Variables. The distinction is that there are many Boolean Expressions that are equivalent to the same Boolean Function, but there are only 2^m Boolean Functions, where the number of Atoms "m" = 2^n, and n = number of Boolean Variables. In the most common example using two Boolean Variables, there are therefore $m = 2^n = 2^2 = 4$ Atoms; and $2^m = 2^4 = 16$ possible Boolean Functions.

Two Boolean Functions are the same if and only if they have the same DBNF (or CBNF). *See*, [Abbott 1969] at 35 and 39.

Whereas each Boolean Function is unique, there may be many different Boolean Expressions that are all equivalent to the same Boolean Function.

For a U_D with "n" Boolean Variables, there are $m=2^n$ Atoms in either DBNF or CBNF; and 2^m unique Boolean Functions.

As discussed in [Abbott 1969] at 212-213, the Set "P_n" of Equivalence Classes of Boolean Functions related to "E_n", the Set of all Boolean Expressions in "n" Variables, is itself a Boolean Algebra. The Elements of P_n are Boolean Polynomials.

Definition: "**Boolean Polynomial**": A "**Boolean Polynomial**" is an Element of the Set "P_n" of Equivalence Classes of Boolean Functions related to "E_n". *See*, [Abbott 1969] at 212 – 213.

To determine whether two Boolean Polynomials are Equivalent, we convert them to either DBNF or CBNF.

Definition: "**Boolean Equation**": A Boolean Equation is an equality based upon one of the equalities that is included in the definition of a Boolean Algebra, together with any variations or transformations obtained by applying the Rule of Substitution. The "**Rule of Substitution**" states that if two Boolean Expressions are equivalent, then we can substitute one for the other in any Boolean Expression or Equation, and the Boolean Expression or Equation is still valid. *See*, **Section 3.5** below.

The fundamental laws of any Boolean Algebra are set forth in detail in **Section 3.2**, and include a number of important equations:

- For Lattice "0" =∅, and Lattice "1":
  - $\emptyset' = 1$
  - $\emptyset = 1'$
- For a Boolean Variable "x":
  - x=x
- Using Union:
  - $x \cup x = x$
  - $x \cup \emptyset = x$
  - $x \cup x' = 1$
  - $x \cup 1 = 1$
- Using Intersection:
  - $x \cap x = x$
  - $x \cap \emptyset = \emptyset$
  - $x \cap x' = \emptyset$
  - $x \cap 1 = x$

Once we introduce the notion of "equality," then, starting with one of the fundamental equations of any Boolean Algebra listed above, we can perform a Substitution and thereby create an infinite number of new Boolean Equations.

In **Section 3.7**, we will see that we can write any Boolean Equation as an equation that is equal to "0", or as an equation that is equal to "1". *See*, [Whitesitt 1960] at 16.

It is easy to show that a "Complete" DBNF Boolean Expression is a "Tautology" equal to "1", where "1" is the Base Set of the Boolean Algebra.

Conversely, a "Complete" CBNF Boolean Expression is a "Contradiction" equal to "0", where "0" is the Empty Set. What about Boolean Expressions that are not "Complete"? Can we create a Boolean Equation? One approach is to note that $(e \cup e') = 1$ and $(e \cap e') = 0$. Therefore, we can create a Boolean Equation from any Boolean Expression by adding (Union) or multiplying (Intersection) the Complement of the Boolean Expression. Similarly, given any Boolean Expression "e", we can create a Boolean Equation by taking the Union of "e" with "1", or the Intersection of "e" with "0":

- $e \cup 1 = 1$
- $e \cap \emptyset = \emptyset$

Table 3-2 summarizes some of the key Attributes of Boolean Expressions, Boolean Functions, Boolean Polynomials, and Boolean Equations.

Table 3-2

	Boolean Expression	Boolean Function	Boolean Polynomial	Boolean Equation
Finite number?	No. There are infinite variations.	Yes. If there are "n" Variables, then there are $m=2^n$ rows in a Truth Table, and 2^m possible Truth Tables. Therefore, there are 2^m possible Boolean Functions.	No. There are, however, 2^m Equivalence Classes of Boolean Polynomials. We can determine the equivalence of any two Boolean Polynomials by converting them to DBNF or CBNF.	No. There are infinite variations. A Tautology is a Boolean Function in Complete DBNF $= 1$. A Contradiction is a Boolean Function in Complete CBNF $= 0$. A Conditional Boolean Function can be used to create a Boolean Equation by adding or multiplying its Complement; or by adding "1" or multiplying "0".
Mapping?	No.	Yes. Each Boolean Expression Maps to one of the 2^m possible Truth Tables.	No.	No.

Fig. 3-4 illustrates the similarities and differences among Boolean Expressions, Boolean Functions, Boolean Polynomials, and Boolean Equations.

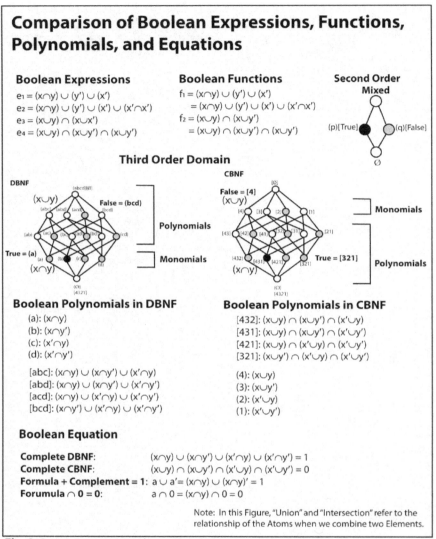

Fig. 3-4

3.4. Normal Formal: Disjunctive and Conjunctive

In this Section, we will explore the well-established principle that any Boolean Expression can be written in Normal Form, including each of the following related forms: DNF, CNF, DBNF, and CBNF.

At an intuitive level, we know that the Operations of Union and Intersection are Closed in any Boolean Algebra, which means that the Sum or Product of any two Elements will be an Element in the Power Set. We know from the Associative Law that we can group Elements any way we want if they are connected by a single Boolean Operation of Union or Intersection. If we are using two Boolean Operations, then we can still group Elements in different ways, but we must apply the De Morgan Laws when we simplify the expression.

The fact that the Operations are Closed, even in long strings of Variables, is significant, because it means that there are a limited number of choices available: a Boolean Algebra with two Atoms has four Elements ($2^n=2^2=4$); a Boolean Algebra with three Atoms has eight Elements ($2^n=2^3=8$); a Boolean Algebra with four Atoms has sixteen Elements ($2^n=2^4=16$) *etc.* This means, for example, that in a Boolean Algebra with four Atoms, we can take any string of Variables (*i.e.*, Atoms) connected by Union and Intersection, and using Complementation, and the result must be equal to one of the 16 Elements in the Power Set. The significance of DBNF and CBNF, defined below, is that the Clauses correspond to the Atoms of a Power Set; and each Boolean Function corresponds to an Element of the Power Set of DBNF Clauses or CBNF Clauses, respectively.

Definition: "**Atomic Formula**": An Atomic Formula is a Boolean Expression consisting of a single Boolean Variable representing an Element of a Boolean Algebra. *E.g.*, "x", where "x" is an Element of $P(X) = (\emptyset, a, b, c, ab, ac, bc, abc)$, where $X = \{ a, b, c \}$. Note that an Atomic Formula can represent *any* Element of the Boolean Algebra, not necessarily an Atom.

Definition: "**Literal**": a "Literal" is an Atomic Formula or the Complement of an Atomic Formula. *E.g.*, " x " or " x' ". In terms of Logic Operations, we use Negation instead of Complementation, and we write the Negation as " $\neg x$ ". We need to exercise care, however, because Complementation and "NOT" do not have exactly the same meaning.

Definition: "**Clause**": A "Clause" is either a Disjunction of Literals, or a Conjunction of Literals. Note that when we speak of a generic Boolean Algebra of Sets, "Disjunction" refers to "Union," and "Conjunction" refers to "Intersection." (Although Union and Disjunction are not identical terms, in this context they operate in the same way. In other words, the "Normal Form" is an Attribute of all Boolean Algebras, not just Propositional Logic.)

Definition: "**Normal Form**": The term "Normal Form" refers to a Boolean Expression that uses only Variables ($x_1, x_2, x_3, \dots$) and their Complements ($x_1', x_2', x_3', \dots$), together with the Operations of Union and Intersection, and parentheses as necessary to group Operations. (Later we will see that Logic Formulas $(x_1, x_2, x_3,...)$ and their Negations $(\neg x_1, \neg x_2, \neg x_3,...)$, together with the Operations of Disjunction (OR) and Conjunction (AND) behave in a similar fashion.)

Since all other Operations may be defined in terms of Negation and Union (Disjunction), all Boolean Expressions and Logic Formulas may be written in Normal Form. *See,* **Chapter 7**.

Definition: "**Disjunctive Normal Form**": A Boolean Expression is in "Disjunctive Normal Form" (DNF) if it is a disjunction of conjunctions of Literals. The following are examples of Boolean Expressions in DNF:

- x
- $x \cup (y \cap z)$
- $x \cup (y \cap z) \cup (x \cap z)$

In essence, DNF is a disjunction of conjunctive Clauses.

Every Boolean Function which contains no Constants is equal to a function in DNF.

Definition: "**Disjunctive Boolean Normal Form**": A Boolean Expression in DBNF is a type of Boolean Expression in DNF where each Clause is a conjunctive Clause which contains each Variable in the Order 3 Domain or its Negation. The following are examples of Boolean Expressions in DBNF:

- **Two Variable DBNF:**
  - $(x \cap y)$
  - $(x \cap y) \cup (x \cap y')$
  - $(x \cap y) \cup (x \cap y') \cup (x' \cap y) \cup (x' \cap y')$

- **Three Variable DBNF:**
  $(x \cap y \cap z) \cup (x \cap y \cap z') \cup (x \cap y' \cap z) \cup$
  $(x' \cap y \cap z) \cup (x \cap y' \cap z') \cup (x' \cap y \cap z') \cup$
  $(x' \cap y' \cap z) \cup (x' \cap y' \cap z')$

The DBNF in "n" Variables that contains 2^n Clauses is called the "Complete Disjunctive Normal Form." [Whitesitt 1960] at 35.

Definition: "**Conjunctive Normal Form**": A Boolean Expression is in "Conjunctive Normal Form" (CNF) if it is a conjunction of disjunctions of Literals. The following are examples of Boolean Expressions in CNF:

- x
- $x \cap (y \cup z)$
- $x \cap (y \cup z) \cap (x \cup z)$

In essence, CNF is a conjunction of disjunctive Clauses.

Every Boolean Function which contains no Constants is equal to a function in CNF.

Definition: "**Conjunctive Boolean Normal Form**": A Boolean Expression in CBNF is a type of Boolean Expression in CNF where each Clause is a disjunctive Clause which contains each Variable in the Order 3 Domain or its Negation. The following are examples of Boolean Expressions in CBNF:

- **Two Variable CBNF:**
    - $(x \cup y)$
    - $(x \cup y) \cap (x \cup y')$
    - $(x \cup y) \cap (x \cup y') \cap (x' \cup y) \cap (x' \cup y')$

- **Three Variable CBNF:**
  $(x \cup y \cup z) \cap (x \cup y \cup z') \cap (x \cup y' \cup z) \cap$
  $(x' \cup y \cup z) \cap (x \cup y' \cup z') \cap (x' \cup y \cup z') \cap$
  $(x' \cup y' \cup z) \cap (x' \cup y' \cup z')$

The CBNF in "n" Variables that contains 2^n Clauses is called the "Complete Conjunctive Normal Form."

Note that the number of Variables in an Order 3 Domain of Logic Formulas is not restricted in any way by the number of Atoms in the Order 1 Domain of Ideas, or Order 2 Domain of Propositions. For example, we can use a one Atom Order 2 Boolean Algebra as a Base for creating Boolean Equations in two, three, four, or more Variables in Order 3. *See,* **Fig. 3-5**.

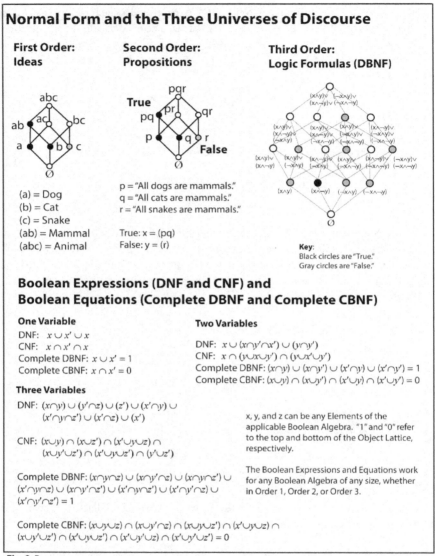

Normal Form and the Three Universes of Discourse

First Order: Ideas

abc
ab ac bc
a b c
∅

(a) = Dog
(b) = Cat
(c) = Snake
(ab) = Mammal
(abc) = Animal

Second Order: Propositions

pqr
True
pq pr qr
p q r
False
∅

p = "All dogs are mammals."
q = "All cats are mammals."
r = "All snakes are mammals."

True: x = (pq)
False: y = (r)

Third Order: Logic Formulas (DBNF)

Key:
Black circles are "True."
Gray circles are "False."

Boolean Expressions (DNF and CNF) and Boolean Equations (Complete DBNF and Complete CBNF)

One Variable

DNF: $x \cup x' \cup x$
CNF: $x \cap x' \cap x$
Complete DBNF: $x \cup x' = 1$
Complete CBNF: $x \cap x' = 0$

Three Variables

DNF: $(x \cap y) \cup (y' \cap z) \cup (z') \cup (x' \cap y) \cup$
$(x' \cap y \cap z') \cup (x' \cap z) \cup (x')$

CNF: $(x \cup y) \cap (x \cup z') \cap (x' \cup y \cup z) \cap$
$(x \cup y' \cup z') \cap (x' \cup y \cup z') \cap (y' \cup z')$

Complete DBNF: $(x \cap y \cap z) \cup (x \cap y' \cap z) \cup (x \cap y \cap z') \cup$
$(x' \cap y \cap z) \cup (x \cap y' \cap z') \cup (x' \cap y \cap z') \cup (x' \cap y' \cap z) \cup$
$(x' \cap y' \cap z') = 1$

Complete CBNF: $(x \cup y \cup z) \cap (x \cup y' \cap z) \cap (x \cup y \cup z') \cap (x' \cup y \cup z) \cap$
$(x \cup y' \cup z') \cap (x' \cup y \cup z') \cap (x' \cup y' \cup z) \cap (x' \cup y' \cup z') = 0$

Two Variables

DNF: $x \cup (x \cap y' \cap x') \cup (y \cap y')$
CNF: $x \cap (y \cup x \cup y') \cap (y \cup x' \cup y')$
Complete DBNF: $(x \cap y) \cup (x \cap y') \cup (x' \cap y) \cup (x' \cap y') = 1$
Complete CBNF: $(x \cup y) \cap (x \cup y') \cap (x' \cup y) \cap (x' \cup y') = 0$

x, y, and z can be any Elements of the applicable Boolean Algebra. "1" and "0" refer to the top and bottom of the Object Lattice, respectively.

The Boolean Expressions and Equations work for any Boolean Algebra of any size, whether in Order 1, Order 2, or Order 3.

Fig. 3-5

An important point to note is that *any* Boolean Expression or Logic Formula can be written in *any* of the following formats: DNF, CNF, DBNF, and CBNF. The advantage to writing formulas in DBNF (or CBNF) is that we can quickly ascertain whether the formulas are equivalent. *See*, [Arnold 1962] at 104; and [Hedman 2004] at 27-29.

3.5. *Manipulating Boolean Expressions, Boolean Functions, Boolean Polynomials, and Boolean Equations*

We have seen that there are four types of Boolean sentences that are relevant to our study of Propositional Logic: Boolean Expressions, Boolean Functions, Boolean Polynomials, and Boolean Equations. In the case of Boolean Expressions, there is an infinite variety, but in each case the Boolean Expression is equivalent to one of a finite number of Boolean Functions. As a result, we tend to focus on Boolean Functions, but this means that we need to become proficient at converting Boolean Expressions to Boolean Functions. We also need to become proficient at transforming Boolean Functions into either DBNF or CBNF. Typically, we use DBNF when we are solving for a "True" Proposition; and CBNF when we are solving for a "False" Proposition. There can be other advantages to one form over the other, but generally speaking we tend to work more in DBNF.

Boolean Equations are also important, because "Theorems" are Tautologies that are always "True" and = 1; "Contradictions" are always "False" and = 0.

In addition to converting to DBNF or CBNF, and creating or checking for Tautologies and Contradictions, we sometimes want to simplify Boolean Functions and Boolean Equations to make them easier to read. As a result, we need to understand the rules that allow us to simplify, factor, or expand Boolean Expressions and Equations.

3.5.1. *The Rule of Substitution*

In MWN, we refer to the Rule of Substitution that allows us to substitute one Boolean Expression for another if the two are equivalent. Some authors, however, make a distinction between different types of substitution. For example, Quine uses the term "substitution" for those situations where we replace each occurrence of a single letter with a Boolean Expression; but Quine uses the term "interchange" for those situations where we replace Boolean Expressions with Boolean Expressions, but not necessarily every occurrence. *See*, [Quine 1982] at 63. As Quine demonstrates, "interchange" (or what we refer to in MWN as "Substitution of equivalent Boolean Expressions") preserves validity, implication, equivalence, and inconsistency, as well as consistency, non-validity, nonimplication, and nonequivalence. *See also*, [Eves 1990] at 251-252.

3.5.2. *De Morgan's Laws: Sign Reversal v. Complementation*

De Morgan's Laws are used in three distinct ways: (1) as a tool to convert complex Boolean Expressions into DBNF or CBNF, (2) to identify the Complement of a Boolean Expression in its Inverse, Dual CBNF or DBNF Domain, as the case may be, and (3) to create a valid Dual Boolean Expression or Theorem (*i.e.*, a Tautology) in the related Inverse, Dual CBNF or DBNF Domain, as the case may be.

De Morgan's Laws state the following:

- $(x \cup y)' = x' \cap y'$
- $(x \cap y)' = x' \cup y'$

We can use De Morgan's Law to simplify any Boolean Expression or Boolean Equation where the Union (OR) or Intersection (AND) Operation is to be distributed across the terms of a Clause in parentheses. (The situation where we convert to a different Domain will be discussed in **Section 3.10** below when we discuss Duality.)

3.5.3. *Other Helpful Equivalences*

Although not always listed as fundamental laws of Boolean Algebras, there are a number of additional equivalences that are particularly useful when we are manipulating the form of a Boolean Expression. Often the goal is to find the quickest way to convert a Boolean Expression to an equivalent Boolean Expression in DBNF or CBNF.

The Boolean Equation $x = y$ is equivalent to the Boolean Equation $xy' + x'y = 0$. *See*, [Whitesitt 1960] at 17. Note the special significance of this Boolean Equation: we cannot simply add "-y" to each side of the equation $x = y$, as we would with ordinary counting numbers.

Examples of helpful equivalences, some old and some new, include the following:

- $x = x''$
- $x = x \cap x$
- $x = x \cup x$
- $x \cap y = y \cap x$
- $x \cap y = (x' \cup y')'$

- $x \cup y = y \cup x$
- $x \cup y = (x' \cap y')'$
- $x \to y = (x \cap y')'$
- $x \to y = x' \cup y$
- $x \leftrightarrow y = (x \to y) \cap (y \to x)$
- $x \leftrightarrow y = (x \cap y')' \cap (y \cap x')'$
- $(x \cap y) \cap z = x \cap (y \cap z)$
- $(x \cup y) \cup z = x \cup (y \cup z)$
- $(x \cap y)' = x' \cup y'$
- $(x \cup y)' = x' \cap y'$

See generally, [Quine 1982] at 60.

While these equivalences apply to any Boolean Algebra of Sets, if we accept that we are going to use Disjunction (OR) in much the way we use Union, and Conjunction (AND) in much the way that we use Intersection, then the same equivalences will apply to Disjunction and Conjunction generally.

3.6. *Strategy for Converting Boolean Expressions to DBNF or CBNF*

When confronted with a Boolean Expression that is not in DBNF or CBNF, as the case may be, we can follow these steps to convert the Boolean Expression to the desired form:

- **Convert other Operations to Complementation (Negation in the case of Logic Formulas), Union (Disjunction), or Intersection (Conjunction)**: *E.g.*, $x \to y = x' \vee y$
- **Simplify any double Complementation**: $x'' = x$
- **Apply De Morgan Laws wherever possible**: If Complementation (Negation) is applied to a Union (Disjunction) or Intersection (Conjunction) of Polynomials, then apply the De Morgan Laws
- **Apply Distributive Laws**: Apply the distributive laws until we have a Disjunction of Conjunctions (DNF), or a Conjunction of Disjunctions (CNF)

Although we do not provide examples here, there are many examples given in the books listed at the end of this Chapter, of converting Boolean Expressions or Logic Formulas to DBNF or CBNF.

3.7. Equations that are Equal to "0" or "1"

In MWN Propositional Logic, Boolean Equations that are equal to the Lattice "1" or Lattice "0" play a special role. In MWN, we use "0" to represent the Empty Set (which is different from a Truth Value concept of falsity). We use "1" to represent the Universal Set, or more often, the Universe of Discourse.

To create these special types of Boolean Equations, we start with one of the universal truths for all Boolean Algebras, such as those provided below, and create other equations using the Rules of Substitution and the De Morgan Laws:

- $(x \cup x') = 1$
- $(x \cap x') = 0$

It is beyond the scope of this book to provide a lot of examples, but the interested learner can find many examples in the books listed at the end of this Chapter.

We can write any Boolean Equation as an equation $= 0$. [Whitesitt 1960] at 16. Therefore, we can also write every Boolean Equation as an equation $= 1$:

- $(\text{Boolean Formula}) = 0$
- $(\text{Boolean Formula})' = 1$

As noted earlier, another helpful equivalence, is that if x=y, then $xy' \cup x'y = 0$. *See,* [Whitesitt 1960] at 16-17.

The important point to remember is that in MWN we use 0 and 1 as the Empty Set and Universal Set (or Universe of Discourse) respectively, but not to mean "True" or "False."

3.8. DBNF Lattices and CBNF Lattices

If we use the Clauses of a "Complete" Boolean Expression in DBNF (or CBNF) as "Atoms," we can create a DBNF Lattice (or CBNF Lattice). *See,*

"A Lattice-Diagram for the Propositional Calculus" at [Evenden 1962].

DBNF Lattices and CBNF Lattices are different from other Lattices in the following ways:

- Assuming an Order 2 Domain of Propositions with one Atom "p", and therefore two Elements "Ø" and "p", in a DBNF Lattice only one Atom is True, and the rest are False; and in a CBNF Lattice, only one Atom is False, and the rest are True.
- The DBNF Lattice and the CBNF Lattice are Inverse Duals.
- The DBNF Atoms correspond to the 2^n distinct areas in a Venn Diagram where n = the number of Variables in the WFF or Boolean Expression.

Fig. 3-6 illustrates DBNF and CBNF Lattices based upon an Order 2 Domain with one Atom X = { A }, and therefore two Elements $P(A) = (Ø, A)$.

Dual DBNF and CBNF Lattices: one Order 2 Atom

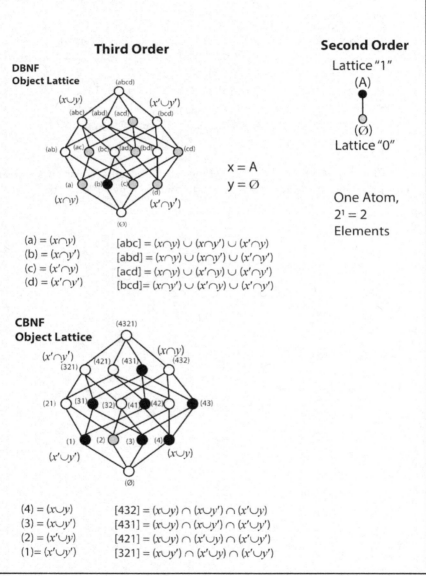

Third Order

DBNF Object Lattice

(abcd)

$(x \cup y)$
(abc) (abd) (acd) (bcd)
$(x' \cup y')$

(ab) (ac) (bc) (ad) (bd) (cd)

(a) (b) (c) (d)
$(x \cap y)$
$(x' \cap y')$

(∅)

$x = A$
$y = \varnothing$

(a) = $(x \cap y)$
(b) = $(x \cap y')$
(c) = $(x' \cap y)$
(d) = $(x' \cap y')$

[abc] = $(x \cap y) \cup (x \cap y') \cup (x' \cap y)$
[abd] = $(x \cap y) \cup (x \cap y') \cup (x' \cap y')$
[acd] = $(x \cap y) \cup (x' \cap y) \cup (x' \cap y')$
[bcd] = $(x \cap y') \cup (x' \cap y) \cup (x' \cap y')$

CBNF Object Lattice

(4321)

$(x' \cap y')$
(321) (421) (431)
$(x \cap y)$
(432)

(21) (31) (32) (41) (42) (43)

(1) (2) (3) (4)
$(x' \cup y')$
$(x \cup y)$

(∅)

(4) = $(x \cup y)$
(3) = $(x \cup y')$
(2) = $(x' \cup y)$
(1) = $(x' \cup y')$

[432] = $(x \cup y) \cap (x \cup y') \cap (x' \cup y)$
[431] = $(x \cup y) \cap (x \cup y') \cap (x' \cup y')$
[421] = $(x \cup y) \cap (x' \cup y) \cap (x' \cup y')$
[321] = $(x \cup y') \cap (x' \cup y) \cap (x' \cup y')$

Second Order

Lattice "1"
(A)

(∅)
Lattice "0"

One Atom,
$2^1 = 2$
Elements

Fig. 3-6

Fig. 3-7 illustrates DBNF and CBNF Lattices based upon an Order 2 Domain with two Atoms X = { A, B }, and therefore four Elements in the Domain $P(A) = (\emptyset, A, B, AB)$. Note that when we Map an Order 2 Value of "$\emptyset$" to an Order 3 Atom, we treat the Truth Value in Order 3 as "False." (Conversely, when we Map an Order 2 Value of "AB" to an Order 3 Atom, we treat the Truth Value in Order 3 as "True.")

Dual DBNF and CBNF Lattices: two Order 2 Atoms

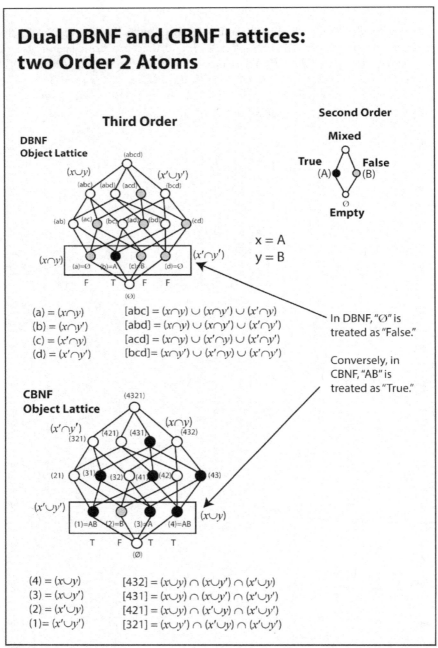

Third Order

DBNF Object Lattice

$(x \cup y)$ $(x' \cup y')$

$(x \cap y)$ $(x' \cap y')$

F   T   F   F

(a) = $(x \cap y)$ [abc] = $(x \cap y) \cup (x \cap y') \cup (x' \cap y)$
(b) = $(x \cap y')$ [abd] = $(x \cap y) \cup (x \cap y') \cup (x' \cap y')$
(c) = $(x' \cap y)$ [acd] = $(x \cap y) \cup (x' \cap y) \cup (x' \cap y')$
(d) = $(x' \cap y')$ [bcd] = $(x \cap y') \cup (x' \cap y) \cup (x' \cap y')$

Second Order

Mixed

True   False
(A)   (B)

Empty

$x = A$
$y = B$

In DBNF, "Ø" is treated as "False."

Conversely, in CBNF, "AB" is treated as "True."

CBNF Object Lattice

$(x' \cap y')$ $(x \cap y)$

$(x' \cup y')$ $(x \cup y)$

T   F   T   T

(4) = $(x \cup y)$ [432] = $(x \cup y) \cap (x \cup y') \cap (x' \cup y)$
(3) = $(x \cup y')$ [431] = $(x \cup y) \cap (x \cup y') \cap (x' \cup y')$
(2) = $(x' \cup y)$ [421] = $(x \cup y) \cap (x' \cup y) \cap (x' \cup y')$
(1) = $(x' \cup y')$ [321] = $(x \cup y') \cap (x' \cup y) \cap (x' \cup y')$

Fig. 3-7

3.9. Duality and the Square of Lattices

In this Subchapter, we explore briefly the concept of Duality, and in particular how it relates to the concept of Complementation.

Principle of Duality: Every Boolean Expression or Boolean Equation deducible from the fundamental laws of Boolean Algebras remains valid if the Operations (+) and (×), and the identity Elements 0 and 1 are interchanged throughout. *See*, [Whitesitt 1960] at 28.

We will see that Negation ("¬") , as used in Traditional Propositional Logic, and Complementation ("_'") as used in Boolean Algebras, are not the same. Negation in Traditional Propositional Logic does result in the Complement (when applied to a Boolean Expression in the Order 3 Domain of Logic Formulas), but it also has the effect of switching Domains from DBNF to CBNF, or *vice versa*. (Complementation normally does not result in switching Domains, but it can have that effect on Logic Formulas when we apply the De Morgan Laws.)

We have seen that any Boolean Expression can be transformed into a formula in DBNF or CBNF. In each case, given "n" Boolean Variables, we can use the 2^n Clauses in DBNF or CBNF as Atoms to create a Boolean Lattice. **Fig. 3-8** shows how we can represent the DBNF Clauses and CBNF Clauses using Venn Diagrams.

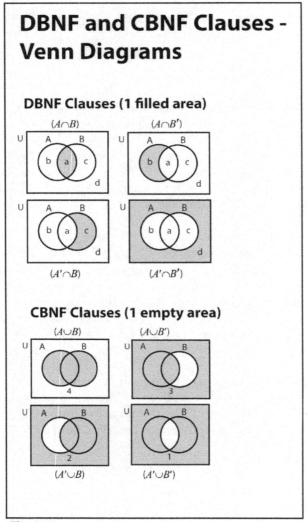

DBNF and CBNF Clauses - Venn Diagrams

DBNF Clauses (1 filled area)

CBNF Clauses (1 empty area)

Fig. 3-8

In **Fig. 3-9**, we see how Complements are formed in each of the three Orders. In Order 1 and Order 2, Complementation is straightforward. In Order 3, however, application of the De Morgan Laws has the unintended consequence of moving from the DBNF Domain to the CBNF Domain, or *vice versa*. Note that this result is the same whether we use the Negation Operation ("$\neg$") or the Complementation Operation ("$\_'$"):

- $(A \cap B)' = (A' \cup B')$
- $\neg(p \wedge q) = (\neg p \vee \neg q)$

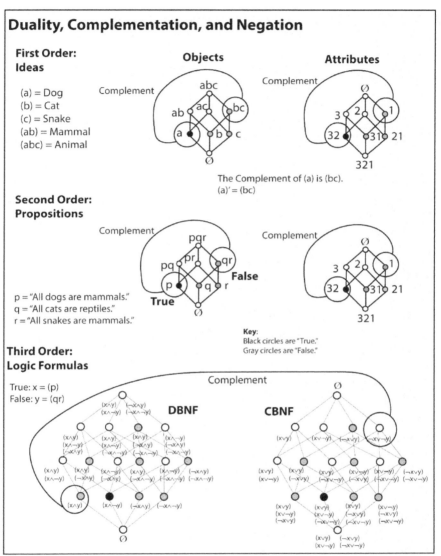

Fig. 3-9

What we see is that there are many possible interpretations of terms such as "Complementation" and "Negation" in the context of Dual Lattices of Logic Formulas. Do we intend to find a Complement in the same Domain, or do we want to switch to the Inverse, Dual Domain? To further complicate matters, we can choose to use either the DBNF Clauses or the

CBNF Clauses as "Atoms." As a result, we have four different, but related Lattices, that form a "Square of Lattices." *See,* **Fig. 3-10**.

Note that there are four common functions mapping the Set of Boolean Polynomials one-to-one onto itself. For example, in the case of the DBNF Atom "$(x \cap y)$", we have the following four functions:

- Identity Function: $f(x, y) = (x \cap y)$
- Complement Function: $(f(x, y))' = f'(x, y) = (x' \cup y')$
- Contradual Function: $f(x', y') = (x' \cap y')$
- Dual Function: $f'(x', y') = (x \cup y)$

Note that the Dual Function and Complement Function have the effect of switching Domains from DBNF to CBNF, or *vice versa*.

This set of functions is closed under composition:

- Complement + Contradual = Dual
- Contradual + Dual = Complement
- Each function is its own inverse
- Identity Function is the Identity

Therefore, the four functions constitute a Group called the Klein four-group. *See,* [Givant and Halmos 2009] at 20-23.

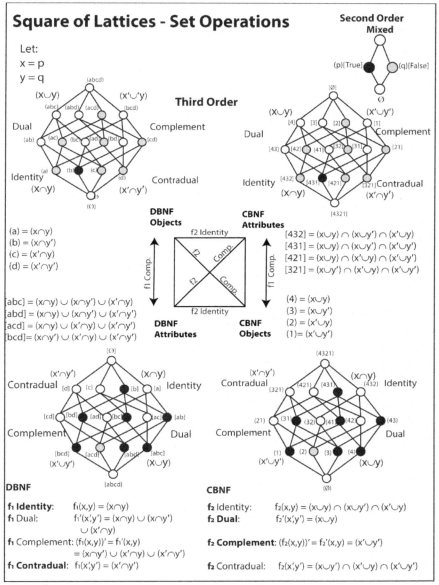

Fig. 3-10

In MWN, however, we extend this concept further to accommodate the fact that we have two Inverse, Dual Lattices. In reality, it is a single Lattice, like two sides of the same coin, but we treat each Lattice as a separate Domain and, as a rule, we do not mix calculations across different Domains. As a result, we have in total eight functions, four with respect to the DBNF

Lattice, and four with respect to the Inverse, Dual CBNF Lattice. In the example of the DBNF Clause "$(x \cap y)$", we have the following eight Functions:

DBNF Domain

- **Identity Function:** $f_1(x, y) = (x \cap y)$
- **Complement Function:**
  $(f_1(x, y))' = f_1'(x, y) = (x' \cap y) \cup (x \cap y') \cup (x' \cap y')$
- **Contradual Function:** $f_1(x', y') = (x' \cap y')$
- **Dual Function:** $f_1'(x', y') = (x \cap y) \cup (x' \cap y) \cup (x \cap y')$

CBNF Domain:

- **Identity Function** Dual:
  $f_2(x, y) = (x \cup y) \cap (x \cup y') \cap (x' \cup y)$
- **Complement Function** Dual: $(f_2(x, y))' = f_2'(x, y) = (x' \cup y')$
- **Contradual Function** Dual:
  $f_2(x', y') = (x \cup y') \cap (x' \cup y) \cap (x' \cup y')$
- **Dual Function** Dual: $f_2'(x', y') = (x \cup y)$

The idea behind the notation is to use "f_1" to indicate that we are in the DBNF Domain and not changing the internal workings of the Atom (assuming that we started in a DBNF Lattice); whereas we use "f_2" to indicate that we are changing the internal values of the Atom, which has the effect of switching the Domain from DBNF to CBNF (assuming that we started in a DBNF Lattice). The easiest way to understand the eight functions is with reference to a Venn Diagram. *See*, **Fig. 3-11.**

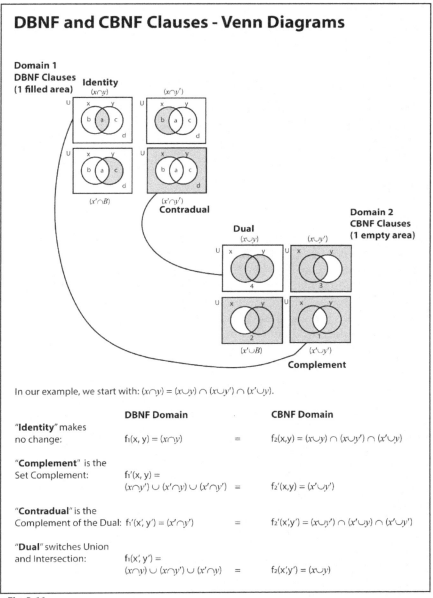

DBNF and CBNF Clauses - Venn Diagrams

In our example, we start with: $(x \cap y) = (x \cup y) \cap (x \cup y') \cap (x' \cup y)$.

	DBNF Domain		CBNF Domain
"Identity" makes no change:	$f_1(x, y) = (x \cap y)$	$=$	$f_2(x,y) = (x \cup y) \cap (x \cup y') \cap (x' \cup y)$
"Complement" is the Set Complement:	$f_1'(x, y) =$ $(x \cap y') \cup (x' \cap y) \cup (x' \cap y')$	$=$	$f_2'(x,y) = (x' \cup y')$
"Contradual" is the Complement of the Dual:	$f_1'(x', y') = (x' \cap y')$	$=$	$f_2'(x',y') = (x \cup y') \cap (x' \cup y) \cap (x' \cup y')$
"Dual" switches Union and Intersection:	$f_1(x', y') =$ $(x \cap y) \cup (x \cap y') \cup (x' \cap y)$	$=$	$f_2(x',y') = (x \cup y)$

Fig. 3-11

We will explore these concepts in more detail as we proceed through the book. For now, we just want to expose the reader to the concepts of Duality, Complementation, and Negation.

3.10.   Do Logic Operations Conform to the Rules of a Boolean Algebra?

As we proceed, we will see that the Logic Operations of "OR, AND, Negation" as used in Traditional Propositional Logic are similar to, but not the same as, the Set Operations of "Union, Intersection, and Complementation." We will be able to create a number of relevant Boolean Algebras, but the task is more complicated than simply substituting the Logic Operations of "OR, AND, Negation" for the Set Operations of "Union, Intersection, and Complementation." In particular, we note the following key differences:

- **Creating Sets v. Assigning Truth Values.** Set "Union" refers to the Binary Operation where we combine Atoms (or Coatoms) from two or more Sets to form a Set with Atoms (or Coatoms) from each component Set. The Disjunction Operation "OR", as used in Traditional Propositional Logic, refers to the "inclusive or" operation where, for example, "$p \vee q$" is "True" if one or the other, or both, p and q are True. The OR operation is different from Union in several material respects:
    - o Union refers to "both" whereas OR refers to "one or the other, or both."
    - o OR (as used in a Logic Formula) is making a statement about a property, also known as an Attribute, *i.e.*, the Truth Value, whereas Union (as used in a Boolean Lattice of Objects) does not make a statement about the Attribute Value of any Mixed Elements.
    - o In fact, OR combines (and perhaps confuses) two distinct functions: creating sets and assigning Truth Values. In MWN, we choose to use $(\vee, \wedge, \neg)$ as Set Operations like $(\cup, \cap, \_')$. Then, we will use a different approach to assigning Truth Values.

(Terms such as Atom and Coatom are defined in [Veatch 2016], which also discusses the application of Binary Operations to Sets of Atoms and Coatoms.)

- **Complementation v. Reversal of an Attribute Value.** In MWN, Set "Complementation" refers to the Complement of an Element within a specified Boolean Lattice Domain. In Traditional Propositional Logic, "Negation" refers to "**Sign Reversal**," *i.e.*, changing the value of an Attribute, for example, from True to False, or from False to True. In a two-Atom Lattice, Complementation and Negation may have the same result, but this is really just a coincidence. In Lattices with more than two Atoms, Complementation (MWN) and Negation (TPL) may yield a different result. Also, Complementation is not speaking to the Truth Value of an Attribute, whereas Negation in Traditional Propositional Logic is speaking of reversing the Truth Value of an Attribute. Note that application of the De Morgan Laws, if we are not careful, can have the (perhaps unintended) consequence of switching Domains from DBNF to CBNF, or *vice versa*. This is the case whether we are applying the De Morgan Laws to Complementation (MWN) or Negation (TPL).

In effect, then, in Traditional Propositional Logic NOT ("$\neg$ ") does two things:

- It creates a Complement, and
- It changes the Domain from DBNF to CBNF, or *vice versa*.

For example, $\neg (x \lor y) = (\neg x \land \neg y)$ is the Complement of $(x \lor y)$, but in a different Domain, *i.e.*, DBNF rather than CBNF. Interestingly, we can use the fact that $(a')' = a$ to take the Complement and then reverse the sign to find the same Element in the other Domain. For example, in a two-Variable Domain:

- $a_{DBNF} = (x \land y) \lor (x \land \neg y)$
- $a'_{DBNF} = (\neg x \land \neg y) \lor (\neg x \land y)$
- $\neg a'_{DBNF} = a_{CBNF} = (x \lor y) \land (x \lor \neg y)$

Fig. 3-12 compares and contrasts "Union" (MWN) and "OR" (TPL) in terms of Truth Tables. The Union Operation does not assign a Truth Value, so "Mixed" Sets of True and False Atoms have an "**Indeterminate**" Truth Value.

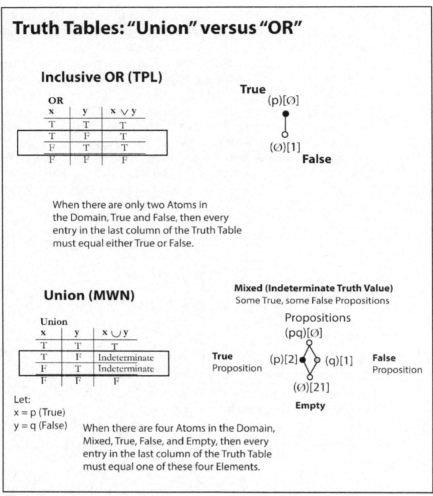

Truth Tables: "Union" versus "OR"

Inclusive OR (TPL)

OR

x	y	x ∨ y
T	T	T
T	F	T
F	T	T
F	F	F

True (p)[∅]

(∅)[1] False

When there are only two Atoms in the Domain, True and False, then every entry in the last column of the Truth Table must equal either True or False.

Union (MWN)

Union

x	y	x ∪ y
T	T	T
T	F	Indeterminate
F	T	Indeterminate
F	F	F

Let:
x = p (True)
y = q (False)

Mixed (Indeterminate Truth Value)
Some True, some False Propositions

Propositions
(pq)[∅]

True Proposition (p)[2]   (q)[1] False Proposition

(∅)[21]

Empty

When there are four Atoms in the Domain, Mixed, True, False, and Empty, then every entry in the last column of the Truth Table must equal one of these four Elements.

Fig. 3-12

Fig. 3-13 compares and contrasts "Intersection" (MWN) and "AND" (TPL) in terms of Truth Tables. The Intersection Operation does not assign a Truth Value, so the Empty Set has an **"Indeterminate"** Truth Value.

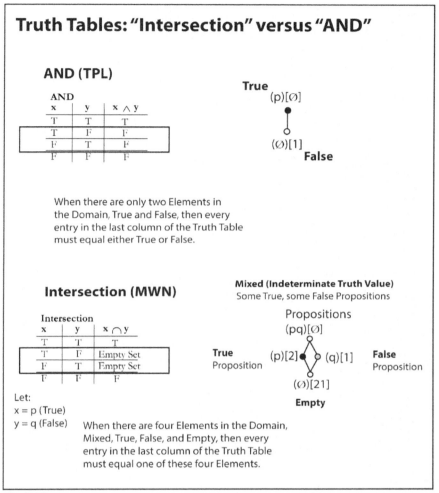

Fig. 3-13

One of the problems we have when we try to reconcile TPL with MWN, is that Sign Reversal can have the unintended consequence of switching Domains. (In fact, we have seen that Complementation can give rise to the same problem when we apply the De Morgan Laws.) However, switching Domains violates a rule of MWN that we should not mix calculations across Domains (unless we are intentionally switching Domains). As a result, in MWN we redefine " ¬ " as follows, using " $(x \wedge y)$ " as an example:

DBNF Domain:

- **Identity Function**: $f_1(x, y) = (x \wedge y)$
- **Complement Function**:
  $\neg(f_1(x, y)) = \neg f_1(x, y) = (x \wedge \neg y) \vee (\neg x \wedge y) \vee (\neg x \wedge \neg y)$
- **Contradual Function**: $f_1(\neg x, \neg y) = (\neg x \wedge \neg y)$
- **Dual Function**: $\neg f_1(\neg x, \neg y) = (x \wedge y) \vee (\neg x \wedge y) \vee (x \wedge \neg y)$

CBNF Domain:

- **Identity Function** Dual:
  $f_2(x, y) = (x \vee y) \wedge (x \vee \neg y) \wedge (\neg x \vee y)$
- **Complement Function** Dual:
  $\neg(f_2(x, y)) = \neg f_2(x, y) = (\neg x \vee \neg y)$
- **Contradual Function** Dual:
  $f_2(\neg x, \neg y) = (\neg x \vee y) \wedge (x \vee \neg y) \wedge (\neg x \vee \neg y)$
- **Dual Function** Dual: $\neg f_2(\neg x, \neg y) = (x \vee y)$

These are equivalent to the functions that we defined earlier for Complementation, except that we are using " $\neg$ " instead of " $\_'$ ". We have defined " $\neg$ " with precision, and we have avoided the problem of switching Domains (unless we affirmatively choose to do so).

In essence, in MWN we redefine " $\neg$ " to make it equivalent to Complementation. Do we need both forms of notation? In MWN, we use Complementation (" $\_'$ ") for any Boolean Algebra, whereas NOT (" $\neg$ ") is used only for a Boolean Algebra consisting of Order 3 Logic Formulas. Therefore, if we see " $\neg$ ", we know that we are in an Order 3 Domain.

Defined in this way, Traditional Propositional Logic is an Order 3 Domain of Logic Formulas, with the further restriction that the Order 2 Domain has one Atom "p", representing all True Propositions, and two Elements, "p" and "Ø". (Traditional Propositional Logic with one Atom in the Order 2 Domain is a subset of a broader MWN Propositional Logic where the Order 2 Domain may have more than one Atom.)

Any Boolean Polynomial will return an Element in the Order 2 Domain, so in Traditional Propositional Logic any Boolean Polynomial will be equal to "True" or "False." This is so because Traditional Propositional Logic uses the Value Map to determine Truth Value.

MWN Propositional Logic is different in that the Order 2 Domain may have 2, 3, 4, or more Atoms, in which case the possible Truth Values are equal to "Mixed," "True," "False," or "Empty." Do we need more than one Atom? The reasons for establishing a Boolean Algebra of Logic with more than one Atom in the Order 2 Domain of Propositions include the following:

- In MWN, False Propositions should be represented by an Atom, and not by the Empty Set.
- Propositions are often related to one another, and have Attributes other than just Truth Value. We need more than one Atom to represent different classes of Propositions, so the we can sort them based on Attributes other than Truth Value.
- Stated another way, Sets of Propositions, as we use them in the social sciences and humanities, are not binary.
- Being able to sort Propositions based upon Attributes other than Truth Value will allow us to give new meaning to the concept of "Material Implication." *See*, **Chapter 13**.

With these key differences in mind, we continue our journey to create a Boolean Algebra of Logic that is consistent with the view of the world as set forth in MWN Vol. 1.

3.11. *Why is a Boolean Algebra So Special?*

There is a wealth of amazing properties that apply to Boolean Algebras. Once a Boolean Algebra is established, there is an equivalent Boolean Ring, Boolean Lattice, and Boolean Topology, as well as a Multiplicative Semigroup and an Additive Group. If we can demonstrate that the Propositional Logic constitutes a Boolean Algebra, then the wealth of knowledge and mathematical rules governing the above structures will apply to our system of Propositional Logic.

Perhaps the most compelling reason to attempt to demonstrate that Propositional Logic constitutes a Boolean Algebra, is the application of the rules and properties concerning Disjunctive Boolean Normal Form (DBNF) and Conjunctive Boolean Normal Form (CBNF). By converting any two Boolean Expressions to DBNF or CBNF, we can quickly determine whether they are Equivalent.

We can also use the Clauses of DBNF and CBNF as Atoms to form Inverse, Dual Boolean Lattices. These are the Lattices that are traditionally used to demonstrate that Traditional Propositional Logic constitutes a

Boolean Algebra. The rules regarding CBNF and DBNF apply to *all* Boolean Algebras, not just the Boolean Algebra of Logic Formulas.

This author, and many others too, have tried to identify substructures that might work as a model for the Mathematics of Ideas. None of the substructures come close, however, to the full range of properties exhibited by a Boolean Algebra. Therefore, rather than trying to find an alternative structure, we embrace the Boolean Algebra structure, and seek a way to make it work within the confines of our intuitive sense of how a Propositional Logic should work.

We found in MWN Vol.1, that Boolean Algebras work in practice as a model for the mathematical structure of an Idea.

3.12.   References, Historical Notes, and Further Reading

For a discussion of Boolean Expressions, Boolean Functions, Boolean Polynomials, and Boolean Equations, see the following:

[Gamut Vol.1 1991] at 35, 41.
[Abbott 1969] at 211-217.
[Whitesitt 1960] at 27 et seq.

Normal Form, including DNF, CNF, DBNF, and CBNF

[Abbott 1969] at 213.
[Ackermann and Hilbert 1937] at 17-21.

Converting Boolean Expressions to DBNF or CBNF

[Hedman 2004] at 30
[Quine 1982] at 83-84.
[Abbott 1969] at 213.

Free Algebras and Generators

[Givant and Halmos 2009].
[Vladimirov 1994] at 68.
[Birkhoff and Mac Lane 1999] at 491-494.

Duality

[Givant and Halmos 2009] at 20 *et seq.*

[Ackermann and Hilbert 1937] at 15-16.

Boolean Lattices of DBNF and CBNF Clauses

[Evenden 1962]

Boolean Algebras generally

[Givant and Halmos 2009]
[Givant and Halmos 1998]
[Vladimirov 1994]]
[Monk and Bonnet 1989]
[Burris and Sankappanavar 1981]
[Curry 1976]
[Sikorski 1964]
[Whitesitt 1960]
[Stone 1936]

4. FREE BOOLEAN ALGEBRAS WITH "N" GENERATORS

Now that we have a basic understanding of Boolean Algebras, we take some time to study what in the field of Universal Algebra is referred to as a Free Boolean Algebra with "n" Generators. What we will see is that a Free Boolean Algebra provides a structure for modeling Logic Formulas not only for the one Atom Domain used in Traditional Propositional Logic, but also for the multiple Atom Domains used in MWN Propositional Logic.

The term "free" is used to refer to the fact that the Boolean Algebra is "free" of any Attributes or restrictions other than those inherent in the definition of a Boolean Algebra. *See*, [Abbott 1969] at 216 and [Gindikin 1972] at 242. We will demonstrate that the Order 3 Boolean Algebra of Logic Formulas constitutes a Free Boolean Algebra with "n" Generators, where "n" is the number of Variables in the Logic Formula. This is a significant point, because there is considerable literature relating to Free Boolean Algebras in the field of Universal Algebra. In other words, the nature of Free Boolean Algebras is well-understood in the field of mathematics. *See*, [Birkhoff and Mac Lane 1999] at 491-494 for a concise discussion, or [Vladimirov 1994] or [Givant and Halmos 2009] for a more in-depth discussion.

In our analysis of Free Boolean Algebras, we will follow the general approach taken in [Vladimirov 1994] and explore topics in the following order:

- Subalgebra generated by an Element of a Boolean Algebra and its Complement
- Subalgebra generated by a Set of two or more Elements

- Canonical representation of an Element of a Subalgebra

The remarkable thing is that the "canonical representation of an Element of a Subalgebra" is precisely what we refer to in Traditional Propositional Logic as Disjunctive Boolean Normal Form (or its Dual, Conjunctive Boolean Normal Form). We see that interpreting Propositional Logic in terms of Free Boolean Algebras supports our proposition in MWN, that we can explain Logic in terms of Set Theory and the laws of Boolean Algebra, as opposed to the other way around. *Cf.*, [Eves 1990] at 257.

Another important consequence of our study of Free Boolean Algebras, is that we come to see that the binary nature of Propositional Logic is more closely linked to the binary nature of an Element of a Power Set and its unique Complement, than to the Order 2 Domain of Propositions. In other words, while in Traditional Propositional Logic the Order 2 Domain has a single Atom, and therefore two Elements, *i.e.*, Lattice "1" and Lattice "0", in MWN Propositional Logic we explore Domains with two or more Atoms that no longer are binary in nature. In each case, however, the Order 3 Logic Formulas are built upon the binary nature of an Element and its unique Complement. Through a deeper understanding of Complementation, we gain a deeper understanding of the true nature of Logic Formulas, particularly as we venture into Domains with more than a single Atom.

4.1. Definition of a "Free Algebra"

The standard definition of a Free Boolean Algebra taken from Universal Algebra is as follows:

> A Boolean Algebra " B " is said to be "Free" (with "n" free generators), provided it contains a set G (of power "n") of free generators of B . A Set "G" of generators of a Boolean Algebra B is said to be a set of Free Generators of B if every Mapping "f" of G into an arbitrary Boolean Algebra " B' " can be extended to a homomorphism "h" of B into " B' ". *See*, [Sikorski 1964] at 42.

This definition, however, is difficult to understand intuitively in the context of Propositional Logic. Therefore, we take a more intuitive approach inspired by [Vladimirov 1994], where we look at Free Boolean Algebras as a technique for generating Subalgebras from randomly selected Elements of a Boolean Algebra. The fascinating discovery is that the Free Algebras expressed as Formulas apply to *any* Boolean Algebra, and are therefore "free" of any Attributes or restrictions specific to any particular Boolean Algebra.

As we will soon see, Free Boolean Algebras are a study in how Complementation operates in a generic Boolean Algebra. Free Boolean Algebras also provide an excellent model for the Boolean Algebra of Logic Formulas.

Attributes of Free Boolean Algebras include the following:

- Every relation between "free generators" expressed using $\vee, \wedge, \neg$ is valid for every Boolean Algebra. [Vladimirov 1994] at 69.

4.2. *Introducing Trivial and Simple Subalgebras; Using a Single Element to Generate a Subalgebra*

Can we use a single Element of a Boolean Algebra to generate a Subalgebra? The answer is "yes." A Subalgebra is defined as a Subset of an Algebra, where the Subset is Closed for the operations of Union, Intersection, and Complementation, has the same Lattice "0" and Lattice "1" Elements. The most significant point for our present purposes is that the Lattice "1" Element remains the same in the Algebra and the Subalgebra. What this means is that the Atoms (or Deemed Atoms, really) in the Subalgebra must constitute a Partition of the Base Set, so that the Union of all the Deemed Atoms is equal to the Base Set of the original Algebra. **Fig. 4-1** illustrates a P_4 Boolean Algebra and a variety of Subalgebras.

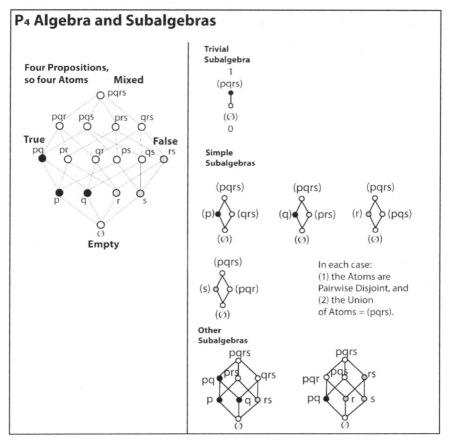

Fig. 4-1

For any given Boolean Algebra $P(X)$, there are two "**Trivial Subalgebras**": $(\emptyset, X)$ and the entire Boolean Algebra $P(X)$.

In addition to the Trivial Subalgebras, we can use any Element "x" in the Boolean Algebra to form a "**Simple Subalgebra**" consisting of the Element, its unique Complement "x'", and the "Lattice 0" and "Lattice 1" Elements: $P(x,x') = (\emptyset, x, x', X)$, where $x, x' \subseteq X$.

The remarkable point to note is that the formula that we have just provided for creating a Simple Subalgebra, works for *any* Element of *any* Boolean Algebra, which we refer to as the Domain. **Fig. 4-2** illustrates this point for several different Domains.

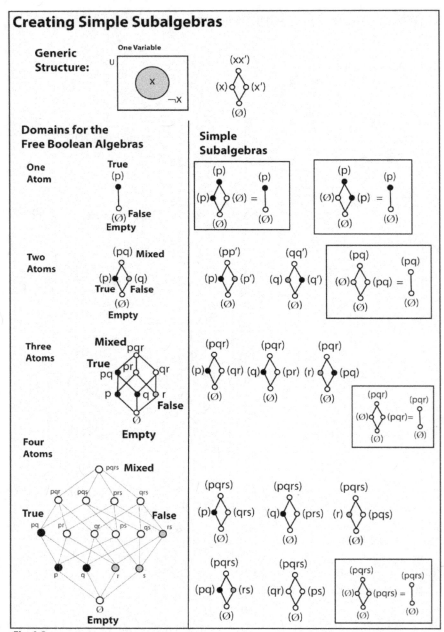

Fig. 4-2

Note that if the number of Atoms in the generated Subalgebra is less than the number of Variables in the Formula, then there will be two or more copies of the Subalgebra. We can simplify by Mapping Elements to a single copy, as illustrated by the Subalgebras enclosed in a box.

4.3. Subalgebras Generated by Two or More Elements

Can we use two or more Elements of a Boolean Algebra to generate a Subalgebra? Again, the answer is "yes." We do so by creating a set of formulas that will work for *any* selection of Elements from *any* Boolean Algebra. (Again, the word "free" reflects the fact that the formulas are a result of the laws of Boolean Algebra alone, and are free from any other restrictions.)

We start with a Subalgebra generated by two Elements of a Domain Boolean Algebra. If we knew for certain that that two Elements selected from the Domain Boolean Algebra were Disjoint, then we could simply use the "Sum of Atoms Approach" to add the two Subalgebras together. *See,* [Veatch 2016] at 226. However, since two Elements of a Boolean Algebra chosen at random may not be Disjoint, we need to create a formula that ensures that our new Subalgebra has Disjoint Atoms (or Pairwise Disjoint Deemed Atoms, really) in the bottom row of the Subalgebra. To do this, we ask: in how many ways may two Elements be related to one another? The answer is suggested by the classic Venn Diagram with two over-lapping circles. *See,* **Fig. 4-3** and **Fig. 4-4**, illustrating how we use two-Variable formulas to generate Subalgebras for *any* Boolean Algebra Domain. **Fig. 4-3** illustrates how the two-Variable formula works for a one-Atom Domain; and **Fig. 4-4** illustrates how the two-Variable formula works for a four-Atom Domain.

Note that in MWN Propositional Logic, the symbol " $\neg$ " is used only with Logic Formulas in an Order 3 Universe of Discourse, and in that context, it is equivalent to Complementation denoted by " $\_'$ ". Therefore, we use the two symbols " $\neg$ " and " $\_'$ " interchangeably. Since we are using " $\neg$ " to mean "Complementation," the rules relating to Free Algebras and Generators apply to all Boolean Algebras, so arguably we should use Complementation " $\_'$ " instead of Logic Negation " $\neg$ ". However, our primary focus in this book is on the use of Free Algebras in the Order 3 Universe of Discourse of Logic Formulas. In that context, it is less confusing if we use the symbols traditionally used in Logic. It is critically important, however, to understand that the rules relating to Free Algebras are based upon Complementation generally, and are not limited to Sign Reversal or concepts of Truth Value.

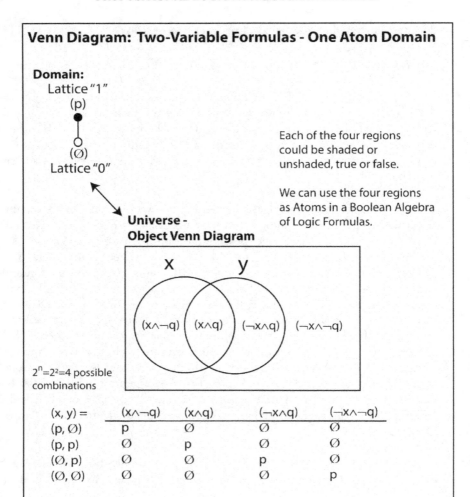

Venn Diagram: Two-Variable Formulas - One Atom Domain

Domain:
Lattice "1"
(p)

(∅)
Lattice "0"

Universe -
Object Venn Diagram

Each of the four regions
could be shaded or
unshaded, true or false.

We can use the four regions
as Atoms in a Boolean Algebra
of Logic Formulas.

x   y

(x∧¬q)   (x∧q)   (¬x∧q)   (¬x∧¬q)

$2^n = 2^2 = 4$ possible
combinations

(x, y) =	(x∧¬q)	(x∧q)	(¬x∧q)	(¬x∧¬q)
(p, ∅)	p	∅	∅	∅
(p, p)	∅	p	∅	∅
(∅, p)	∅	∅	p	∅
(∅, ∅)	∅	∅	∅	p

There are certain rules that are unique to the one-Atom, two-Element Domain:
(1) only one of the four Atoms is True; and three are False.
(2) every Atom maps to either "Lattice 1" or "Lattice 0."

Fig. 4-3

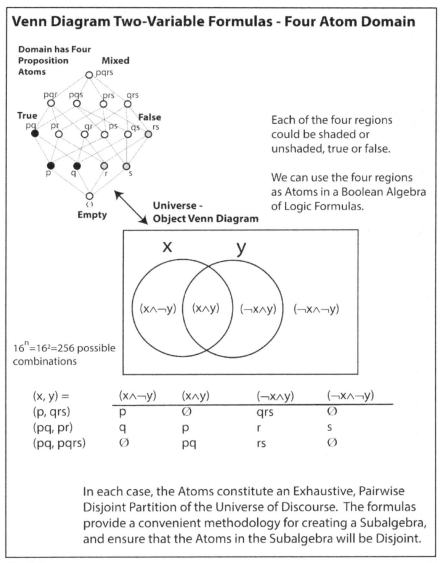

Fig. 4-4

We see that any two Elements represented by "x" and "y" selected from the Domain Boolean Algebra may be related to each other in one of four ways: $(x \wedge y),(x \wedge y'),(x' \wedge y),(x' \wedge y')$; or equivalently $(x \wedge y),(x \wedge \neg y),(\neg x \wedge y),(\neg x \wedge \neg y)$. As with any Venn Diagram representation of two Sets, the diagram shows all possible relationships between the particular Sets, but some or all of the possibilities may be Empty. By using the four possible relationships as Atoms for a new Boolean Algebra, we can generate a Lattice representing all possible combinations. To generate a Subalgebra, we simply select any two Elements from the Boolean Algebra Domain, and solve the Boolean Expressions. For Subalgebras with less than four distinct Atoms, the result is a repeating pattern of a given Subalgebra.

Fig. 4-5 illustrates how a three-Variable formula works for a one-Atom Domain; and **Fig. 4-6** illustrates how a three-Variable formula works for a four-Atom Domain.

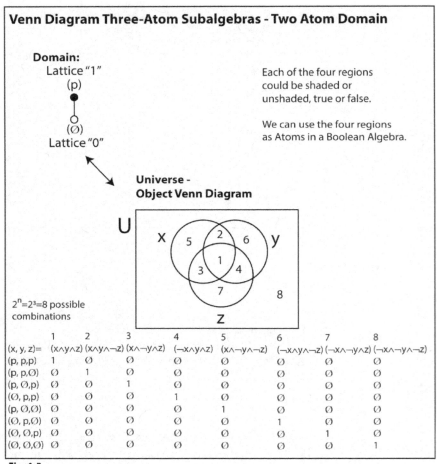

Venn Diagram Three-Atom Subalgebras - Two Atom Domain

Domain:
Lattice "1"
(p)

(Ø)
Lattice "0"

Each of the four regions could be shaded or unshaded, true or false.

We can use the four regions as Atoms in a Boolean Algebra.

**Universe -
Object Venn Diagram**

$2^n=2^3=8$ possible combinations

	1	2	3	4	5	6	7	8
$(x, y, z)=$	$(x{\wedge}y{\wedge}z)$	$(x{\wedge}y{\wedge}\neg z)$	$(x{\wedge}\neg y{\wedge}z)$	$(\neg x{\wedge}y{\wedge}z)$	$(x{\wedge}\neg y{\wedge}\neg z)$	$(\neg x{\wedge}y{\wedge}\neg z)$	$(\neg x{\wedge}\neg y{\wedge}z)$	$(\neg x{\wedge}\neg y{\wedge}\neg z)$
(p, p,p)	1	Ø	Ø	Ø	Ø	Ø	Ø	Ø
$(p, p,Ø)$	Ø	1	Ø	Ø	Ø	Ø	Ø	Ø
$(p, Ø,p)$	Ø	Ø	1	Ø	Ø	Ø	Ø	Ø
$(Ø, p,p)$	Ø	Ø	Ø	1	Ø	Ø	Ø	Ø
$(p, Ø,Ø)$	Ø	Ø	Ø	Ø	1	Ø	Ø	Ø
$(Ø, p,Ø)$	Ø	Ø	Ø	Ø	Ø	1	Ø	Ø
$(Ø, Ø,p)$	Ø	Ø	Ø	Ø	Ø	Ø	1	Ø
$(Ø, Ø,Ø)$	Ø	Ø	Ø	Ø	Ø	Ø	Ø	1

Fig. 4-5

Venn Diagram Three-Variable Subalgebras - Four Atom Domain

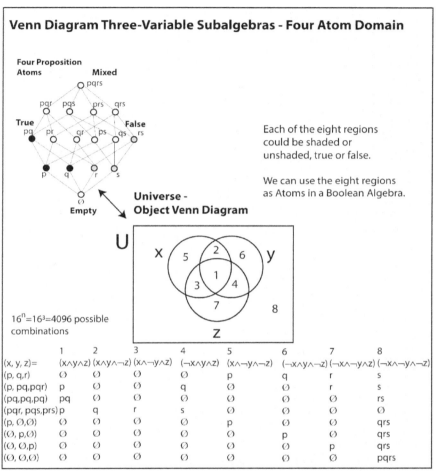

Each of the eight regions could be shaded or unshaded, true or false.

We can use the eight regions as Atoms in a Boolean Algebra.

Universe - Object Venn Diagram

$16^n=16^3=4096$ possible combinations

$(x, y, z)=$	1 $(x{\wedge}y{\wedge}z)$	2 $(x{\wedge}y{\wedge}{\neg}z)$	3 $(x{\wedge}{\neg}y{\wedge}z)$	4 $({\neg}x{\wedge}y{\wedge}z)$	5 $(x{\wedge}{\neg}y{\wedge}{\neg}z)$	6 $({\neg}x{\wedge}y{\wedge}{\neg}z)$	7 $({\neg}x{\wedge}{\neg}y{\wedge}z)$	8 $({\neg}x{\wedge}{\neg}y{\wedge}{\neg}z)$
(p, q,r)	∅	∅	∅	∅	p	q	r	s
(p, pq,pqr)	p	∅	∅	q	∅	∅	r	s
(pq,pq,pq)	pq	∅	∅	∅	∅	∅	∅	rs
(pqr, pqs,prs)	p	q	r	s	∅	∅	∅	∅
$(p, ∅,∅)$	∅	∅	∅	∅	p	∅	∅	qrs
$(∅, p,∅)$	∅	∅	∅	∅	∅	p	∅	qrs
$(∅, ∅,p)$	∅	∅	∅	∅	∅	∅	p	qrs
$(∅, ∅,∅)$	∅	∅	∅	∅	∅	∅	∅	pqrs

Fig. 4-6

4.4. Canonical Representation of an Element of a Subalgebra; Relationship to Disjunctive and Conjunctive Boolean Normal Form

There are many equivalent representations for an Element of a Subalgebra. We saw this earlier in **Chapter 3**, where we saw there was an infinite number of Boolean Expressions, but only 2^n distinct Boolean Functions. In order to simplify the situation, there is a so-called "canonical representation," which is a standard format used for writing a formula representing an Element of a Subalgebra. The standard format uses a simple formula "x", its Complement "x'", and the Operations Union "$\cup$" and Intersection "$\cap$". *See*, [Vladimirov 1994] at 44-45.

We can write equivalent formulas using either the notation of Set Theory (with Complementation) or Logic Formulas (with Negation), so long as we keep in mind that in MWN, Negation is defined only for Order Three Logic Formulas:

- Canonical Representation (DBNF):

  "Lattice 1" = $\bigcup (x_1^i \cap x_2^i \cap ... x_n^i)$, where i = 0, 1 and

  $x^0 = x, x^1 = x'$, and "n" is the number of Variables in the formula.

- Disjunctive Boolean Normal Form:

  "Lattice 1" = $\vee (x_1^i \wedge x_2^i \wedge ... x_n^i)$, where i = 0, 1 and

  $x^0 = x, x^1 = \neg x$, and "n" is the number of Variables in the formula.

Each Term "x_j^i", sometimes referred to as a Clause, is an Atom in the Boolean Algebra of formulas. Each Atom contains, respect to each Variable, either the Variable or its Complement. There are 2^n Atoms, where "n" is the number of Variables. If the number of Atoms in the Subalgebra is less than the number of Variables, then a repeating Map of the Subalgebra is created which we can simplify to a single copy.

Table 4-1 illustrates the formulas for one, two, and three Variables in their Canonical Representation and in DBNF.

Table 4-1

No. of Var.	Canonical Representation (DBNF)	DBNF
1	$(x),(x')$	$(x),(\neg x)$
2	$(x \cap y),(x \cap y'),$ $(x' \cap y),(x' \cap y')$	$(x \wedge y),(x \wedge \neg y),$ $(\neg x \wedge y),(\neg x \wedge \neg y)$
3	$(x \cap y \cap z),(x \cap y \cap z'),$ $(x \cap y' \cap z),(x' \cap y \cap z),$ $(x \cap y' \cap z'),(x' \cap y \cap z'),$ $(x' \cap y' \cap z),(x' \cap y' \cap z')$	$(x \wedge y \wedge z),(x \wedge y \wedge \neg z),$ $(x \wedge \neg y \wedge z),(\neg x \wedge y \wedge z),$ $(x \wedge \neg y \wedge \neg z),(\neg x \wedge y \wedge \neg z),$ $(\neg x \wedge \neg y \wedge z),(\neg x \wedge \neg y \wedge \neg z)$

We can also write a Dual formulation for Conjunction Boolean Normal Form:

- Canonical Representation (CBNF):

  "Lattice 0" $= \bigcap (x_1^i \cup x_2^i \cup ... x_n^i)$, where i = 0, 1 and

  $x^0 = x, x^1 = x'$, and "n" is the number of Variables in the formula.

- Conjunctive Boolean Normal Form:

  "Lattice 0" $= \bigwedge (x_1^i \vee x_2^i \vee ... x_n^i)$, where i = 0, 1 and

  $x^0 = x, x^1 = \neg x$, and "n" is the number of Variables in the formula.

Table 4-2 illustrates the formulas for one, two, and three Variables in their Canonical Representation and in CBNF.

Table 4-2

No. of Var.	Canonical Representation (CBNF)	CBNF
1	$(x),(x')$	$(x),(\neg x)$
2	$(x \cup y),(x \cup y'),$ $(x' \cup y),(x' \cup y')$	$(x \vee y),(x \vee \neg y),$ $(\neg x \vee y),(\neg x \vee \neg y)$
3	$(x \cup y \cup z),(x \cup y \cup z'),$ $(x \cup y' \cup z),(x' \cup y \cup z),$ $(x \cup y' \cup z'),(x' \cup y \cup z'),$ $(x' \cup y' \cup z),(x' \cup y' \cup z')$	$(x \vee y \vee z),(x \vee y \vee \neg z),$ $(x \vee \neg y \vee z),(\neg x \vee y \vee z),$ $(x \vee \neg y \vee \neg z),(\neg x \vee y \vee \neg z),$ $(\neg x \vee \neg y \vee z),(\neg x \vee \neg y \vee \neg z)$

4.5. Any Boolean Algebra Can Serve as the Domain of Any Free Boolean Algebra of Formulas in Canonical or Normal Form

Although we are studying Propositional Logic in this book, and we are looking for a mathematical model to apply to the Boolean Algebra of Logic Formulas, it is important to understand how broad the concept of a Free Boolean Algebra really is. It works well as a model for Logic Formulas where the Domain is a Boolean Algebra of Propositions, but it applies equally to a Boolean Algebra of Ideas, or any other Boolean Algebra. *See*, **Fig. 4-7**.

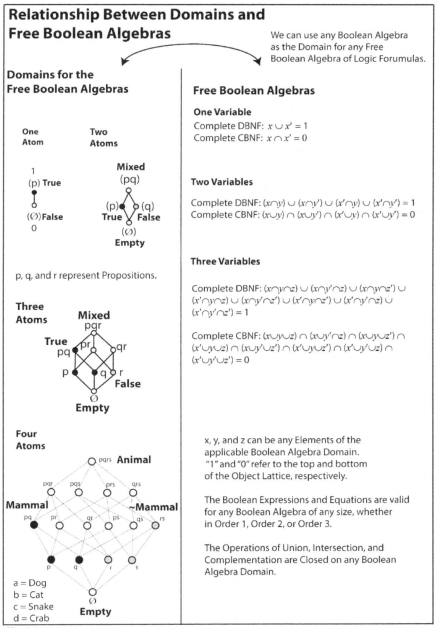

Relationship Between Domains and Free Boolean Algebras

We can use any Boolean Algebra as the Domain for any Free Boolean Algebra of Logic Forumulas.

Domains for the Free Boolean Algebras

p, q, and r represent Propositions.

a = Dog
b = Cat
c = Snake
d = Crab

Free Boolean Algebras

One Variable

Complete DBNF: $x \cup x' = 1$
Complete CBNF: $x \cap x' = 0$

Two Variables

Complete DBNF: $(x \cap y) \cup (x \cap y') \cup (x' \cap y) \cup (x' \cap y') = 1$
Complete CBNF: $(x \cup y) \cap (x \cup y') \cap (x' \cup y) \cap (x' \cup y') = 0$

Three Variables

Complete DBNF: $(x \cap y \cap z) \cup (x \cap y' \cap z) \cup (x \cap y \cap z') \cup (x' \cap y \cap z) \cup (x \cap y' \cap z') \cup (x' \cap y \cap z') \cup (x' \cap y' \cap z) \cup (x' \cap y' \cap z') = 1$

Complete CBNF: $(x \cup y \cup z) \cap (x \cup y' \cap z) \cap (x \cup y \cup z') \cap (x' \cup y \cup z) \cap (x \cup y' \cup z') \cap (x' \cup y \cup z') \cap (x' \cup y' \cup z) \cap (x' \cup y' \cup z') = 0$

x, y, and z can be any Elements of the applicable Boolean Algebra Domain. "1" and "0" refer to the top and bottom of the Object Lattice, respectively.

The Boolean Expressions and Equations are valid for any Boolean Algebra of any size, whether in Order 1, Order 2, or Order 3.

The Operations of Union, Intersection, and Complementation are Closed on any Boolean Algebra Domain.

Fig. 4-7

Any Boolean Algebra can serve as the Domain for any Free Algebra with "n" Generators. There is no required relationship between the number of Atoms in the Domain and the number of Variables in the Free Algebra. As noted previously, if the number of unique Atoms in the generated Subalgebra is less than the number of Variables, multiple copies of the Subalgebra will be generated, but we can simplify to a single copy.

4.6. Creating Boolean Algebras and Boolean Lattices from the Logic Formula Atoms

As illustrated in **Fig. 4-8**, the 2^n Clauses in DBNF or CBNF, as the case may be, formed from the Variables and their Complements, can be used to create a Boolean Algebra or Boolean Lattice. *See*, [Evenden 1962].

Free Algebras with Generators

The Domain for the Variables or Generators x, y, z, ... can be the Elements of any Boolean Algebra, whether Ideas, Propositions, or something else.

Zero Variables

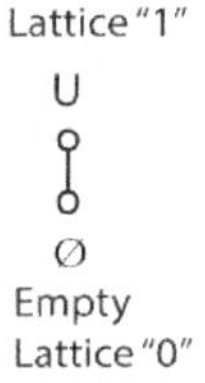
Lattice "1"
U
∅
Empty
Lattice "0"

Generators: n = 0, Zero Variables
Atoms: $m = 2^n = 2^0 = 1$ Atom
Boolean Polynomials: $2^m = 2^1 = 2$ Elements

One Variable

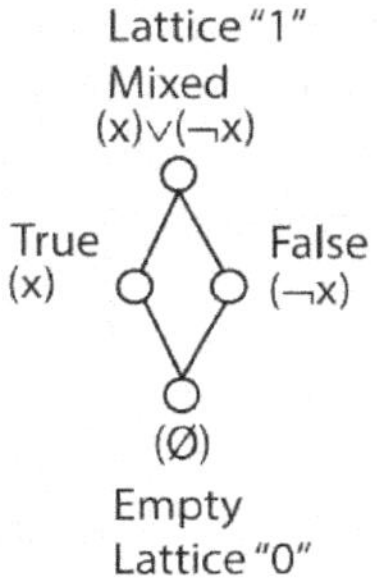
Lattice "1"
Mixed
(x)∨(¬x)
True
(x)
False
(¬x)
(∅)
Empty
Lattice "0"

Generators: n = 1, One Variable
Atoms: $m = 2^n = 2^1 = 2$ Atoms
Boolean Polynomials: $2^m = 2^2 = 4$ Elements

Two Variables - DBNF

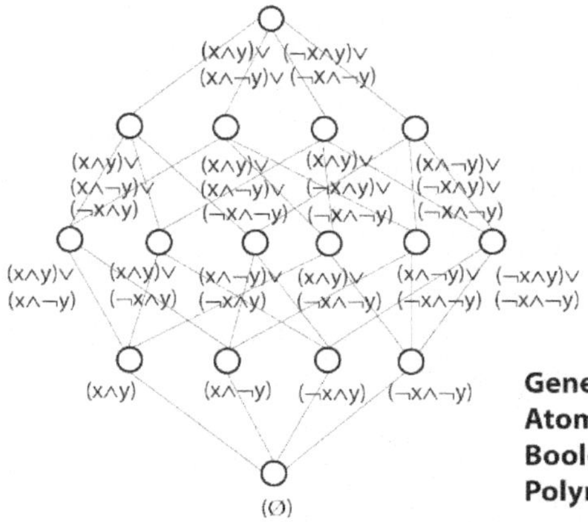
(x∧y)∨ (¬x∧y)∨
(x∧¬y)∨ (¬x∧¬y)
(x∧y)∨ (x∧¬y)∨ (¬x∧y)
(x∧y)∨ (x∧¬y)∨ (¬x∧¬y)
(x∧y)∨ (¬x∧y)∨ (¬x∧¬y)
(x∧¬y)∨ (¬x∧y)∨ (¬x∧¬y)
(x∧y)∨ (x∧¬y)
(x∧y)∨ (¬x∧y)
(x∧¬y)∨ (¬x∧y)
(x∧y)∨ (¬x∧¬y)
(x∧¬y)∨ (¬x∧¬y)
(¬x∧y)∨ (¬x∧¬y)
(x∧y)
(x∧¬y)
(¬x∧y)
(¬x∧¬y)
(∅)

Generators: n = 2, Two Variables
Atoms: $m = 2^n = 2^2 = 4$ Atoms
Boolean Polynomials: $2^m = 2^4 = 16$ Elements

Fig. 4-8

4.7. *Value Maps and Subalgebras*

If we solve the Boolean Formulas in our Free Boolean Algebra, we get what we refer to as an **"Order Two Value Map"** or simply a **"Value Map."** The Lattice of Logic Formulas is an Order 3 Lattice, but the Values are Mapped from the Order 2 Domain in the process of creating a Subalgebra.

In Traditional Propositional Logic, the Value Map is used as a Lattice of Truth Values for the Logic Formulas. In MWN Propositional Logic, however, we take a different approach to Truth Value. We use the Order Two Value Map to determine the Truth Values of Atoms in Order Three, but then we use the regular MWN techniques to determine the Truth Values of the Compound Elements in the Lattice.

What we learn through our study of Free Boolean Algebras, is that a Value Map is really a reflection of a Subalgebra generated by the selection of any "n" Elements from any Domain Boolean Algebra. The Value Map is based upon Complementation relationships and arguably has nothing to do with Truth Values at all.

While it is true that the Value Map assigns a "Lattice 1" or "lattice 0" Element to each Logic Formula if we are using a Domain with one Atom, as soon we use a Domain with more than one Atom, this is no longer the case. Rather, we generate a Subalgebra that may contain multiple copies of the Elements: (Mixed, True, False, Empty).

The implication is that, arguably, it is a mere coincidence that the Value Map appears to coincide with Truth Values in Traditional Propositional Logic. Therefore, we must look deeper to determine whether there is an alternative means of assigning Truth Values, that applies whether the Order Domain has 1, 2, 3, or more Atoms.

4.8. *Every Boolean Expression is Equivalent to One of the 2^m Boolean Functions, where m = 2^n*

It is well-established in the study of Propositional Logic, that every Boolean Expression is equivalent to one of the 2^m Boolean Functions, where m = 2^n and "n" is the number of Variables. *See*, [Abbott 1969] at 216-217. For this reason, we are justified in focusing our attention on Boolean Formulas written in DBNF or CBNF.

4.9. Examples of Free Algebras

In **Fig. 4-9** through **Fig. 4-14**, we provide examples of Free Algebras with two Generators, but where the Order 2 Domains have 1, 2, 3, or 4 Atoms.

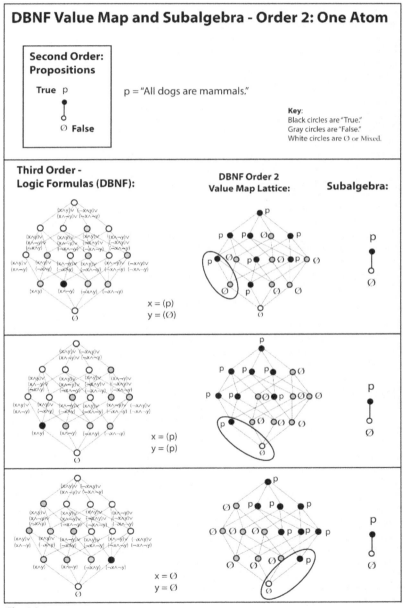

Fig. 4-9

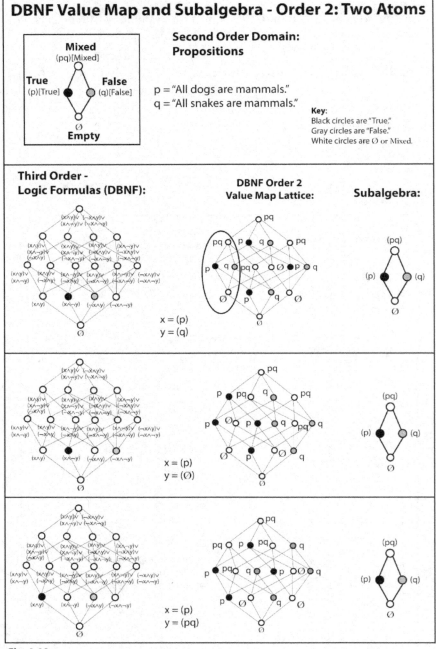

Fig. 4-10

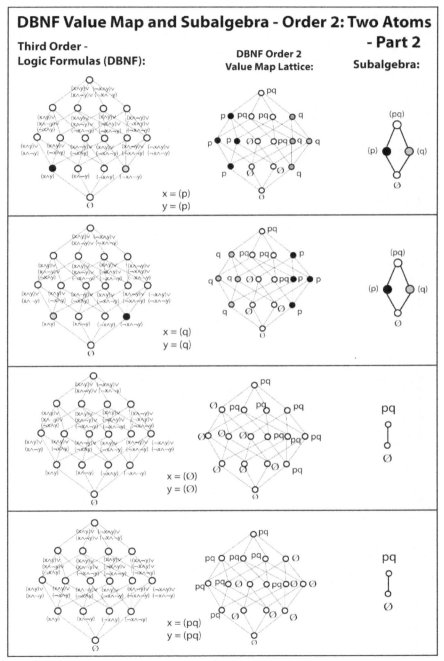

Fig. 4-11

DBNF Value Map and Subalgebra –
Order 2: Two Atoms – Part 3

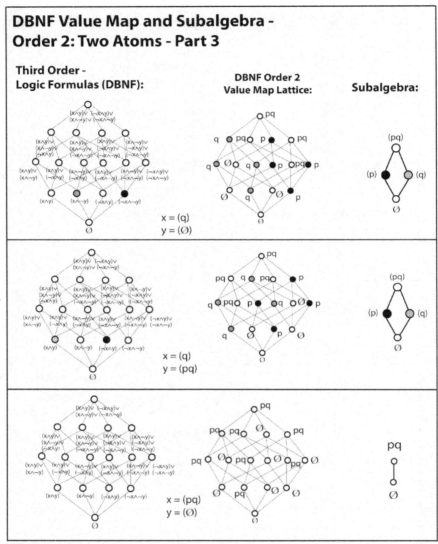

Fig. 4-12

114

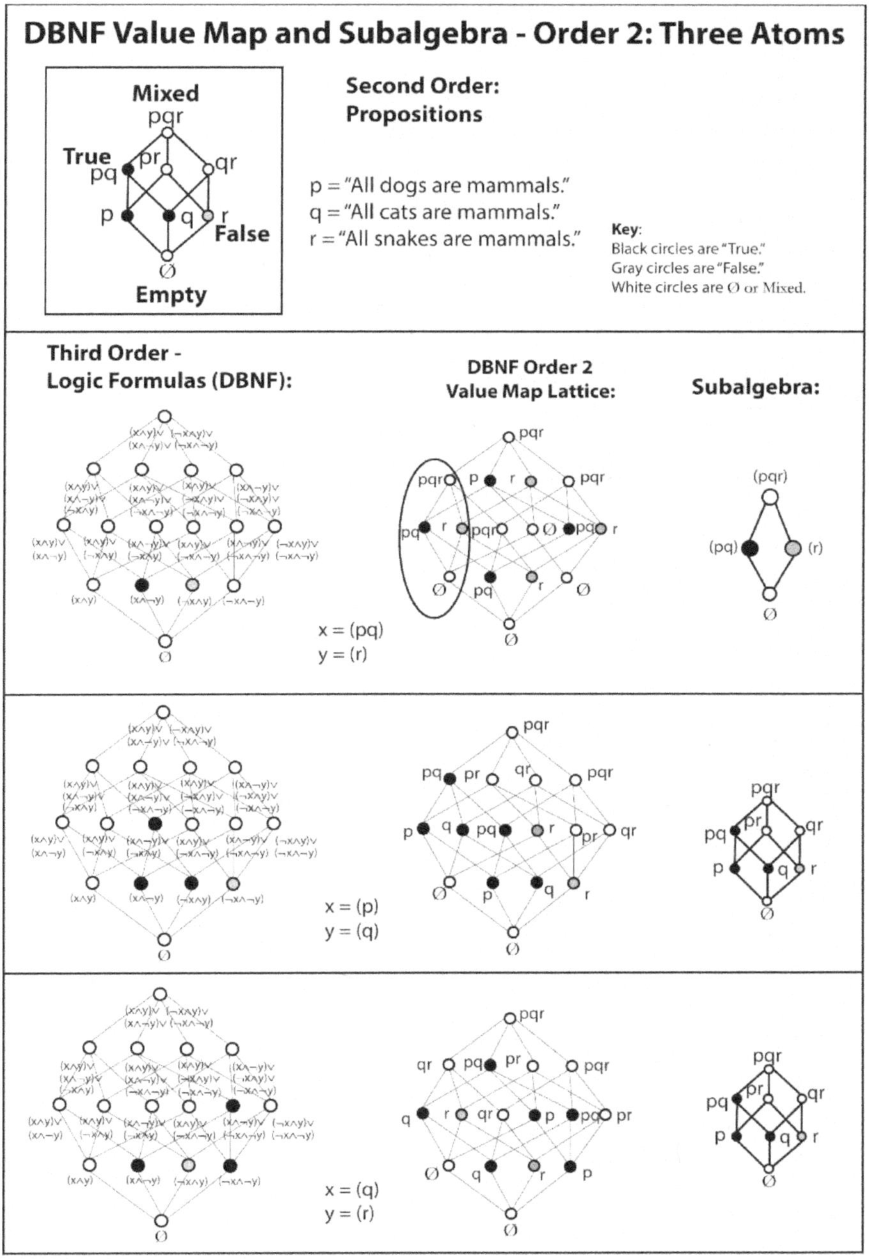

DBNF Value Map and Subalgebra - Order 2: Three Atoms

Mixed
pqr

True
pq   pr   qr

p   q   r
False

Ø
Empty

Second Order:
Propositions

p = "All dogs are mammals."
q = "All cats are mammals."
r = "All snakes are mammals."

Key:
Black circles are "True."
Gray circles are "False."
White circles are O or Mixed.

Third Order -
Logic Formulas (DBNF):

DBNF Order 2
Value Map Lattice:

Subalgebra:

x = (pq)
y = (r)

x = (p)
y = (q)

x = (q)
y = (r)

Fig. 4-13

115

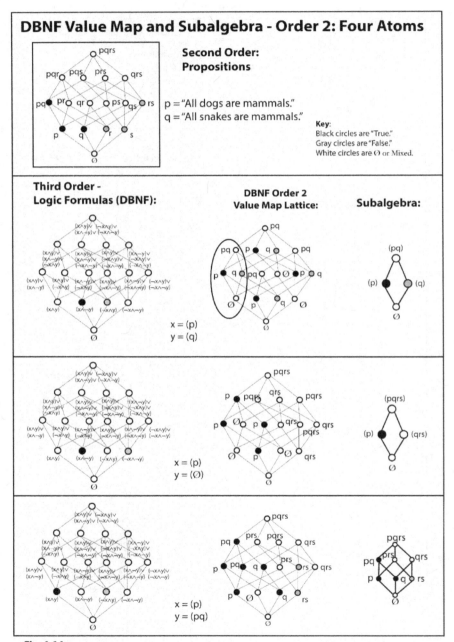

Fig. 4-14

4.10.   *References, Historical Notes, and Further Reading*

For a discussion of Free Boolean Algebras, *see*:

[Birkhoff and Mac Lane 1999] at 491-493.

[Vladimirov 1994] at 68-69.

[Abbott 1969] at 216-217.

5. UNIVERSE OF DISCOURSE: IDEAS (FIRST ORDER)

In this Chapter, we examine the Universe of Discourse of Ideas generally, as it is the source of Subjects and Predicates that combine to form Propositions.

In MWN, we are interested in Propositional Logic as it relates to the study of the Mathematics of Ideas generally, not just as a standalone field of study. In order to understand what role Propositional Logic plays in the overall Mathematics of Ideas, it is important to understand that the foundation of Propositions is built from Ideas. We speak of Ideas as being of the **"First Order"** or **"Order 1"**. A Proposition is a True/False Declarative Sentence about the relationship between two Ideas, so we speak of Propositions as being of the **"Second Order"** or **"Order 2"**. A Logic Formula is a Set of Propositional Variables and their Negations (*e.g.*, "x" and "NOT x" or "$\neg$ x") connected by AND ($\wedge$) and OR ($\vee$), which determine the Truth Value of the Logic Formula as a function of the Truth Value of the Propositions. We speak of Logic Formulas as being of the **"Third Order"** or **"Order 3"**. An important theme in MWN is that we need to understand the relationships among the underlying Ideas that constitute the Subjects and Predicates of Propositions to truly understand Propositional Logic.

5.1. Three Related Universes of Discourse: Ideas, Propositions, and Logic Formulas

Fig. 5-1 illustrates the three primary Universes of Discourse that we use in MWN in the study of Propositional Logic. The first is the U_D of Ideas that are the subject matter of the Propositions. While not a Propositional

Logic in itself, the U$_D$ of Ideas is important because the Set relationships among the Ideas determine the Truth Value of any Propositions that we create regarding those Ideas. The second U$_D$ is the Universe of True/False Propositions. We can view this as a U$_D$ consisting of a single True and a single False Proposition, or as a U$_D$ where all Propositions are consolidated into two Deemed Atoms, although later we will see that we can subdivide each Deemed Atom as desired. The Third U$_D$ is the Universe of Logic Formulas using Propositional Variables representing True/False Propositions and their Negations (*e.g.*, x and ¬ x), along with Logic Operations AND (∧) and OR (∨). We will see that the Truth Values of the Propositions will in turn determine the Truth Values of the Logic Formulas.

In **Fig. 5-1**, each Element of the Lattice of Logic Formulas is either Homogeneous or Heterogeneous as to any particular Attribute, *i.e.*, in this case the Attributes "True" and "False." The Homogeneous Elements shaded black consist of Atoms all of which inherit the Attribute True; the Homogeneous Elements shaded gray consist of Atoms all of which inherit the Attribute False. The unshaded white Heterogeneous Elements, other than the Empty Set (∅), are Mixed Elements with an Indeterminate Truth Value.

Relationships Among Universes of Discourse of Ideas, Propositions, and Logic Formulas

In Propositional Logic, we use three prinicpal Universes of Discourse: Ideas, Propositions, and Logic Formulas. The Set relationships in the Uᴅ of Ideas determine the Truth Value of the Propositions in the Uᴅ of Propositions, which in turn determine the Truth Values of the Logic Formulas in the third Uᴅ.

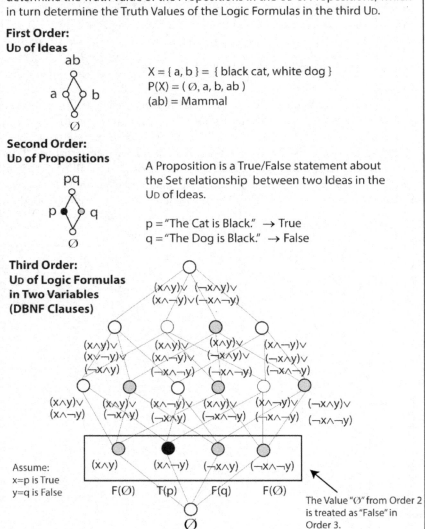

First Order:
Uᴅ of Ideas

ab

a b

Ø

$X = \{ a, b \} = \{$ black cat, white dog $\}$
$P(X) = (Ø, a, b, ab)$
$(ab) = $ Mammal

Second Order:
Uᴅ of Propositions

pq

p q

Ø

A Proposition is a True/False statement about the Set relationship between two Ideas in the Uᴅ of Ideas.

p = "The Cat is Black." → True
q = "The Dog is Black." → False

Third Order:
Uᴅ of Logic Formulas
in Two Variables
(DBNF Clauses)

$(x∧y)∨ (¬x∧y)∨$
$(x∧¬y)∨(¬x∧¬y)$

$(x∧y)∨$
$(x∨¬y)∨$
$(¬x∧y)$

$(x∧y)∨$
$(x∧¬y)∨$
$(¬x∧¬y)$

$(x∧y)∨$
$(¬x∧y)∨$
$(¬x∧¬y)$

$(x∧¬y)∨$
$(¬x∧y)∨$
$(¬x∧¬y)$

$(x∧y)∨$
$(x∧¬y)$

$(x∧y)∨$
$(¬x∧y)$

$(x∧¬y)∨$
$(¬x∧y)$

$(x∧y)∨$
$(¬x∧¬y)$

$(x∧¬y)∨$
$(¬x∧¬y)$

$(¬x∧y)∨$
$(¬x∧¬y)$

$(x∧y)$ $(x∧¬y)$ $(¬x∧y)$ $(¬x∧¬y)$

Assume:
x=p is True
y=q is False

F(Ø)   T(p)   F(q)   F(Ø)

Ø

The Value "◌" from Order 2 is treated as "False" in Order 3.

Fig. 5-1

5.2. *Individual Ideas are the Source of Subjects and Predicates that Form Propositions*

In MWN, the Universe of Ideas is the source of "Subjects" and Predicates" that combine to form "Propositions." Since in MWN we are interested in eventually Mapping the entire Universe of Ideas to a Lattice-based Knowledge Representation Structure, it is critical that we understand Propositional Logic in the overall context of the Universe of Ideas. Although such a Knowledge Representation Structure has not yet been created, in theory every Idea that we are capable of thinking could be mapped to a single lattice.

5.3. *Any Two Ideas are Related by One of the Five Two-Set Relationships*

Any two Ideas in a lattice-based Knowledge Representation Structure are related to each other in one of five ways. We will define Propositions in **Section 6.2**, but for now the important point to understand is that a Proposition describes the Set Relationship between two Ideas. We discuss the philosophical nature of Ideas in detail in MWN Vol. 1, but the key point for our present purposes is that we make certain simplifying assumptions that allow us to manipulate Ideas more easily in mathematical terms, including the following:

- We assume that Atomic Ideas exist, and that every Idea is either an Atomic Idea or a Compound made up of Atomic Ideas.
- We assume that the number of Atoms is Finite.

Of course, any time that we make an assumption, we need to exercise care, and regularly revisit the assumption to ensure that it remains valid. For example, an Idea that we assumed was an Atom may later turn out to be a Compound. If so, we can update our list of Atoms to take this into account. The good news here is that the mathematics of Power Sets and Boolean Algebras allows us to Subdivide and Consolidate Atoms as we deem necessary, and in effect create Deemed Atoms, all without detriment to our overall Knowledge Representation Structure. This is one of the primary motivations for developing the MWN system upon a foundation of Boolean Algebra.

We now understand that a Proposition sets forth the relationship between two Ideas. How many relationships are possible between any two Ideas? It turns out that there are only five possible "**Two-Set Relationships**," where the order of the Ideas is relevant in the case of subsets and supersets, *i.e.*, (a, ab) is different from (ab, a). *See*, **Fig. 5-2**.

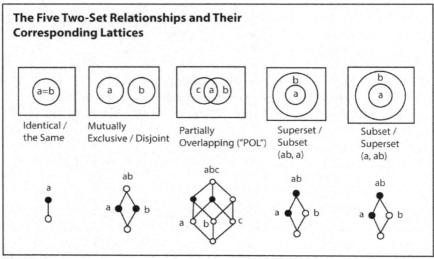

The Five Two-Set Relationships and Their Corresponding Lattices

Identical / the Same   Mutually Exclusive / Disjoint   Partially Overlapping ("POL")   Superset / Subset (ab, a)   Subset / Superset (a, ab)

Fig. 5-2

This is a significant point, because it means that to have mathematical precision in any analysis of the Truth Values of Propositions, we need to understand which of the five Two-Set Relationships governs the Subject and Predicate of any given Proposition.

Table 5-1 lists the symbols that we use in MWN to represent the five Two-Set Relationships.

Table 5-1

Set Relationship	Symbol
Identical	=
Subset-Superset	⊂
Superset-Subset	⊃
Disjoint	Ω
Partially-Overlapping (POL)	Π

5.4. Objects v. Attributes; Duality

We know from our study of Propositions that a Proposition refers to the relationship between two Sets. In this Section we will demonstrate that Propositions refer only to the five Two-Set Relationships between Object Sets, as opposed to Attribute Sets. While the five Two-Set Relationships apply equally to Sets of Objects and Sets of Attributes, we will see that "Propositions" refer to the relationships between Object Sets, not Attribute Sets. Attribute Sets, however, are particularly helpful to illustrate the inheritance of Attributes.

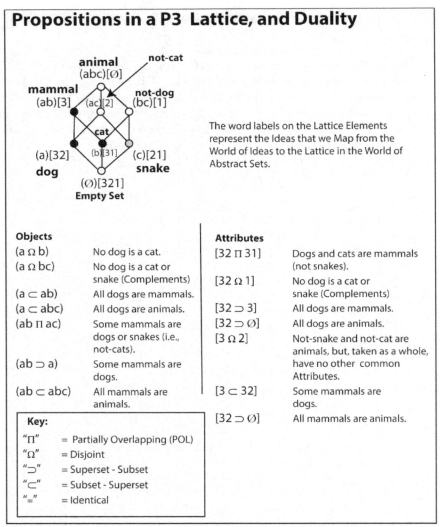

Propositions in a P3 Lattice, and Duality

The word labels on the Lattice Elements represent the Ideas that we Map from the World of Ideas to the Lattice in the World of Abstract Sets.

Objects		Attributes	
(a Ω b)	No dog is a cat.	[32 Π 31]	Dogs and cats are mammals (not snakes).
(a Ω bc)	No dog is a cat or snake (Complements)	[32 Ω 1]	No dog is a cat or snake (Complements)
(a ⊂ ab)	All dogs are mammals.	[32 ⊃ 3]	All dogs are mammals.
(a ⊂ abc)	All dogs are animals.	[32 ⊃ Ø]	All dogs are animals.
(ab Π ac)	Some mammals are dogs or snakes (i.e., not-cats).	[3 Ω 2]	Not-snake and not-cat are animals, but, taken as a whole, have no other common Attributes.
(ab ⊃ a)	Some mammals are dogs.		
(ab ⊂ abc)	All mammals are animals.	[3 ⊂ 32]	Some mammals are dogs.
		[32 ⊃ Ø]	All mammals are animals.

Key:

"Π"	= Partially Overlapping (POL)	
"Ω"	= Disjoint	
"⊃"	= Superset - Subset	
"⊂"	= Subset - Superset	
"="	= Identical	

Fig. 5-3

In **Fig. 5-3**, for example, the Object Signature "(a)" does not tell us anything about the Attributes of "a". We can, however, calculate the Attribute Signature of (a) in P_3 as [32]. The Attribute Signature tells us that (a) inherits the Attributes of each of [3], [2], and [Ø] (if we are working within a Universe of Discourse).

Fig. 5-3 also illustrates how we can derive Propositions from the Set relationships exhibited in the lattice. **Table 5-2** lists several such Propositions sorted by the applicable Two-Set Relationships.

Table 5-2

	Object Sets	Attribute Sets	(A+O) or (E+I)	Proposition
1	(a Ω b)	[32 Π 31]	E	**Object**: No dog is a cat. **Attribute**: Dogs and cats are mammals (not snakes).
2	(a Ω b)	[32 Π 31]	O	**Object**: Some dogs are not cats. **Attribute**: Dogs and cats are mammals.
3	(a Ω bc)	[32 Ω 1]	E	**Object**: No dog is a cat or snake (*i.e.*, not-dog). **Attribute**: Same.
4	(a Ω bc)	[32 Ω 1]	O	**Object**: Some dogs are not cats or snakes (*i.e.*, not-dog). **Attribute**: Same.
5	(a ⊂ ab)	[32 ⊃ 3]	A	**Object**: All dogs are mammals. **Attribute**: All dogs are mammals.
6	(a ⊂ ab)	[32 ⊃ 3]	I	**Object**: Some dogs are mammals. **Attribute**: All dogs are mammals.
7	(ab ⊃ a)	[3 ⊂ 32]	I	**Object**: Some mammals are dogs. **Attribute**: Some mammals are dogs.
8	(ab ⊃ a)	[3 ⊂ 32]	O	**Object**: Some mammals are not dogs. **Attribute**: Some mammals are dogs.
9	(ab Π ac)	[3 Ω 2]	I	**Object**: Some mammals are not-cats. **Attribute**: Mammals (not-snake) and not-cat are animals, but, taken as a whole, have no other common Attributes exhibited by all Elements.
10	(ab Π ac)	[3 Ω 2]	O	**Object**: Some mammals are cats (*i.e.*, not not-cats). **Attribute**: Not-snake and not-cat are animals, but, taken as a whole, have no other common Attributes exhibited by all Elements.

Note the Duality between Subset-Superset ($\subset$) and Superset-Subset ($\supset$) in lines five through eight. *I.e.*, if we switch from Object Sets to Attribute Sets, we substitute "$\subset$" for "$\supset$", and *vice versa*.

Disjoint pairs and POL pairs are also duals, except in the case where the Elements are Set Complements, in which case the pair of Elements is Disjoint whether expressed as Objects or as Attributes. Therefore, the pairs in lines 1, 2, 9, and 10 are Duals, whereas in lines 3 and 4 the pairs are Disjoint, whether expressed as Objects or Attributes.

If we look at the Propositions in **Table 5-2** to determine whether the Proposition reflects the Set Relationship of Objects and Attributes, we see that the Object relationships always match the Proposition. Some Propositions such as "Some dogs are not cats" are considered "True" in Classical Logic, although the Disjoint Set Relationship makes it clear in lines 1 and 2 that "No dog is a cat" is a stronger result. Similarly, the Proposition in line 4 is not as strong as the Proposition in line 3; and line 6 is not as strong as line 5.

In the case of Attribute Sets, however, the Propositions in **Table 5-2** do not match up as well with the Set Relationships. For example, in lines 1 and 2 the Sets are Disjoint, yet the Attributes are Partially Overlapping (POL) because "cats" and "dogs" share the Attribute of being "mammals." Similarly, in lines 9 and 10 the Sets are Partially Overlapping, yet the Attributes are Disjoint. (In this last case, the Attributes are POL in the sense that Mammals and not-Cats share the Attribute [$\varnothing$], which represents the Attribute "animal" for all Elements in the U_D.)

We could develop rules for reconciling Attribute Sets with Propositions, but for now it is easier simply to think of Propositions as relating to the Set relationships between Sets of Objects.

In summary, we can make the following observations about the Lattice in **Fig. 5-3**:

- A Proposition more accurately reflect the Set Relationship between two "Objects," or the "extension" in philosophical terms, as opposed to Attributes, or "intension." For example, [$32 \sqcap 31$] does not reflect the "Disjoint" Propositional relationship between "a" and "b".
- Although the five Two-Set Relationships apply to Attribute Sets, it is more helpful to think of Attribute Sets as displaying the

Inheritance of Attributes. For example, any Element with [3] in its Attribute Signature is a "mammal."

- In terms of Duality, we can make the following observations:
  - o " ⊂ " and " ⊃ " are Duals, if we also exchange the Object Signature and the Attribute Signature.
  - o " Π " and " Ω " are sometimes Duals, if we also exchange the Object Signature and the Attribute Signature, but not where the two Sets being compared are Complements.
  - o Where two Sets are Complements in the applicable Lattice, both the Object and Attribute Two-Set Relationships are Disjoint (" Ω ").

5.5. We Assert that a Set Relationship is True When We Map Ideas from the World of Ideas to a Lattice in the World of Abstract Sets

In Propositional Logic, much confusion arises if we are not careful to specify the precise point in time when we are asserting that a Set Relationship is True or False, which in turn determines the Truth Values of any related Propositions. In MWN, we assert a Set Relationship and the related Propositional Truth Values when we create a Map from the World of Ideas to a Lattice in the World of Abstract Sets. *See*, **Fig. 5-4**.

Assertion of Attribute Values and Truth Values: Mapping Attributes

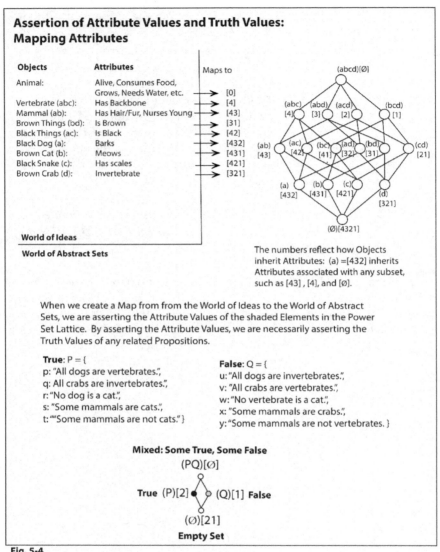

Objects	Attributes		Maps to
Animal:	Alive, Consumes Food, Grows, Needs Water, etc.	→	[0]
Vertebrate (abc):	Has Backbone	→	[4]
Mammal (ab):	Has Hair/Fur, Nurses Young	→	[43]
Brown Things (bd):	Is Brown	→	[31]
Black Things (ac):	Is Black	→	[42]
Black Dog (a):	Barks	→	[432]
Brown Cat (b):	Meows	→	[431]
Black Snake (c):	Has scales	→	[421]
Brown Crab (d):	Invertebrate	→	[321]

World of Ideas

World of Abstract Sets

The numbers reflect how Objects inherit Attributes: (a) =[432] inherits Attributes associated with any subset, such as [43] , [4], and [∅].

When we create a Map from from the World of Ideas to the World of Abstract Sets, we are asserting the Attribute Values of the shaded Elements in the Power Set Lattice. By asserting the Attribute Values, we are necessarily asserting the Truth Values of any related Propositions.

True: P = {
p: "All dogs are vertebrates.",
q: All crabs are invertebrates.",
r: "No dog is a cat.",
s: "Some mammals are cats.",
t: ""Some mammals are not cats." }

False: Q = {
u: "All dogs are invertebrates.",
v: "All crabs are vertebrates.",
w: "No vertebrate is a cat.",
x: "Some mammals are crabs.",
y: "Some mammals are not vertebrates. }

Mixed: Some True, Some False

(PQ)[∅]

True (P)[2] ◆ ◇ (Q)[1] **False**

(∅)[21]

Empty Set

Fig. 5-4

Typically, we start by mapping the Atomic Ideas in the World of Ideas to the Atoms in the lattice. In this case, we map Black Dog, Brown Cat, Black Snake, and Brown Crab to the Atoms a, b, c, and d in the Power Set Lattice in the World of Abstract Sets. Then, we Map Sets of Atoms that share common Attributes to Compound Elements in the Power Set Lattice. In the example in **Fig. 5-4**, this means that we create the following Maps:

- Animal $\rightarrow$ (abcd)[Ø]
- Vertebrate $\rightarrow$ (abc)[4]
- Mammal $\rightarrow$ (ab)[43]
- Brown objects $\rightarrow$ (bd)[31]
- Black objects $\rightarrow$ (ac)[42]
- Black Dog $\rightarrow$ (a)[432]
- Brown Cat $\rightarrow$ (b)[431]
- Black Snake $\rightarrow$ (c)[421]
- Brown Crab $\rightarrow$ (d)[321]

5.6. *Attribute Values*

When we map an Attribute in the World of Ideas to an Element of a Lattice in the World of Abstract Sets, we are asserting that the Element (the "**Attribute Element**") represents that Attribute, as well as every Element in the Down Set of the Attribute Element. For example, in the World of Ideas, dog, cat, and snake are Vertebrates, so we map the Attribute "Vertebrate" to the Element of the Lattice with the Idea Signature (abc)[4]. For convenience, we use the Attribute Signature [4] to represent the Attribute, although the Object Signature (abc) is equivalent, like two sides of the same coin. The advantage to using [4] to represent the Attribute is that we can see the inheritance of [4] in the Down Set; every Element that has [4] in the Attribute Signature "is a Vertebrate." **Fig. 5-5** shows the Down Set of each of the nine Attributes we observed in **Fig. 5-4**.

Attribute Values - Expressed Using Object Signatures

For each of the nine Attributes below, the uppermost Element shaded Black represents the Union of the Atoms that exhibit the Attribute in question (the "**Attribute Element**"). We label the Attribute Element with the name of the Attribute. Each Element in the Downset of that Element also exhbits that Attribute, and is also shaded Black.

The uppermost Element shaded Gray represents the Complement of the Attribute Element. Each Element in the Downset of that Element also fails to exhbit that Attribute, and is also shaded Gray.

Elements that remain White (other than the Empty Set) are Mixed or Hetergeneous Elements made up of some Atoms that exhibit the Attribute and some that do not.

The Empty Set, as a technical matter, exhibits both the Attribute and the not-Attribute, which is impossible, so the Empty Set has no Object Atoms.

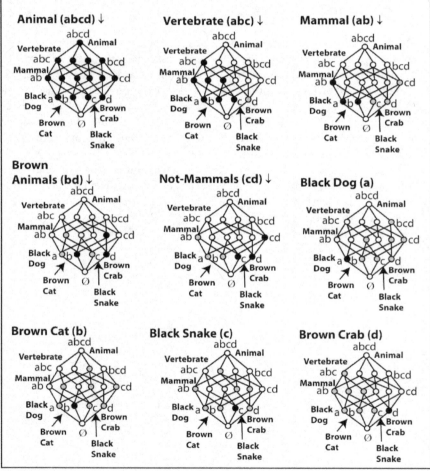

Fig. 5-5

The Complement of the Attribute Element represents the "not-Attribute" Set, and the Down Set is the Set of all Elements that do not have that Attribute, shown in gray in **Fig. 5-5**. The Elements that remain white (other than the Empty Set) do not have the "Attribute Value" or the "not-Attribute Value." This is an extremely important point in that MWN approach to Propositional Logic. They represent **"Mixed"** or **"Heterogeneous"** Elements, where some Atoms exhibit the Attributes and some do not. But the mixed Element as a whole cannot be said to "have" or "not have" the Attribute in question.

Another key point is that the Empty Set (Ø), as a technical matter, inherits both the "Attribute" and the "not-Attribute," which is impossible, which is another way to understand the meaning of the Empty Set; there are no Object Atoms in the Empty Set.

Alternatively, we can express the Down Sets of Attribute Elements using the Attribute Signature, rather that the Object Signature. *See*, **Fig. 5-6**. Remember, it is the exact same Lattice, but here we are using the Attribute Signature rather than the Object Signature. For example, in a P_3 Lattice the Atom "a" has the following Idea Signature:

Idea Signature = (Object Signature "a") [Attribute Signature "32"].

The advantage to using Attributes is that we can see the inheritance of Attributes from the numbers used in the Attribute Signature.

Attribute Values - Expressed Using Attribute Signatures

The diagrams below are the same as in **Fig. 5-5**, except that we use the Attribute Signature (i.e., the Coatom numbering) rather than the Object Signature (i.e., the Atom lettering). The advantage to using the Attribute numbering is that we can see the inheritance of the Attribute in the Downset, i.e., each Element in the Downset of [4] has the number "4" in it. This allows, for example, a computer to calculate the inheritance of Attributes.

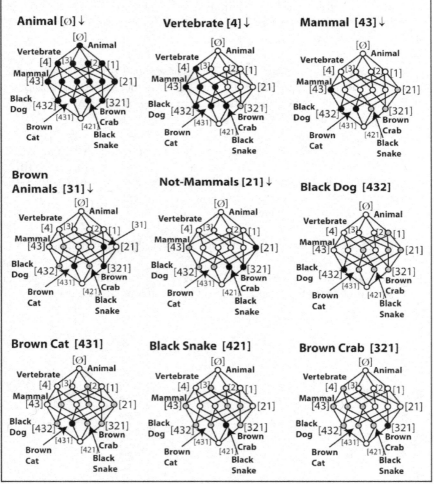

Fig. 5-6

5.7. References, Historical Notes, and Further Reading

See generally, [Veatch 2016].

6. UNIVERSE OF DISCOURSE: PROPOSITIONS (SECOND ORDER)

In this Chapter, we examine the Universe of Discourse of Propositions. In essence, a Proposition states the relationship between two Ideas cast as the Subject and the Predicate of a special type of declarative sentence. The critical Attribute of a Proposition is that it has a binary Truth Value of either True or False. Given that in MWN we interpret Ideas as Sets, to understand when a Proposition is True or False we need to understand what makes a Proposition True or False in terms of the Set relationship between the Subject and the Predicate.

We will see that not all declarative sentences qualify as "True/False Propositions." There are, however, techniques that we can use to ensure that a declarative sentence will have an unambiguous Truth Value, thereby qualifying as a Proposition. We will demonstrate that the Set of all Propositions, together with the Operations of Union, Intersection, and Complementation, constitutes a Boolean Algebra. In addition, in **Chapter 7** we will specify rules for creating Logic Formulas consisting of symbols representing Propositions (*e.g.*, "x") and their Negations (*e.g.*, "NOT x" or "¬ x") along with specific rules for combining Propositional Variables and their negations into a formula using OR ($\lor$) and AND ($\land$). The U_D of Logic Formulas will form a second Boolean Algebra of Propositional Logic. *See*, **Fig. 6-1**.

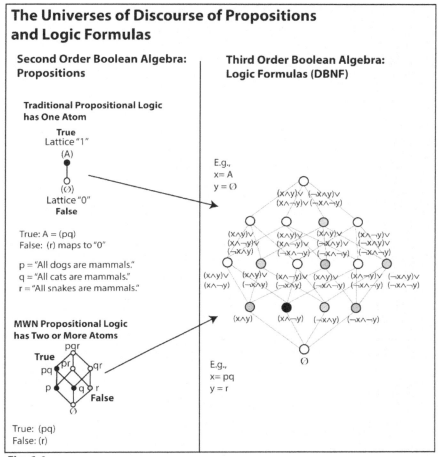

Fig. 6-1

6.1. *Combining Two Ideas to Create a New "Proposition Atom"; A Proposition States the Relationship Between Two Sets of Ideas*

In this Section, we examine how we can create a new category of **"Proposition Atoms"** from the Ideas that we examined in the previous Chapter. As we begin to work with new types of Second Order Atoms, and later Third Order Atoms, it is important to remember that we cannot mix Elements from one Order with Elements from another Order. The primary example of this will be the Negation Operation ("¬"), which, in MWN, is not defined in Second Order calculations using Propositions, but will play a prominent role in Third Order calculations using Logic Formulas.

To begin, we need to define what we mean by a Proposition. A Proposition is defined as a Declarative Sentence consisting of a Subject and a Predicate, connected by a Copula, *i.e.*, a form of the verb "to be." Not all sentences are Declarative; other types of sentences include: interrogative sentences, imperative sentences, exclamatory sentences, and perfomatory sentences. *See*, [Kreeft 2010] at 139. Here are some examples:

- All dogs are mammals.
- No dog is a cat.
- Some mammals are cats.

Note the use of a "Quantifier" (*i.e.*, "all," "no," or "some") before the Subject.

The most important Attribute of a Proposition, however, is that it is by definition either True or False. This assumption that a Proposition is either True or False is so important, that we take some time to examine it more closely. The issue is that not all Declarative Sentences have a fixed and determinable Truth Value. In **Section 6.4**, we will see that we can ensure that a Declarative Sentence had a fixed and determinable Truth Value through "Quantification of the Subject," *i.e.*, by modifying the Subject of the Sentence (in the affirmative or the negative) by "some S are..." or "all S are ...", or "some S are not" or "no S ... are." In this way, we see that Propositions are in fact a Subset of the class of Declarative Sentences, which is in turn a Subset of the broader class of Sentences of all types.

We see that a Proposition states the relationship between two Sets of Ideas. We know that every Idea has associated with it both a Set of Objects and a Set of Attributes, so does it matter which type of Set we use to create Propositions? The answer is "yes," Propositions as used in Propositional Logic relate more accurately to the Two-Set Relationships between Object Sets, not Attribute Sets. (We discussed this previously in **Section 5.4**.) Therefore, in our discussion of Propositions and the five Two-Set Relationships, we will focus primarily on Object Sets rather than Attribute Sets.

Any two Sets may be related to each other in one of five ways, *i.e.*, the five "**Two-Set Relationships**." *See*, **Fig. 6-2**.

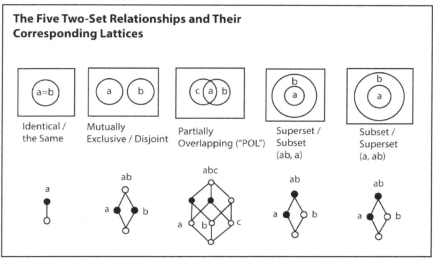

The Five Two-Set Relationships and Their Corresponding Lattices

Fig. 6-2

We can also use symbols to specify these relationships as set forth in **Table 6-1**.

Table 6-1

Name	Formula	Description
Identical	$(x=y)$	x and y are equal or equivalent, *i.e.*, they represent the same Set.
Disjoint	$(x \, \Omega \, y)$	x and y are Disjoint.
Subset-Superset	$(x \subset y)$	x is a Subset of y.
Superset-Subset	$(x \supset y)$	x is a Superset of y.
Partially Overlapping (POL)	$(x \, \Pi \, y)$	x and y are Partially Overlapping

When we write a Declarative Sentence, it may not be obvious what the Set relationship is between the Subject and the Predicate. For example, if we write "Mammals are black," the Set relationship and Truth Value may not be obvious at first. If, however, we specify our Base Set X = { a, b } = { Black Cat, White Dog } and the related Power Set P(X) = (Ø, a, b, ab) = (Ø, Black Cat, White Dog, Mammals), we can see that a Black Cat is a Subset of Mammals: "Black Cat ⊂ Mammals." Not all Mammals are "Black," however, so the statement "Mammals are black" is not True. The statement is not False either, because some Mammals are Black. This is an example of a Declarative Sentence that is neither True nor False. One way to specify the

Set Relationship and an unambiguous Truth Value is to use the Set Relationship symbols as follows:

- "Mammal ⊃ Black Cat." → True.
- "Black Cat ⊂ Mammal." → True.
- "Black Cat Ω White Dog." → True.
- "Mammal Ω Black Cat." → False.
- "Mammal Π Black Cat." → False.
- "Mammal ⊂ Black Cat." → False.
- "Mammal = Black Cat." → False.

Each of the above statements specifies the exact Set Relationship and is True or False based upon the relationships of the Ideas in the Base Set specified above.

6.2. Sentence Types and the Definition of a "Proposition"

Before we go further, we need to understand the difference between a Proposition as used in Propositional Logic, and other types of Sentences. Also, in MWN we use these terms differently from the way that they are used in other books on Logic, so the reader must exercise care when comparing this book to other books on Propositional Logic. For example, some books on Symbolic Logic define a "sentence" to mean the same thing as a Proposition. In MWN, however, we use the terms differently. *See*, **Fig. 6-3**.

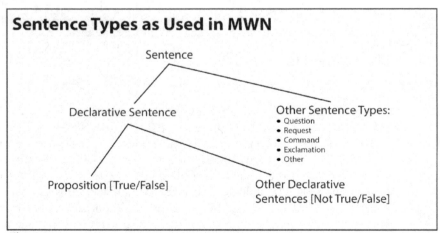

Sentence Types as Used in MWN

Sentence

Declarative Sentence

Other Sentence Types:
- Question
- Request
- Command
- Exclamation
- Other

Proposition [True/False]

Other Declarative Sentences [Not True/False]

Fig. 6-3

We start with the class of all Sentences, defined in much the way that we would define a Sentence for purposes of the study of grammar. The sentence type that we are interested in here is a "**Declarative Sentence**," where the sentence makes a statement about the relationship between two Ideas. Other types of Sentences such as questions, requests, commands, exclamations, *etc.* are not of interest to us at the moment.

6.3. *Using Partitions to Sort Sets of Propositions*

The most important Attribute of a Proposition is its Truth Value, where Truth Value $_{PE}$ = (True + False). ("PE" refers to "Partition Equation." *See*, MWN Vol. 1.) There are, however, other Attributes that are relevant, including the A, E, I, and O classification scheme of Classical Logic, the five-type classification scheme articulated by John Venn in the 1890's, the five Two-Set Relationships, and the relative position of the Subject and Predicate in a P_3 Lattice. In this **Section 6.3**, we will provide a broad overview and introduction to the topic, and then we will look at each of these classification schemes in detail.

One of our goals will be to identify Partition Sets that constitute a Partition of the Set of all possible Propositions. We will see that there are at least six principal ways to do this:

- **Truth Value**: (True + False)
- **(A+O)**: A and O Propositions of Classical Logic,
- **(E+I)**: E and I Propositions of Classical Logic,
- **Five Venn Propositions**: The five Venn Propositions: ($A_{V1} + A_{V2} + I_{V1} + I_{V2} + E_V$),
- **Five Two-Set Relationships**: Specifying the Two-Set Relationship: Identical (=), Disjoint (Ω), Subset-Superset ($\subset$), Superset-Subset ($\supset$), or Partially Overlapping (POL or Π), and
- **P_3 Lattice Position - Ten P_3 Lattice Pairs**: Specifying one of the ten Pairs of non-Isomorphic relative Lattice Positions of the two Ideas in a P_3 Lattice: (a,a), (a,b), (a,ab), (a,bc), (a,abc), (ab,ac), (ab,abc), (ab,a), (abc,a), and (abc,ab).

For Propositions constructed in one of these six ways, the Truth Value of the Proposition will always be fixed and determinable as either True or False, depending upon whether the Proposition accurately reflects that Map that we created from the World of Ideas to the World of Abstract Sets. Note that each category of Attributes forms a Partition of the Set of all Propositions.

We can also state the five Partitions in the form of a Partition Equation as follows:

Propositions $_{PE}$ =
$$(A+O)\times$$
$$(E+I) \times$$
$$(A_{V1}+A_{V2}+I_{V1}+I_{V2}+E_V) \times$$
$$(\text{"="}+ \subset + \supset + \Pi + \Omega\ ) \times$$
$$((a,a)+(a,b)+(a,ab)+(a,bc)+(a,abc)+(ab,ac)+(ab,abc)+$$
$$(ab,a)+(abc,a)+(abc,ab))$$

In other words, each of the five terms in the above Partition Equation constitutes a Partition of the Set of all Propositions. Given a Partition Equation, there are a number of things we can do. For example, we can create a Hierarchy Tree or Nested Partition Lattice, although as the number of Atoms grows, it becomes easier to draw Hierarchy Trees as compared to Nested Partition Lattices. The key point to remember is that each is equivalent to the other, and that they are simply different representations of the same Partition Equation. *See*, [Veatch 2016] at 202 *et seq.*

The diagrams in **Fig. 6-4** illustrate the relationships among the five different Partitions of the Universe of Discourse consisting of all Propositions.

Partition Equation of X = {True/False Propositions}, Represented by Hierarchy Trees

Partition Equation:

X   = Propositions
      = (10 non-Isomorphic P₃ Lattice Relationships)
      = (A+O) x (E+I) x (Av₁+Av₂+Iv₁+Iv₂+Ev) x ("="+⊂+⊃+Ω+Π)

We let the Partition Set with the largest number
of elements constitute a Set of Deemed Atoms of a U_D.
Then, we use the remaining four Partition Sets to
create Levels in a Hierarchy Tree.

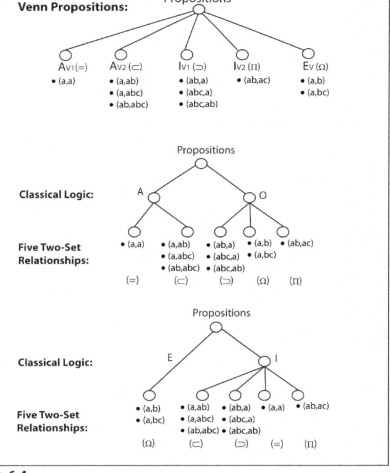

Fig. 6-4

To create Hierarchy Trees, we start by creating a Universe of Discourse using the largest Partition Set, in this case X = ((a,a)+(a,b)+(a,ab)+(a,bc)+(a,abc)+(ab,ac)+(ab,abc)+(ab,a)+(abc,a)+(abc,ab)), as a source of Deemed Atoms. Then, we can use some or all of the remaining four Partition Sets, applied in any order, to create Hierarchy Trees. As mentioned above, we could represent the Hierarchy Trees as equivalent Nested Partition Lattices, but for this example we choose to use Hierarchy Trees instead.

6.4. The A, E, I, and O Propositions of Classical Logic

One of the most common approaches to clarifying the Truth Value of a Declarative Sentence is to "quantify the Subject" using "some" or "all", stated in the affirmative or the negative, as in following four types of Propositions in Classical Logic:

- A: All x are y.
- E: No x are y. (Alternatively: "All x are not y.")
- I: Some x are y.
- O: Some x are not y.

The Propositions of Classical Logic are related to the five Two-Set Relationships as set forth in **Fig. 6-5**. Note that each of the A, I, and O forms of Propositions is ambiguous, in that they each have more than one interpretation in terms of the five Two-Set Relationships. Another important point to note from **Fig. 6-5** is that A and O form a Partition of the Set of Propositions; and E and I form a Partition of the Set of Propositions. As a reminder, by a Partition, we mean an Exhaustive Partition of the Base Set of Atoms into Mutually Exclusive (*i.e.*, Pairwise Disjoint) Subsets. In other words, each Proposition must fall into one and only one of the Equivalence Classes of the Partitions. Given that we have two Partitions, *i.e.*, (A+O) and (E+I), this also means that every Proposition will constitute two types of Proposition under the rules of Classical Logic, *i.e.*, AI, OE, or OI.

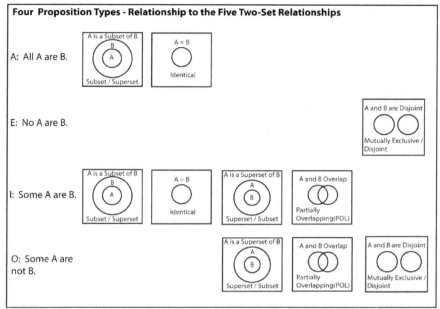

Fig. 6-5

Although the Set Relationship of the Subject and Predicate in a Proposition of Classical Logic is ambiguous, the Truth Value is not. By quantifying the Subject, we have clarified the Truth Value as seen in the following examples:

- A: "All Mammals are Black." →False.
- E: "No Mammals are Black." →False.
- I: "Some Mammals are Black." →True.
- O: "Some Mammals are not Black." →True.

In Classical Logic as well as in MWN, we use Inductive Logic to develop a Set of Propositions where each Proposition consists of a Subject and a Predicate connected by a form of the verb "to be." A sentence such as "Mammals are White" is ambiguous, because we cannot tell whether the intent is to say "All Mammals are White" or "Some Mammals are White." As a result, in Classical Logic we must use one of following four forms of Proposition where we quantify the Subject:

- A: All [Subject] are [Predicate].
- E: No [Subject] are [Predicate].

- I: Some [Subject] are [Predicate].
- O: Some [Subject] are not [Predicate].

Although the content of the Propositions is relevant in Classical Logic, for our present purposes the only Attribute that we are concerned with is the fact that a Proposition must be either True or False.

Fig. 6-6 uses a P_5 Lattice to illustrate the relationship of the four Proposition types of Classical Logic to the five Two-Set Relationships.

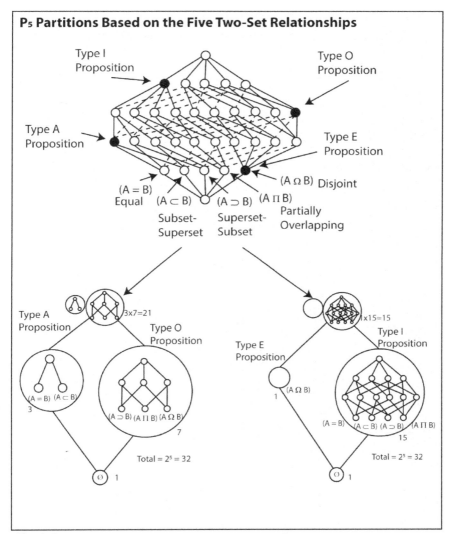

Fig. 6-6

Note that although three of the four Proposition types of Classical Logic, A, I, and O, are ambiguous in terms of the five Two-Set Relationships, the four Proposition types are unambiguous in terms of their Truth Values. It is this fact that allows us to use the Propositions of Classical Logic as Atomic Formulas for purposes of Propositional Logic.

6.5. The Square of Opposition: Relationships Among A, E, I, and O Propositions

Before moving, we take a moment to look at the **"Square of Opposition"** from Classical Logic. In this Section, we see that the Square of Opposition can best be understood by looking at the related Two-Set Relationships. *See,* **Fig. 6-7**.

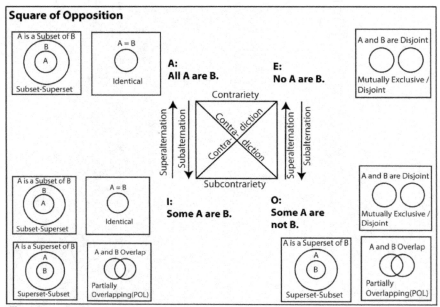

Fig. 6-7

Each Proposition type is represented by one or more of the five Two-Set Relationships as follows:

- A: Subset-Superset, or Identical.
- E: Disjoint.
- I: Subset-Superset, Identical, Superset-Subset, or Partially Overlapping
- O: Identical, Superset-Subset, Partially Overlapping

Table 6-2 illustrates how we can reconcile the Classical Logic rules relating to the Square of Opposition, with principles of Math Without Numbers (MWN). The five Two-Set Relationships make it easy to see the relationships among the A, E, I, and O Propositions.

Table 6-2

Principle	Related Types	Rule
Contrariety	A-E	No Proposition can be both A and E.
Subalternation	A-I, E-0	All A Propositions are also I Propositions. All E Propositions are also O Propositions.
Superalternation	I-A, O-E	Some I Propositions are A Propositions. Some O Propositions are E Propositions.
Subcontrariety	I-O, O-I	Some I Propositions are O Propositions. Some O Propositions are I Propositions.
Contradiction	A-O, E-I	A and O form a Partition of the Set of Propositions, *i.e.*, a Proposition is one or the other, but cannot be both Type A and O. E and I form a Partition of the Set of Propositions, *i.e.*, a Proposition cannot be both Type E and I.

6.6. *The Five Two-Set Relationships Expressed as Propositions – Venn Propositions and Quantification of the Predicate*

Can we create Propositions expressed in words that relate to the five Two-Set Relationships? We saw in the previous Section that the four A, E, I, and O Propositions of Classical Logic are ambiguous in terms of which of the five Two-Set Relationships applies. There is a way, however, to make the Propositions unambiguous by "quantifying the Predicate," a technique written about by John Venn as early as 1881. *See,* [Venn 1894] at 8.

The concept is to start with ambiguous sentences about two Sets, and then add words that eliminate the ambiguity. First, we create A, E, I, and O Propositions by quantifying the Subject; and then we create what we refer to as "Venn Propositions" by quantifying the Predicate. *See,* **Table 6-3**.

Table 6-3

Ambiguous Sentences	Same	Sub-Super	Super-Sub	POL	Disjoint
S are P.	X	X	X	X	
S are not P.		X	X	X	X
Classical Logic – Quantify the Subject					
A: All S are P.	X	X			
E: No S are P.					X
I: Some S are P.	X	X	X	X	
O: Some S are not P.			X	X	X
Venn Propositions – Quantify the Predicate					
A_{V1}: All S are all P.	X				
A_{V2}: All S are some P.		X			
I_{V1}: Some S are all P.			X		
I_{V2}: Some S are some P.				X	
E_V: No S are any P.					X

The subscript "V" is in recognition of the fact that John Venn, writing in 1881-1894, wrote about the five Two-Set Relationships and the Principle of Quantification of the Predicate, and identified these five forms of Propositions as relating to the five Two-Set Relationships.

Note that the Quantified Predicate version is different from the regular A, E, I, and O forms in several ways:

- Quantifying the Predicate eliminates the ambiguity in the A, I, and O Propositions,
- In A_{V2}, I_{V1}, and I_{V2}, "some" means "some not all," and
- We do not need the "O" form of Proposition.

Whereas in the case of Classical Logic Propositions each of the five Two-Set Relationships is associated with two Proposition Types, in the case of Venn Propositions each of the five Two-Set Relationships is associated with only one Proposition Type.

See, [Venn 1894] at 8, 11 *et seq.* for a discussion of the Principle of Quantification of the Predicate, and how logicians interpret the various permutations of "all/some" and "are/are not".

Table 6-4 provides an example of the impact of Quantification on the Attributes that we are most interested in: Truth Value, Two-Set Relationships, and P_3 Lattice Position. If all we need is a fixed and determinable Truth Value, then Quantification of the Subject is sufficient. If, however, we also want to have a fixed and determinable Two-Set Relationship, then we need to quantify the Predicate as well.

Table 6-4

	Example	Truth Value	Two-Set Relationship	P_3 Lattice Position
No Quantification	Dogs are black.	Indeterminate "i"	i	i
Quantify the Subject	Some dogs are black.	True	Identical, POL, Subset-Superset, Superset-Subset	i
Quantify the Predicate	Some dogs are some black things.	True	POL	(ab, ac)

The difficulty that we have in everyday speech, is that we normally do not "Quantify the Predicate," so it sounds odd to say: "Some dogs are some black things." The above analysis serves a purpose, however, in that it helps us to understand the ambiguities and limitations of ordinary speech. In cases where we need to be more precise, we can find a way to Quantify the Predicate and remove ambiguities. In some instances, we may want to go even further and specify the P_3 Lattice Position, because some Two-Set Relationships, such as Subset-Superset and Superset-Subset, have more than one corresponding Pair of Elements in the P_3 Lattice. Once we specify the P_3 Lattice Position, we have removed all ambiguities.

6.7. Lattice Position and the Logic of Lattices

Another way to clarify the Set Relationships among Ideas and Truth Values of Propositions is to specify the position of the Ideas in a Lattice. A Lattice has the advantage of showing all of the Set Relationships in a clear manner. We use a P_3 Lattice as an example in **Fig. 6-8**, because the P_2 Lattice does not contain an example of Partially Overlapping (POL) Sets. We show the P_3 Lattice in the context of the whole Universe of Ideas in order to illustrate why the P_3 Lattice has three Objects X = { a, b, c }, whereas the inverse P_3 Lattice has four Attributes Y = [4, 3, 2, 1]. This is explained in detail in MWN Vol. 1 at 90 *et seq.*

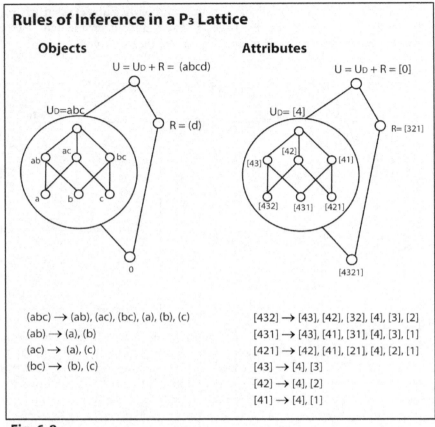

Fig. 6-8

Based upon the Lattice in **Fig. 6-8**, we can make a number of statements, including the following:

- "ab ⊃ a" → True.
- "a ⊂ ab" → True.
- "a Ω b" → True.
- "ab Π b" → False.
- "ab ⊂ a" → False.
- "ab = a" → False.
- A: "All ab are a." → False.
- E: "No ab are a." → False.
- I: "Some ab are a." → True.
- O: "Some ab are not a." → True.

- A$_V$: "All ab are some a." → False.
- E$_V$: "No ab are any a." → False.
- I$_{V1}$: "Some ab are all a." → True.
- I$_{V2}$: "Some ab are some a." → False.

The above statements are possible because of the principle that any time we Assert the existence of a Set of Objects or Attributes, we are also Asserting the existence of each Element of the Set. In this context, we use "x → y" to mean that Asserting "x" means that we are also necessarily Asserting "y". For example, if we Assert the existence of (ab), then we are asserting the existence of (a), as well as the Two-Set Relationship "ab ⊃ a" or "a ⊂ ab". We can Map statements that are in accordance with the Lattice structure to "True," and statements that are not in accordance with the Lattice structure to "False." For example, the statement "ab ⊂ a" is clearly False.

We have a number of choices as to how to write the Propositions, including by specifying the Two-Set Relationship, the A, E, I, or O Proposition of Classical Logic, or the Venn Proposition where we have Quantified the Predicate.

Clearly, there is a Logic of Ideas inherent in the Lattice structure, which in turn gives rise to a fixed number of True Propositions. Once we have created a Map from the World of Ideas to a Lattice in the World of Abstract Sets, we can list a fixed number of True (or False) Propositions based upon the Logic inherent in the Lattice structure. For example, based upon the example in **Fig. 6-9**, we can discern a number of True Propositions, including the following:

- All Black Dogs are Mammals. ([432] → [43]; a ⊂ ab)
- No Black Dog is a White Cat. (a Ω b)
- Some Mammals are Black Dogs. (ab ⊃ a; a ⊂ ab)
- Some Mammals are not Black Dogs. (ab ⊃ b; b ⊂ ab; a Ω b)

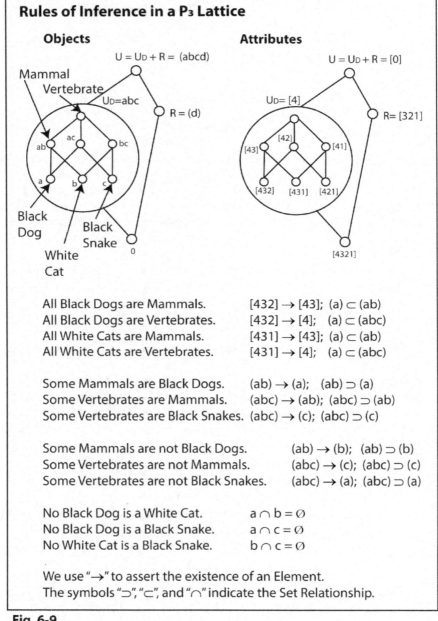

Rules of Inference in a P₃ Lattice

All Black Dogs are Mammals.	[432] → [43]; (a) ⊂ (ab)
All Black Dogs are Vertebrates.	[432] → [4]; (a) ⊂ (abc)
All White Cats are Mammals.	[431] → [43]; (a) ⊂ (ab)
All White Cats are Vertebrates.	[431] → [4]; (a) ⊂ (abc)
Some Mammals are Black Dogs.	(ab) → (a); (ab) ⊃ (a)
Some Vertebrates are Mammals.	(abc) → (ab); (abc) ⊃ (ab)
Some Vertebrates are Black Snakes.	(abc) → (c); (abc) ⊃ (c)
Some Mammals are not Black Dogs.	(ab) → (b); (ab) ⊃ (b)
Some Vertebrates are not Mammals.	(abc) → (c); (abc) ⊃ (c)
Some Vertebrates are not Black Snakes.	(abc) → (a); (abc) ⊃ (a)
No Black Dog is a White Cat.	a ∩ b = ∅
No Black Dog is a Black Snake.	a ∩ c = ∅
No White Cat is a Black Snake.	b ∩ c = ∅

We use "→" to assert the existence of an Element.
The symbols "⊃", "⊂", and "∩" indicate the Set Relationship.

Fig. 6-9

We will review the logic inherent in Lattices (the "**Logic of Lattices**") exhaustively in MWN Vol. 2 – Logic, but for purposes of this book we just want to introduce the concept of logic relationships being inherent in the Lattice structure.

Armed with the above information about what a Proposition is in terms of Set relationships, we can look more closely at the concepts of Truth and Falsity to determine when a Proposition can be said to be either "True" or "False".

The Logic of Lattices

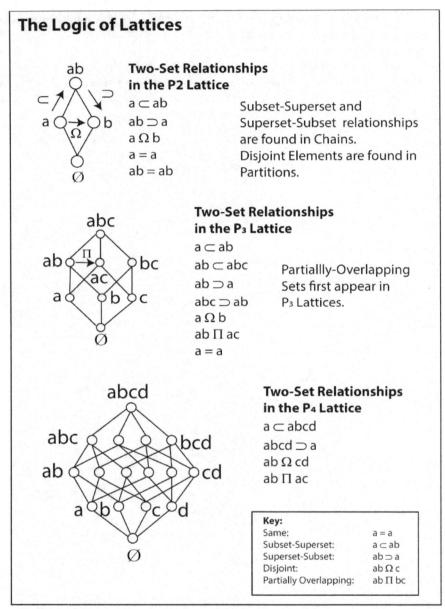

Two-Set Relationships in the P2 Lattice

a ⊂ ab
ab ⊃ a
a Ω b
a = a
ab = ab

Subset-Superset and Superset-Subset relationships are found in Chains. Disjoint Elements are found in Partitions.

Two-Set Relationships in the P₃ Lattice

a ⊂ ab
ab ⊂ abc
ab ⊃ a
abc ⊃ ab
a Ω b
ab Π ac
a = a

Partiallly-Overlapping Sets first appear in P₃ Lattices.

Two-Set Relationships in the P₄ Lattice

a ⊂ abcd
abcd ⊃ a
ab Ω cd
ab Π ac

Key:	
Same:	a = a
Subset-Superset:	a ⊂ ab
Superset-Subset:	ab ⊃ a
Disjoint:	ab Ω c
Partially Overlapping:	ab Π bc

Fig. 6-10

Fig. 6-10 illustrates the Two-Set Relationships inherent in the P₂, P₃, and P₄ Lattices. In **Tables 6-5** and **6-6**, we show how the five Two-Set Relationships in the P₂ and P₃ Lattices relate to the A, E, I, and O Propositions of Classical Logic.

Table 6-5

Two-Set Relationships in a P_2 Lattice	Isomorphic Pairs	Examples of Equivalent A, E, I, O Propositions
(a)=(a)	(b, b), (ab, ab)	A: All dogs are dogs. I: Some dogs are dogs.
(a) $\subset$ (ab)	(b, ab)	A: All dogs are mammals. I: Some dogs are mammals.
(ab) $\supset$ (a)	(ab, b)	I: Some mammals are dogs. O: Some mammals are not dogs.
(a) Ω (b)	(b) Ω (a)	E: No dogs are cats. O: Some dogs are not cats.

In the P_2 Lattice, there are three non-Empty Elements: (a), (b), and (ab). The maximum number of combinations of pairs of Elements where order matters and where there are three Elements, is $3 \times 3 = 9$. This includes all combinations, including where the same two Elements are combined in a different order.

The Combinatorics formula for calculating the number of ways that we can choose "r" Elements from a Set with "n" Elements, where order is *not* important, is as follows:

- (n choose r) = n!/(r! (n-r)!)

Using the formula for a set where n=3 and r=2, we get:

- 3! / (2!(3-2)!) = 6 / 2 = 3.

Since order matters only for the Subset-Superset and Superset-Subset relationships, we know that the number of relevant Pairs lies somewhere between 3 and 9.

The three possible combinations are (a, b), (a, ab), and (b, ab). Note that we excluded the Empty Set ("∅"), because we are interested only in non-empty Sets. For that reason, we have n=3, rather than n=4.

If we allow for Elements to be the same, we would add three more Elements. Also, order makes a difference for Subset-Superset, so that adds two more Elements for a total of 8.

Order does not matter for the "Disjoint" relation, but that would provide one more combination, for a total of 9.

Table 6-5 assumes that each of the two Sets being compared is non-empty. The last column in **Table 6-5** illustrates the equivalent A, E, I, and O Propositions of Classical Logic.

In the P_3 Lattice, there are seven non-Empty elements: a, b, c, ab, ac, bc, and abc. The maximum number of combinations of pairs of Elements where order matters and there are seven Elements, is $7 \times 7 = 49$. This includes all combinations, including where the same two Elements are combined in a different order.

The Combinatorics formula for calculating the number of ways that we can choose "r" Elements from a Set with "n" Elements, where order is *not* important, is as follows:

- (n choose r) = n!/(r! (n-r)!)

Using the formula for a set where n=7 and r=2, we get:

- (7 choose 2) = 7! /(2!(7-2)!) = 42 / 2 = 21.

Since order matters only for the Subset-Superset and Superset-Subset relationships, we know that the number of relevant Pairs lies somewhere between 21 and 49.

Note that we chose "n=7" rather than "n=8", because we are assuming that both of the Ideas that we are comparing are non-empty.

Table 6-6

Primary Combinations	Isomorphic Combinations	No.	Set Relationships
(a,b)	(a,c), (b,c)	3	Disjoint
(a,ab)	(a,ac), (b,ab), (b,bc), (c,ac), (c,bc)	6	Sub-Super
(a,bc)	(b,ac), (c,ab)	3	Disjoint
(a,abc)	(b,abc), (c,abc)	3	Sub-Super
(ab,ac)	(ba,bc), (ca,cb)	3	POL
(ab,abc)	(ac,abc), (bc,abc)	3	Sub-Super
	Total:	21	

If Order mattered, we would have 2 x 21 = 42. If we include an Element added to itself, we would have 42 + 7 = 49. This result is consistent with 7 x 7 = 49.

If we ignore the isomorphic variations and start with the six lines in **Table 6-6**, but include *one* example where an Element is added to itself and *three* examples where order matters for " $\subset$ ", then we see that there are only 10 forms of Two-Set Relationships in the P_3 Lattice. *See*, **Table 6-7**, where the Set Relationships are based upon the P_3 Lattice in **Fig. 6-9**.

Table 6-7

Two-Set Relationships in a P₃ Lattice	Isomorphic Pairs	No.	Examples of Equivalent A, E, I, O Propositions
(a)=(a)	(b, b), (c, c), (ab, ab), (ac, ac), (bc, bc), (abc, abc)	7	All dogs are dogs. (Some dogs are dogs.)
(a) ⊂ (ab)	(b,ab), (a,ac), (c,ac), (b,bc), (c,bc)	6	All dogs are mammals. (Some dogs are mammals.)
(a) ⊂ (abc)	(b,abc), (c,abc)	3	All dogs are vertebrates. (Some dogs are vertebrates.)
(ab) ⊃ (a)	(ab,b), (ac,a), (ac,c), (bc,b), (bc,c)	6	Some mammals are dogs. Some mammals are not dogs.
(abc) ⊃ (a)	(abc,b), (abc,c)	3	Some animals are dogs. Some animals are not dogs.
(abc) ⊃ (ab)	(abc,bc), (abc,ac)	3	Some animals are mammals. Some animals are not mammals.
(a) Ω (bc)	(b,ac), (c,ab) (bc,a), (ac,b), (ab,c)	6	No dogs are cats or snakes. (Some dogs are not cats or snakes.)
(a) Ω (b)	(a,c), (b,c), (b,a), (c,a), (c,b)	6	No dogs are cats. (Some dogs are not cats.)
(ab) ⊂ (abc)	(ac,abc), (bc,abc)	3	All mammals are vertebrates. Some mammals are vertebrates.
(ab) Π (ac)	(ab,bc), (ac,bc) (ac,ab), (bc,ab), (bc,ac)	6	Some mammals are not-cats. Some are mammals are dogs (*i.e.*, not not-cats).
	Total:	49	

Can we demonstrate that there is no need to look at a P_4 Lattice with respect to Idea Pairs? The argument is that through Consolidation, we can show that the extra Two-Set combinations in P_4 as compared to P_3, are redundant.

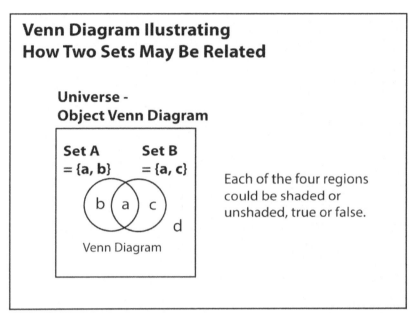

Venn Diagram Ilustrating
How Two Sets May Be Related

Universe -
Object Venn Diagram

Set A   Set B
= {a, b}   = {a, c}

b (a) c
         d

Venn Diagram

Each of the four regions could be shaded or unshaded, true or false.

Fig. 6-11

Looking at the Object Venn Diagram in **Fig. 6-11**, imagine what would happen if we added additional Atoms d, e, f, ... to the Sets A and B in the diagram. Each such additional Atom would have to appear next to one of the existing Atoms a, b, or c, because there is no place else for them to go, unless we create a third Set. We are assuming, however, that there are only two Sets. Using the principles of Consolidation and Subdivision, we know that we can Consolidate the Atoms that appear within any particular Equivalence Class. (*See,* MWN Vol. 1 at Chapter 12.) Similarly, we can Subdivide an Element at any time if we want to return to the larger number of Atoms. Therefore, we can see from the Venn Diagram in **Fig. 6-11**, that we will never need more than three Atoms to represent any combination of two Sets. Of course, we may need more than three Atoms to represent more than two Sets, but for purposes of representing a single Proposition, a P_3 Lattice with three Atoms will always be sufficient.

The Logic of Lattices - Examples

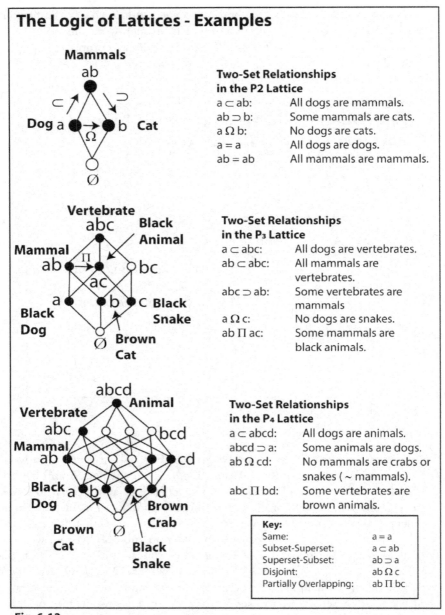

Two-Set Relationships in the P2 Lattice

a ⊂ ab:	All dogs are mammals.
ab ⊃ b:	Some mammals are cats.
a Ω b:	No dogs are cats.
a = a	All dogs are dogs.
ab = ab	All mammals are mammals.

Two-Set Relationships in the P3 Lattice

a ⊂ abc:	All dogs are vertebrates.
ab ⊂ abc:	All mammals are vertebrates.
abc ⊃ ab:	Some vertebrates are mammals
a Ω c:	No dogs are snakes.
ab Π ac:	Some mammals are black animals.

Two-Set Relationships in the P4 Lattice

a ⊂ abcd:	All dogs are animals.
abcd ⊃ a:	Some animals are dogs.
ab Ω cd:	No mammals are crabs or snakes (~ mammals).
abc Π bd:	Some vertebrates are brown animals.

Key:	
Same:	a = a
Subset-Superset:	a ⊂ ab
Superset-Subset:	ab ⊃ a
Disjoint:	ab Ω c
Partially Overlapping:	ab Π bc

Fig. 6-12

Fig. 6-12 provides some examples of Propositions based upon the Logic that is inherent in Lattices.

6.8. *Any Order 2 U_D Lattice of Propositions is Isomorphic to a P_2 Lattice*

Any time we are examining a single binary Attribute of the Elements of a Boolean Algebra, such as the Truth Value of the Elements of an Order 2 Boolean Algebra of Propositions, we can create a P_2 Attribute Lattice highlighting that Attribute. We do so by consolidating all Yes/True Propositions into one Atom, and all No/False Propositions into a second Atom. *See,* **Fig. 6-13**.

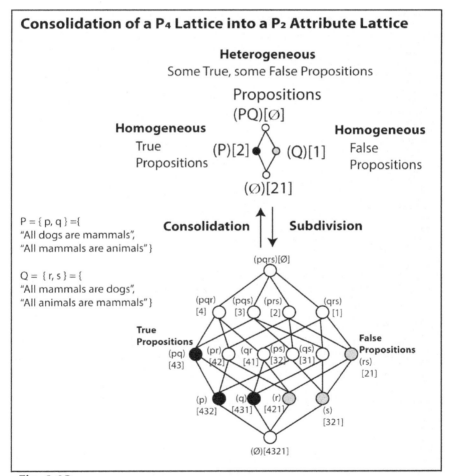

Fig. 6-13

6.9. The Attribute Value of the Subject Determines the Truth Value of the Proposition

We have seen that whether a Proposition is True or False depends upon whether or not it accurately reflects the Two-Set Relationship between the Subject and the Predicate in the Proposition. Traditional Propositional Logic does not look at *how* to determine whether a Proposition is True or False, but rather starts out with a given Truth Value. In MWN Propositional Logic, however, we do look at the underlying Two-Set Relationships of Subjects and Propositions.

An important point to note, however, is that a Proposition may True, but still be ambiguous as to the exact Two-Set Relationship governing the Subject and Predicate. We saw in **Section 6.6** that we can eliminate the ambiguity through "Quantification of the Predicate," as suggested by John Venn in the late 1890's. Classical Logic, however, purposefully leaves the Predicate unquantified. In fact, while beyond the scope of this book, it is important to understand that many of the conclusions of the Syllogisms of Classical Logic are possible only if we leave the quantity of the Predicate ambiguous.

In any event, we can move forward with our study of Propositional Logic, but we need to keep in mind that although we know the Truth Value of the Proposition, depending upon the level of specificity of the Proposition and whether the Predicate has been quantified, we may not know the exact Two-Set Relationship between the Subject and Predicate.

6.10. When Does the Subject have a Fixed and Determinable Attribute Value? - Atoms v. Sets

In MWN Propositional Logic, we place another limitation upon Truth Values, namely that in order for the Subject to have a fixed and determinable Attribute Value (which in turn determines the Truth Value of the related Proposition), the Subject must be an "Atom" not a "Set." The argument is that if the Subject is a Set, then we must examine each individual Atom to see if such Atom exhibits the Attribute in question. There are three possible outcomes:

- Homogeneous - Yes: All Atoms exhibit the Attribute.
- Homogeneous – No: No Atoms exhibit the Attribute.

- Heterogeneous – Mixed Yes/No: Some Atoms exhibit the Attribute, and some do not.

If the Set is Homogeneous, then we have a rational basis for deeming the Set to be a Deemed Atom. If Heterogeneous, however, we have to make a judgment call. Does enough of the Set exhibit the Attribute for us to consider the Set as a whole to have the Attribute? The test we apply will depend upon the circumstances. Sometimes we will require that all Atoms exhibit the Attribute; other times only 50% or 66 2/3%. While this may not seem like a satisfactory result at first, it does in fact reflect how we make decisions in daily life. The answer to questions is often not a clear choice between black and white, but rather there are shades of gray and we must make a judgment call. While mathematics cannot make the decision for us, it can help us understand the nature of the decision and how to communicate it to others, and in the process, narrow the scope of discretion that we must exercise in order to make the decision.

We begin by examining Attribute Values of Ideas generally. The Truth Value of a Proposition depends upon the Attribute Value of the Subject of the Proposition. In other words, in a Proposition consisting of a Subject and a Predicate, the Proposition is a statement about whether an Object (the Subject) exhibits a particular Attribute (the Predicate). Therefore, before we look at Truth Value of Propositions, we need to look at the Attribute Value of a single Atom.

A fundamental premise and assumption of Logic in the MWN system is the following: An Atom either has or does not have any given Attribute. An easy way to illustrate this is to look at a Lattice based upon the Base Set X = { a, b, c, d }. An Attribute is a characteristic that we identify in the World of Ideas, and Map to some Element in the Power Set of Atoms, $P(X)$, in the World of Abstract Sets. We determine which Element to Map the Attribute to by asking of each Atom in the Base Set: does the Atom exhibit the characteristic, Yes or No? For purposes of our example, we choose to Map to (a,b), and label it "Yes" as to the Attribute "Y", meaning that the Atoms "a" and "b" each exhibited the Attribute "Y". Conversely, the Atoms "c" and "d" each did not exhibit the Attribute "Y", so we label the Complement of (ab), *i.e.*, (cd) "No". *See,* **Fig. 6-14**. An important point to note here is that the moment we designate an Element as the "Yes" Element for an Attribute (the "**Attribute Element**"), we are automatically designating the Set Complement as the "No" Element (the "**not-Attribute Element**").

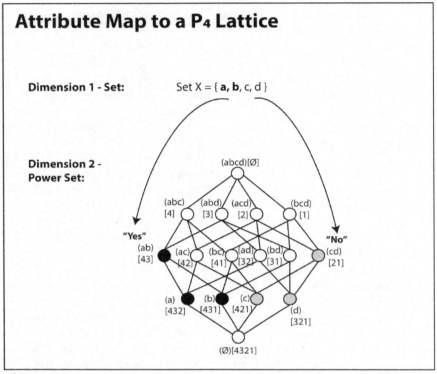

Fig. 6-14

6.11. *What if an Atom is Really a Deemed Atom, i.e., a Set?*

What if we classified an Atom as such and determined a Set of Attributes exhibited by the Atom, and it turns out later that the Atom is in fact a Set? The first question that we must ask as to each Attribute is whether the Set is Homogeneous or Heterogeneous as to that Attribute. If Homogeneous as to each Attribute, then no harm has been done by considering the Set to be a "Deemed Atom." On the other hand, if the Set is Heterogeneous, then we must determine what test to apply (*e.g.*, 100%, 50%, 66 2/3 %, or something else) and whether the choice of Attributes is still valid.

What this demonstrates is that we must recognize that our choice of Atoms is an "assumption," and like any assumption, we must revisit it regularly to test whether our assumption is still valid.

Is there any reason to question whether this assumption is true, *i.e.*, whether Atoms must either exhibit or not exhibit any given Attribute? Well, there is one possible challenge to our assumption, and that is to question whether or not Atoms exist at all. Certainly, we are justified in making simplifying assumptions about the existence of Deemed Atoms in many day-to-day decisions, but it probably is just an assumption. Even the existence of a physical object can be broken down into its existence over smaller and smaller, infinitely divisible units of time. Recall from the development of the foundations of MWN, that whether or not Atoms really exist is an open question. *See*, MWN Vol.1 at 253. We assume that Atoms exist for the convenience of simplifying mathematical operations, and because it is difficult, if not impossible to understand the concept of infinity, but it is merely an assumption. Going forward, we will continue to assume that Atoms exist, but the problem is real and important to keep in mind, particularly when we choose to use Deemed Atoms. As we will soon see, unlike individual Atoms, a Set of multiple Atoms may not have a fixed and determinable Attribute Value governing the entire Set, so if a Deemed Atom is really a Set of Atoms, we may not be justified in assuming that the Deemed Atom in fact has a fixed and determinable "Yes/No" Attribute Value. Once again, we see the importance of regularly checking our assumptions to see if they remain valid, and our choice of Deemed Atoms is one such critical assumption.

We have seen that we can Map individual Atoms in the World of Ideas, to Atoms in a Power Set in the World of Abstract Sets, and that we label one Set in the Power Set "Yes" and its complement "No," to reflect those Homogeneous Sets of Atoms that either all exhibit or do not exhibit a particular Attribute. But what about the other Sets that appear in the Power Set Lattice? By looking at **Fig. 6-14**, we can see that the other non-Empty Sets in the Lattice, *i.e.*, the unshaded Elements other than the Empty Set, are a mixture of "Yes" and "No" Atoms. We see that there are in fact four categories of Sets: Mixed Yes/No, Yes, No, and the Empty Set.

No matter how many Atoms are in our Base Set, we can represent the "Yes" and "No" Attribute Values, together with the Mixed Elements and the Empty Set, using a P_2 Lattice. **Fig. 6-15** illustrates the generic Attribute Lattice that should be familiar by now. We form this P_2 Lattice by Consolidating all of the "Yes" Atoms into a single Deemed Atom "A", and all of the "No" Atoms into a single Deemed Atom "B". For more information on Subdivision and Consolidation of Atoms, *see* MWN Vol. 1 at 63-64.

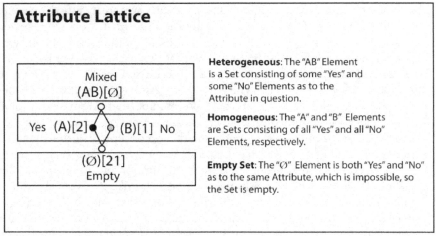

Fig. 6-15

Whether we look at the P_4 Lattice in **Fig. 6-14** or the P_2 Lattice in **Fig. 6-15**, we note that in addition to the "Yes" Elements and the "No" Elements, there are Mixed / Heterogeneous Elements that do not have a single Attribute Value, as well as the Empty Set which represents Elements that exhibit both "Yes" and "No" at the same time, which is not possible, so the Set is Empty. These four categories of Attribute Values: Mixed, Yes, No, and Empty, form the foundation of Propositional Logic in the MWN system of Logic.

6.12.   *When Does a Declarative Sentence Have a Truth Value? – Quantification of the Subject*

Now that we understand better how Attribute Values work generally, we look at the Attributes of a special type of Atom: a Proposition. In fact, we will look at three of the principal Attributes of every Proposition:

- **Truth Value**: (True + False)
- **Two-Set Relationship**: (Identical + Subset-Superset + Superset-Subset + Disjoint + Partially-Overlapping)
- **P_3 Lattice Position**: ((a,a) + (a,ab) + (ab,a) + (a,abc) + (abc,a) + (ab,abc) + (abc,ab) + (a,bc) + (ab,ac) + (a,b))

To illustrate what it takes to form a valid Proposition, we start with an example of a Declarative Sentence that does not qualify as a True/False Proposition: p = "Mammals are dogs." Is this sentence True or False? We could argue that implicitly we are saying "*All* mammals are dogs." If so, then the sentence is clearly False, because there are mammals such as "cats" that are not dogs. That would lead to the conclusion that " ¬ p", or "It is not the case that: mammals are dogs," is True. This, however, does not seem correct either, because some mammals *are* dogs. The problem that we have highlighted here is that not all Declarative Sentences qualify as True/False Propositions. Soon, we will see that the problem is that "Mammal" is Heterogeneous as to the Attribute "Dog," meaning simply that some Mammals are Dogs and some are not.

The solution used in Classical Logic to create valid True/False Propositions is to Quantify the Subject. This means that we modify the Subject, "Mammal" in this case, with either "some" or "all". For completeness, we can also state the Proposition in the Affirmative or the Negative:

- A: All S are P.
- E: No S are P. (This form is preferred to "All S are not P.")
- I: Some S are P.
- O: Some S are not P.

Applied to our Sentence "Mammals are dogs," we have the following four variations:

- "All mammals are dogs" → False.
- "No mammals are dogs" → False.
- "Some mammals are dogs" → True.
- "Some mammals are not dogs" → True.

Quantifying the Subject in this way is sufficient to make the Truth Value of the Proposition fixed and determinable. As we noted in **Section 6.4**, however, the A, E, I, and O Propositions of Classical Logic are ambiguous when it comes to the five Two-Set Relationships. Is there a way to make Propositions unambiguous as to which of the five Two-Set Relationships they relate to? The answer is "yes." As we discussed in **Section 6.6**, we can make the Propositions unambiguous in terms of the five Two-Set Relationships by Quantifying the Predicate as in the following Venn Propositions:

- **Identical** (=): A_{V1}: All S are all P.
- **Subset-Superset** (⊂): A_{V2}: All S are some P.
- **Superset-Subset** (⊃): I_{V1}: Some S are all P.

- **Partially Overlapping** (POL)(Π): I $_{v2}$: Some S are some P.
- **Disjoint** (Ω): E $_{v1}$: No S are any P.

What about the third Attribute of Propositions, *i.e.*, the P$_3$ Lattice Position? Since there are 10 possible non-Isomorphic Pairs of Elements in the P$_3$ Lattice, clearly the five Venn Propositions do not tell us the P$_3$ Lattice Position of the Sets. For many purposes, however, the Classical Logic Propositions or the Venn Propositions are sufficient.

Table 6-8 summarizes what we have learned so far about creating valid Propositions.

Table 6-8

Determinable?:	Truth Value	Two-Set Relationship	P$_3$ Lattice Position
No Quantification: "Mammals are dogs."	No	No	No
Quantification of the Subject: "Some mammals are dogs."	Yes (True)	No	No
Quantification of the Predicate: "Some mammals are all dogs."	Yes (True)	Yes (Superset-Subset)	No
State P$_3$ Lattice Position: "(ab, a): Some mammals are all dogs."	Yes (True)	Yes (Superset-Subset)	Yes (ab, a)

If all we are concerned about is creating a fixed and determinable Truth Value, then the Classical Logic Propositions are perfectly adequate.

6.13. *The Principle of Bivalence, the Law of the Excluded Middle, and the Principle of Non-Contradiction*

When studying Traditional Propositional Logic, we often start with the premise that our Domain consists of a Set of "Propositions," meaning Declarative Sentences that are by definition either True or False. Stated another way, we assume that the Principle of Bivalence applies, meaning that every Proposition is either True or False. *See*, [Lukasiewicz 1957] at 82.

There are, in fact, three related principles in Traditional Propositional Logic concerning Truth Values:

- **Principle of Bivalence**: Every proposition is either True or False. (For example, there is no third option and no absence of a Truth Value.)

  (In MWN, we clarify this principle slightly to say that: Every Proposition or Logic Formula that is an Atom is either True or False. This is important, because a "Set" may not have a fixed and determinable Truth Value.)

- **Law of the Excluded Middle**: For any Proposition "p", either p or not-p is True. Sometimes written as: $(p \vee \neg p)$, *i.e.*, either "p" is True or "$\neg p$" is True, but we assume that there is no other possibility. (Note that "OR" ($\vee$) means "one or the other or both.") *See*, [Copi 1973] at 192.

  (In MWN, we clarify this principle slightly to say that: Every Proposition or Logic Formula that is an Atom, is either True or False. This is an important distinction, because in MWN Propositional Logic a "Set" may be True, False, or have a Mixed Truth Value if there are both True and False Atoms.)

- **Principle of Non-Contradiction**: No Proposition can be True and False at the same time. The principle of Non-Contradiction is sometimes written: $(p \wedge \neg p = 0)$ or $(p \wedge p')' = \neg(p \wedge \neg p)$. (This principle clarifies that "or both" is not an option.)

  (In MWN, we clarify this principle slightly to say that: No Atom can be True and False at the same time. This becomes an important concept if we subdivide a Deemed Atom into two Atoms; for example: $p = (p \wedge q) \vee (p \wedge \neg q)$. Now, if we view the Deemed Atom "p" as the Union of two Atoms, then "p" is half True, half False.)

See, [Shenefelt and White 2013] at 88-91, and 290. *See also*, [Couturat 1914] 23-25, and [Eves 1990] at 248.

But how do we know whether a Declarative Sentence is in fact either True or False? Are there Declarative Sentences that do not qualify as True/False Propositions?

Upon investigation, we find that this is not a new question. In fact, Aristotle had questioned the assumption that every Declarative Sentence is either True or False. *See*, [Kneale and Kneale 1971] at 46-47 and [Aristotle 350 BCE] at Metaphysics, Bk. IV: Ch. 6 (1011b at 23 *et seq.*). For example, in the writings of Aristotle, there is discussion of the doctrines of Heraclitus and Anaxagoras and the problem that when things are mixed, the mixture is neither good nor not-good, so that it is difficult to say that anything is true. [Aristotle 350 BCE] at Metaphysics, Bk. IV: Ch. 7 (1012a at 24-29). This provides a clue to how we will treat Truth and Falsity in MWN, *i.e.*, we need to distinguish between Atoms and Sets of Atoms, because Sets of Atoms may contain a mixture of Attribute Values.

In MWN, we identify the following principles that are important to our study of Propositional Logic:

- A Mapping from the World of Ideas to the World of Abstract Sets is in essence an assumption, and assumptions should be regularly revisited and are always subject to change.
- Inductive Logic is inherently flawed, since we can never check every possible scenario before making a generalization. To the extent that Deductive Logic relies upon Inductive Logic as a source of Mappings and related Propositions, Deductive Logic is also inherently flawed.
- Once a Mapping of Attributes to a Lattice is created (usually by applying Inductive Logic), a number of Propositions flow from the Lattice structure.
- First, we must distinguish between (i) whether an "Idea", or Element of a Lattice, exhibits an Attribute and (ii) whether a "Proposition about an Idea exhibiting an Attribute" is True or False.
- We can ensure that a Proposition has a distinct Truth Value by ensuring that we "quantify the Subject" with "all," "no," "some", or "some ... are not...", as in the A, E, I, and O Propositions of Classical Logic. The Set Relationship, however, will still be ambiguous in the case of the A, I, and O Propositions.
- We also can ensure that a Proposition has a distinct Truth Value by specifying which of the five Two-Set Relationships applies.

In any event, before we continue our detailed discussion of whether Propositional Logic forms a Boolean Algebra, we need to have a clear understanding of what we mean by a Proposition. What we see it is that in MWN, not all Declarative Sentences qualify as True/False Propositions that satisfy the Principle of Bivalence. Rather, in order to qualify as a Proposition, the Subject of the Proposition must either be an Atom or a Homogeneous Set of Atoms. In MWN, a Declarative Statement about a Heterogeneous Set will not qualify as a True/False Proposition. By "**Homogeneous**," we mean that all Atoms in the given Set have the same Attribute Value for the Attribute in question; by "**Heterogeneous**," we mean that *not* all Atoms in the given Set have the same Attribute Value for the Attribute in question. The easiest way to visualize this distinction is with a P_2 Lattice as shown in **Fig. 6-16**.

Propositions and the Law of the Excluded Middle

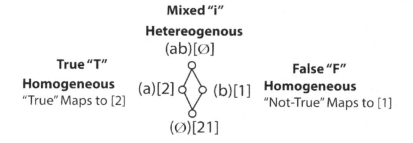

Mixed "i"
Hetereogenous
(ab)[∅]

True "T"   False "F"
Homogeneous   (a)[2]   (b)[1]   Homogeneous
"True" Maps to [2]   "Not-True" Maps to [1]

(∅)[21]

We can assert that (a) is True (and Map "True" to [2]), and conversely we can assert that (b) is False (and Map "False" to [1]).

The Element (ab), however, is a mixture of True and False, and does not have a Truth Value. We can label it "i" for Indeterminate.

The Element (∅) is the Empty Set, and does not have a Truth Value.

Fig. 6-16

Fig. 6-16 illustrates a generic P_2 Lattice structure. With respect to the Attribute [2], the Element (a) can be said to be "True" or to exhibit the

Attribute [2]. Since the Element (b) is the Complement of (a), we can say that (b) represents "not-[2]". In the case of the Element (ab), however, (ab) contains neither the Attribute True [2], nor the Attribute Not-True = [1]. Therefore, we take the position that (ab) is a "mixed" or Heterogenous Element such that it is neither True nor False as to the Attribute [2]. This is an example of the Truth Value of an Element that is neither True nor False, but rather is indeterminable. The Element "(ab)[∅]" does not exhibit any of the Attributes [2] or [1] consistently for all Atoms constituting such Element, so, for example, "(ab)[∅]" is neither True nor False with respect to the Attributes represented by [2] and [1].

We could, however, create a Proposition such as "All (ab) are True/[2]" and the Truth Value would be False. This illustrates how an Element may not have a Truth Value, but a False Proposition to that effect qualifies as a Proposition. (Note that the Proposition "All (ab) are False/[1]" would also be False.)

Another way to interpret **Fig. 6-16** is as a Partition. The Elements "a", and "b" create an Exhaustive, Pairwise Disjoint Partition of (ab):

- (ab) $_{Part}$ = (a + b)

As such, "a" and "b" are Contradictories, meaning that the Principle of Non-Contradiction applies, such that an Object cannot be both "a" and "b" at the same time.

To give an example that is a little bit easier to understand, in **Fig. 6-17** we have a P_2 Lattice based on the Base Set X = Mammals = { Black Cat, White Dog }. The key point that we are trying to make here is that while we can assert that "the cat is black" and "the dog is white," we would not normally say that "Mammals are Black" or "Mammals are Not-Black." The Idea "Mammals" is an example of a Set that is Heterogeneous as to the Attribute "Black." Some Mammals are Black and some are Not-Black. Some scholars might argue that we could make the statement about Mammals a proper True/False Proposition by rephrasing it as "all Mammals are Black," which would be False. However, we choose not to take this approach, because the meaning of the original Sentence was in fact unclear: do we mean that "all Mammals are Black," "no Mammals are Black," or "some Mammals are Black"? The approach that we take in MWN is to recognize that a Set may be Mixed when it comes to the Attribute Value of any particular Attribute, and therefore may not have a fixed and determinable Attribute Value.

Truth Values of Hetergeneous Sets

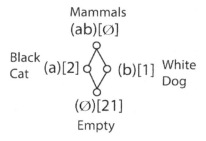

With reference to the Base Set X = Mammal = { a, b } =
{ Black Cat, White Dog }, we can make the following "True"
Declarative Statements:

"The Cat is Black."
"The Dog is White."

We cannot, however, say "Mammals are Black" or "It is not
the case that: Mammals are Black." The Attribute Signature for
Mammal is (ab)[Ø], where [Ø] indicates that there are no "required"
Attributes, meaning that a Mammal could be Black or Not-Black.

Fig. 6-17

What happens if we have a more complicated P_4 Lattice?

The P4 Lattice and the Law of the Excluded Middle

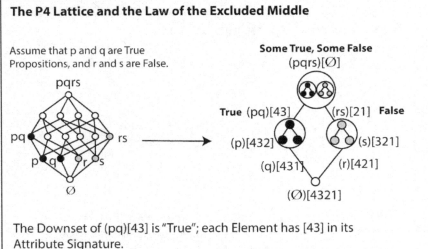

Assume that p and q are True Propositions, and r and s are False.

Some True, Some False
(pqrs)[Ø]

True (pq)[43]   (rs)[21] **False**

(p)[432]   (s)[321]

(q)[431]   (r)[421]

(Ø)[4321]

The Downset of (pq)[43] is "True"; each Element has [43] in its Attribute Signature.
The Downset of (rs)[21] is "False"; each Element has [21] in its Attribute Signature.
(Note that (pq)[43] and (rs)[21] are Complements.)
The remaining nine Elements are "Mixed" or Hetereogenous and are neither True nor False.

Fig. 6-18

From **Fig. 6-18**, we can see that (pq + rs) forms a Partition of the Base Set X = { p, q, r, s }. Each Element in the Down Set of (pq) (*i.e.*, the Elements below (pq) on a path down to 0=Ø) are also True; each Element in the Down Set of (rs) is False. "True" Maps to [43] and each Element in the Down Set of (pq) contains [43]; "False" Maps to [21] and each Element in the Down Set of (rs) contains [21]. Mapping Attributes in this way allows us to look at an "Idea Signature" such as "(p)[432]" and immediately know what Attributes apply. (Also, a computer can search the Attribute numbers, thereby automating the process.)

By selecting Elements that constitute a valid Partition, we are assured that the Law of the Excluded Middle will apply, *i.e.*, each Atom in the U_D will belong to one Equivalence Class or the other, but there is no room for a third option: $(a+a') = 1$

Note that as to the mixed, Heterogeneous Elements, they will contain varying degrees of whatever Attribute we are measuring. If the Attribute in question in "Black", then the Heterogeneous Elements in a P_4 Lattice could be one-third Black, half-Black, or two-thirds Black.

If we have a large number of Atoms relating to tangible Objects in the Physical World, and all but one are Black in color, can we say that the Set of Objects as a whole is Black? *See*, **Fig 6-19**.

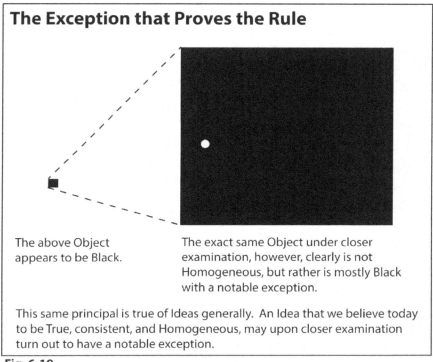

The Exception that Proves the Rule

The above Object appears to be Black.

The exact same Object under closer examination, however, clearly is not Homogeneous, but rather is mostly Black with a notable exception.

This same principal is true of Ideas generally. An Idea that we believe today to be True, consistent, and Homogeneous, may upon closer examination turn out to have a notable exception.

Fig. 6-19

While beyond the scope of this book to discuss this concept in detail, the idea is that we can apply a rule of simplification, an assumption really, that allows us to make a generalization. If the square is "mostly" black, "more than two-thirds" black, or "almost entirely" black, then we say that it is black. The important point to remember is that any time we make an assumption, we need to remember that the assumption may or may not be warranted. As a result, we need to regularly revisit our assumptions to see if they remain valid.

When working with Boolean Expressions, we often apply an "OR" or "AND" rule. With "OR," if at least one DBNF Clause is True, the whole Boolean Expression is True. With "AND" if at least one CBNF Clause is False, the whole Boolean Expression is False. With Ideas generally, however, we do not simply apply AND as in CBNF, or OR as in DBNF, because (1) sometimes a single exception is not sufficient to say "no" (AND rule), and (2) sometimes a single True value is not sufficient to say "all True" (OR rule).

6.14. Summary of Ways to Ensure that a Proposition Has a Fixed and Determinable Truth Value

There are three ways to ensure that a Proposition has a fixed and determinable Truth Value:

- **Quantify the Subject**: This is the approach used in Classical Logic, where we quantify the Subject to form an A, E, I, or O Proposition. The A, I, and O Propositions are still ambiguous as to which of the five Two-Set Relationships applies, but this ambiguity is intentional.

- **State the Two-Set Relationship/Quantify the Predicate**: Stating the Two-Set Relationship, or Quantifying the Predicate, creates an unambiguous Truth Value. The Two-Set Relationship may be stated using symbols $(=, \subset, \supset, \Pi, \Omega)$ or using Venn Propositions.

- **State the Lattice Relationship**: Stating the Lattice position in a P_3 Lattice, and the relationship of any two Ideas provides us with complete information, subject only to the extent of the Mappings that we have created from the World of Ideas to the World of Abstract Sets.

6.15. References, Historical Notes, and Further Reading

Square of Opposition
[Kreeft 2010]

Principle of Bivalence
[Shenefelt and White 2013] at 88-91.
[Kneale and Kneale 1971] at 47-48, 52.

Law of Excluded Middle
[Copi 1973] at 192.
[Kneale and Kneale 1971] at 47.

Law of Non-Contradiction
[Eves 1990] at 248.
[Kneale and Kneale 1971] at 46.

7. UNIVERSE OF DISCOURSE: LOGIC FORMULAS (THIRD ORDER)

In this Chapter, we form a new type of Atom, a Logic Formula, where the Domain for the formulas is the Boolean Algebra of Propositions that we studied in the previous Chapter. We refer to a Logic Formula as being of the Third Order, because it is created from Variables, where the Domain of the Variables consists of the Elements of the Order 2 Boolean Algebra of Propositions. The structure of a Boolean Algebra of Logic Formulas, however, is that of a Free Boolean Algebra with "n" Generators, where "n" is the number of Propositional Variables, so in theory any Boolean Algebra could serve as the Domain. (This may be a good time to review **Chapter 4** regarding Free Boolean Algebras.)

As we will soon discover, there are two types of Order 2 Domains that are relevant for purposes of generating Logic Formulas, those with one Atom and those with more than one Atom. Traditional Propositional Logic uses a Domain with a single Atom representing the consolidation of all True Propositions into a single Atom, whereas MWN Propositional Logic explores Domains with more than one Atom. In MWN, if we are examining a single Attribute and a Domain has more than two Atoms, we can always Consolidate Atoms to arrive at a P_2 Attribute Lattice that highlights the single Attribute that we are interested in. As a result, if we want to compare and contrast Traditional Propositional Logic and MWN Propositional Logic, we can focus on the P_1 Lattice of Traditional Propositional Logic and a P_2 Lattice of MWN Propositional Logic.

7.1. *Logic Formulas Constitute a Free Boolean Algebra; Any Boolean Algebra Can Serve as the Domain*

Before we proceed with our study of Logic Formulas, we review some of principles that we have learned in previous Chapters that form a foundation for our understanding of Logic Formulas.

(1) We create Logic Formulas with a string of Propositional Variables (x, y, z,...) and their Negatives ($\neg$ x, $\neg$ y, $\neg$ z, ...) joined by any combination of Conjunction ($\wedge$) and Disjunction ($\vee$).

(2) With minimal restrictions in place, Conjunction is equivalent to Intersection, Disjunction is equivalent to Union, and Negation is equivalent to Complementation. (The restrictions are that we use Logic Operations only in the Order 3 Universe of Discourse of Logic Formulas, and the Domain for the formulas must have a single Atom representing all True Propositions, if we want to preserve the behavior we are used to seeing in Traditional Propositional Logic. We also use a modified approach to determining Truth Value.)

(3) Any Logic Formula, no matter how long or convoluted, can be written in a standard Canonical Representation (Set Theory) or equivalent Normal Form (Logic), where the form depends solely upon the number of Variables (Order 3), and not the number of Atoms in the Domain (Order 2).

(4) There are $m = 2^n$ Atoms in Normal Form, where "n" is the number of Variables; and 2^m Elements in the Power Set of Logic Formula Atoms. Therefore, any Logic Formula in two Variables is equivalent to one of 16 Logic Functions; any Logic Formula in three Variables is equivalent to one of 256 Logic Functions; *etc.*

(5) The Boolean Algebra of Logic Formulas constitutes a Free Algebra with "n" Generators, where "n" is the number of Variables.

(6) *Any* Boolean Algebra may serve as the Domain for *any* Free Boolean Algebra of Logic Formulas. There is no required relationship between the number of Atoms in the Domain and the number of Variables in the Logic Formulas.

The above principles were discussed in detail earlier in the book, so we do not repeat the discussion here. It is important, however, to have a firm foundation in the principles of a Free Boolean Algebra before proceeding further.

7.2. *Creating an Atomic Logic Formula or One-Variable "Logic Formula Atom"*

As discussed in **Chapter 4** regarding Free Boolean Algebras, we can create a single Propositional Variable "x", where the Domain consists of the Elements of a Boolean Algebra. In this case the Domain is the Order 2 Boolean Algebra of Propositions. We interpret "x" to be a Partition of Unity, that is, a Partition of the Base Set of Propositions into two parts. Since "x" is a Partition, there is always a second Variable "¬x" representing the Complement of "x". **Fig. 7-1** provides an example of how a single Propositional Variable creates $m=2^1 = 2$ Atoms, which in turn creates a Boolean Lattice with $2^m = 4$ Elements.

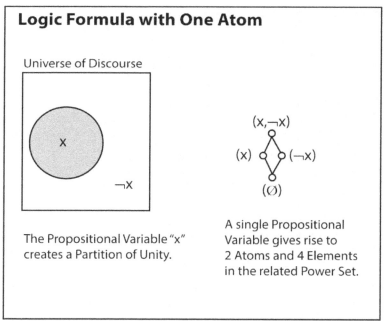

Logic Formula with One Atom

Universe of Discourse

The Propositional Variable "x" creates a Partition of Unity.

A single Propositional Variable gives rise to 2 Atoms and 4 Elements in the related Power Set.

Fig. 7-1

A Boolean Algebra formed from a single Variable is sometimes referred to as a Simple Subalgebra.

7.3. *Creating a Two-Variable "Logic Formula Atom"*

In this Section, we explore how we can use Atomic Logic Formulas to form **"Compound Logic Formulas."** To create a Logic Formula in two

Variables, we combine two Simple Subalgebras in accordance with specific rules.

The issue we have in combining two Simple Subalgebras, each of which is a Partition of Unity, is that the Sets created by the two Partitions may overlap. To create a Boolean Algebra that is Atomic in nature (and a finite Boolean Algebra is always Atomic), however, we need Atoms that are Pairwise Disjoint. The solution, as discussed in detail in **Chapter 4**, is to use a Venn Diagram and related Canonical Representation (or formula in DBNF or CBNF) to create Atoms that by definition are Pairwise Disjoint. (This is a remarkable tool that we will use frequently to combine two Boolean Algebras where the Atoms are not necessarily Pairwise Disjoint across the two Boolean Algebras.) *See*, **Fig. 7-2**.

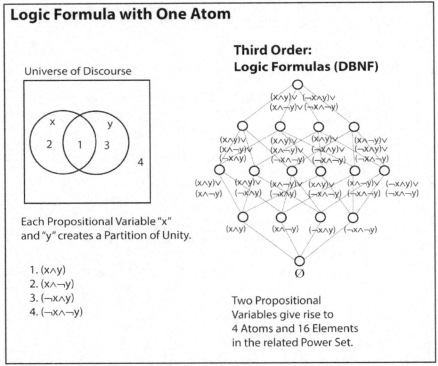

Logic Formula with One Atom

Fig. 7-2

The two Sets of Atoms generated by two Propositional Variables are the following:

- **DBNF Clauses**: $((x \wedge y), (x \wedge \neg y), (\neg x \wedge y), (\neg x \wedge \neg y))$
- **CBNF Clauses**: $((x \vee y), (x \vee \neg y), (\neg x \vee y), (\neg x \vee \neg y))$

Once again, we generate 2^n Logic Formula Atoms, where "n" equals the number of Variables. For example, two Variables generate $2^n = 2^2 = 4$ Atoms in the new U_D. The Atoms may be based upon AND ($\wedge$), in which case we refer to the Atoms as "DBNF Clauses" because they are equivalent to the Clauses of a formula in Disjunctive Boolean Normal Form; or OR ($\vee$), in which case we refer to the Atoms as "CBNF Clauses" because they are equivalent to the Clauses of a formula in Conjunctive Boolean Normal Form.

Throughout our discussion, we always keep in mind:

(1) Logic Formulas (Order 3) relate to a Domain of Propositions (Order 2), which in turn reflect the Set Relationships among Ideas (Order 1). The number of Propositional Variables in Order 3 is not limited, however, by the number of Atoms in the Order 2 Domain. (Technically, the Logic Formulas can use *any* Boolean Algebra for a Domain, but in the context of Propositional Logic we use an Order 2 Universe of Discourse of Propositions.)

(2) Once we Map an Idea in the World of Ideas to an Element of a Lattice in World of Abstract Sets, we have Asserted the Attribute Value of that Element and all Elements in its Down Set in the Lattice. We cannot change the Attribute Value unless we go back to change the Map. The symbol "$\neg$" changes the Attribute Value from "Yes to No" or "No to Yes" for purposes of the Logic Formula, but has no impact on the Map that we created.

(3) If the Attribute in question is the Truth Value of a Proposition, then we speak of "Truth Value" instead of "Attribute Value," and "True/False" instead of "Yes/No", but Truth Values follow the exact same rules that apply to any Attribute Value.

(4) There are five principal Attributes of Propositions, as represented by the following Partition Sets:

    a. **Truth Value**: (True + False).

    b. **Classification of Propositions in Classical Logic**:
        i. (A+O).
        ii. (E+I).

    c. **Five Two-Set Relationships**:
        i. By name: (Identical, Subset-Superset, Superset-Subset, Partially Overlapping, Disjoint).
        ii. As symbols: ($=$, $\subset$, $\supset$, Π, Ω).
        iii. As Venn Propositions: (A_{V1}, A_{V2}, I_{V1}, I_{V2}, E_V).

d. **P₃ Lattice Position**: ((a,a), (a,b), (a,ab), (a,bc), (a,abc), (ab,ac), (ab,abc), (ab,a), (abc,a), (abc,ab)).

e. **Identity of the Subject or Predicate**: The identities of the two Sets comprising the Subject and Predicate of the Proposition: ((a, b) | a, b ⊂ P(U), where U is the Set of all Atoms in the Universe of Ideas, and P(U) is the Power Set of such Atoms consisting of all Atomic and Compound Ideas). We can create a Partition of the Set of Propositions based upon either the Subject or the Predicate.

7.4. The 16 Equivalence Classes of Two Variable Propositional Logic

Although we often speak of "five" Logic Operations (*i.e.*, ∨, ∧, ¬, →, and ↔), there are in fact 16 possible Binary Operations in a Two-Propositional Variable, Four-Atom Universe of Discourse of Logic Formulas. One way to visualize the 16 Operations is by using a Venn Diagram as set forth in **Fig. 7-3**. Given four regions in the Venn Diagram, each region has two possible values, *i.e.*, occupied or empty; shaded or not shaded. *See generally*, [Abbott 1969] at 49 for a full discussion of this approach. To interpret the Venn Diagram, think of a shaded region as the region that we are trying to describe in terms of "x" and "y". Note, however, that Disjunction is not quite the same as Set Union, although they may appear the same in the Venn Diagram. In Traditional Propositional Logic, "Disjunction" gives rise to a Truth Value of "True" if one or the other or both of the "x" and "y" sections are shaded, whereas "Union" requires that both be shaded.

Venn Diagram Ilustrating How Two Sets May Be Related

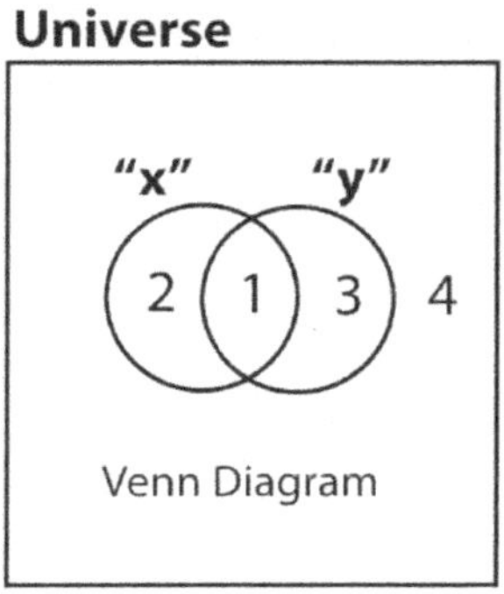

Universe

"x" "y"

2 (1) 3) 4

Each of the four regions could be shaded or unshaded, true or false.

Venn Diagram

Fig. 7-3

Fig. 7-4 illustrates the 16 Operations as Venn Diagrams. As we discuss in **Section 7.10**, Negation in the sense of "Sign Reversal" is not the same concept as Set Complementation. The principal distinction between the Set Operations $(\cup, \cap, \_')$ and the Logic Operations in Traditional Propositional Logic $(\vee, \wedge, \neg)$, is that the Set Operations do not directly calculate Truth Values. Rather, in MWN we Map Ideas in the World of Ideas, to an Element of a Lattice (the "**Attribute Element**") in the World of Abstract Sets. In mathematical terms, every Element in the Down Set of the Attribute Element in the Lattice will share the Attribute in question. In the case of Logic Operations on the other hand, we apply either an AND rule (in the case of CBNF Clauses) or an OR rule (in the case of DBNF Clauses) to calculate the Truth Value. In other words, Set Operations do just one thing: combine sets or their Complements using Union and Intersection; whereas Logic Operations do two things: (1) combine Sets or their Negatives using Disjunction and Conjunction (which work in exactly the same way as Complementation, Union, and Intersection) and (2) calculate Truth Values using an OR or an AND rule.

For purposes of MWN, we elect to treat the Logic Operations $(\vee, \wedge, \neg)$ as substantially equivalent to the Set Operations $(\cup, \cap, \_')$. We can do this as to the combination of Set Elements, because the Operations of Union and Intersection operate in the same way as Disjunction and

Conjunction in respect of how Set Elements and their Complements combine to form new Sets. However, we elect not to apply the OR and AND Operations to the calculation of Truth Value. Instead, we will apply the same approach to calculating the Attribute "Truth Value" that we would apply to any other Attribute of Ideas generally.

Operation Name	Symbol	Venn Diagram
Conjunction, And, Intersection	$x \wedge y$	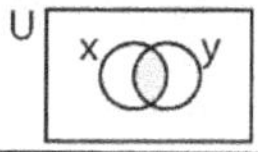
Disjunction, Either-Or, Union	$x \vee y$	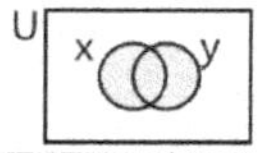
L-R or 1st Implication, Conditional, If-Then	$x \rightarrow y$	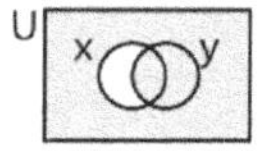
R-L or 2nd Implication, Conditional, If-Then	$x \leftarrow y$	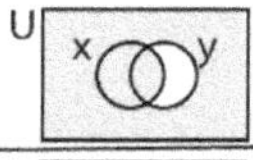
Equivalence, Biconditional	$x \leftrightarrow y$	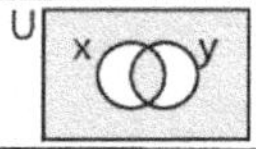
Not p, First Complement	$\neg x$	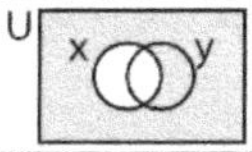
Not q, Second Complement	$\neg y$	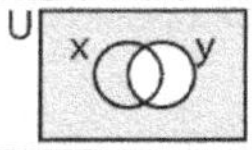
Joint Denial	$x \downarrow y$	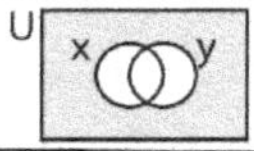
Alternative Denial, Sheffer Stroke	$x \mid y$	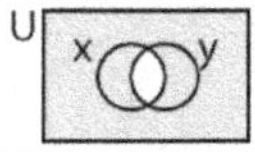
Exclusive Disjunction, Symmetric Diff.	$x \nleftrightarrow y$	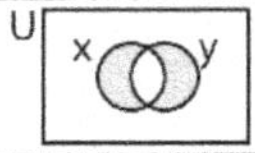
1st Difference	$x \nrightarrow y$	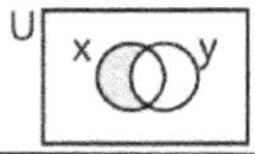
2nd Difference	$x \nleftarrow y$	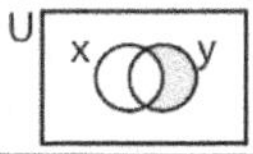
First Selector	x	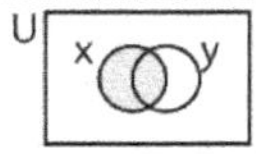
Second Selector	y	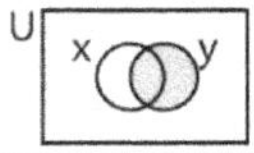
Universal Set, Tautology	U or 1	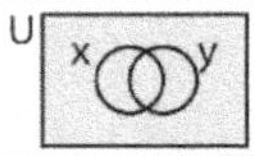
Empty Set, Contradiction	$\emptyset$ or 0	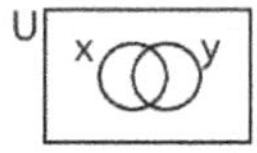

Fig. 7-4

Another approach to understanding the 16 Logic Operations is to look at Truth Tables. *See*, **Table 7-1**. Each row in the Truth Table corresponds to an area in the Venn Diagram that we saw in **Fig. 7-3**.

Table 7-1

x	y	pRq
T	T	[two choices, T or F]
T	F	× [two choices, T or F]
F	T	× [two choices, T or F]
F	F	× [two choices, T or F]
		= total of 2^4 = 16 possible Truth Tables

Fig. 7-5 illustrates how each distinct area in the Venn Diagram corresponds to a row in the Truth Table.

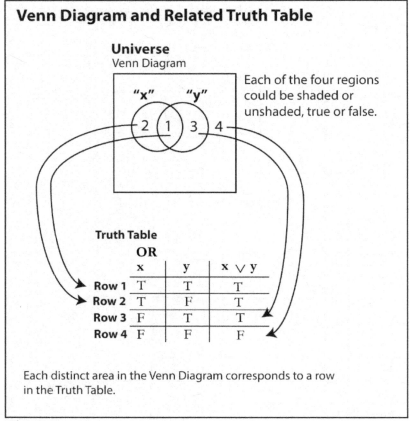

Venn Diagram and Related Truth Table

Universe
Venn Diagram

Each of the four regions could be shaded or unshaded, true or false.

Truth Table
OR

	x	y	x ∨ y
Row 1	T	T	T
Row 2	T	F	T
Row 3	F	T	T
Row 4	F	F	F

Each distinct area in the Venn Diagram corresponds to a row in the Truth Table.

Fig. 7-5

Given that there are four rows, and two choices in the final column for each row, there are $2^4 = 16$ possible Truth Tables. *See*, **Fig. 7-6**.

The 16 Truth Tables

AND

x	y	x ∧ y
T	T	T
T	F	F
F	T	F
F	F	F

OR

x	y	x ∨ y
T	T	T
T	F	T
F	T	T
F	F	F

L-R Implication

x	y	x → y
T	T	T
T	F	F
F	T	T
F	F	T

Equivalence

x	y	x ↔ y
T	T	T
T	F	F
F	T	F
F	F	T

Joint Denial

p	y	x ↓ y
T	T	F
T	F	F
F	T	F
F	F	T

Scheffer Stroke

p	y	x | y
T	T	F
T	F	T
F	T	T
F	F	T

Symmetric Difference

x	y	x ↮ y
T	T	F
T	F	T
F	T	T
F	F	F

1st Difference

x	y	x ↛ y
T	T	F
T	F	T
F	T	F
F	F	F

R-L Implication

x	y	x ← y
T	T	T
T	F	T
F	T	F
F	F	T

2nd Difference

p	y	x ↚ y
T	T	F
T	F	F
F	T	T
F	F	F

Not x

x	y	¬ x
T	T	F
T	F	F
F	T	T
F	F	T

Not y

x	y	¬ y
T	T	F
T	F	T
F	T	F
F	F	T

Tautology / Universe

x	y	T
T	T	T
T	F	T
F	T	T
F	F	T

Contradiction / Empty Set

p	y	F
T	T	F
T	F	F
F	T	F
F	F	F

1st Selector

x	y	x
T	T	T
T	F	T
F	T	F
F	F	F

2d Selector

x	y	y
T	T	T
T	F	F
F	T	T
F	F	F

Fig. 7-6

While the above approach to analyzing and counting the number of Truth Tables works for a simple binary True/False Order 2 Domain, we have a problem if the Domain has more than two Elements. How do we reconcile the fact that we still have 16 Truth Tables, when there may be four or more choices for Values in the final column of the Truth Table? The answer is that we must return to the theory of "Free Algebras with "n" Generators," where Logic Formulas written in DBNF are equivalent to Elements in a Power Set where the Atoms are in the following form: $(x \wedge y), (x \wedge \neg y), (\neg x \wedge y), (\neg x \wedge \neg y)$. The key point for our present purposes is that there are four Atoms in a Free Algebra with two Generators or Variables, but the Domain can be *any* Boolean Algebra with *any* number of Atoms. Therefore, we can maintain a Truth Table with four rows, each representing an Atom in a Free Algebra with two Generators, but the Domain can have 2, 4, 8, or more Elements.

Rewriting the Truth Table to conform to the theory of Free Algebras, we get a Truth Table as set forth in **Fig. 7-7**, where each pair of Elements selected from the Boolean Algebra Domain Maps to a unique Element of the same Boolean Algebra Domain. *See,* **Fig. 7-7**.

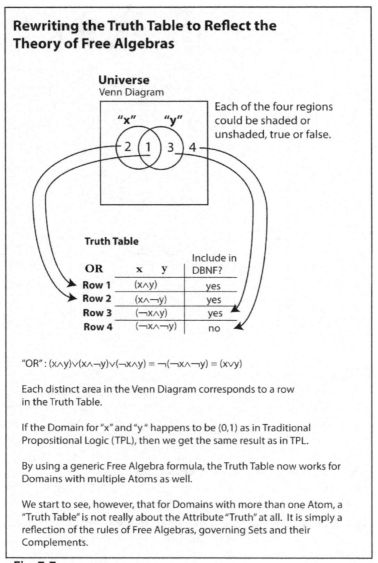

Rewriting the Truth Table to Reflect the Theory of Free Algebras

Universe
Venn Diagram

Each of the four regions could be shaded or unshaded, true or false.

"x"   "y"

2 1 3 4

Truth Table

OR	x y	Include in DBNF?
Row 1	(x∧y)	yes
Row 2	(x∧¬y)	yes
Row 3	(¬x∧y)	yes
Row 4	(¬x∧¬y)	no

"OR" : (x∧y)∨(x∧¬y)∨(¬x∧y) = ¬(¬x∧¬y) = (x∨y)

Each distinct area in the Venn Diagram corresponds to a row in the Truth Table.

If the Domain for "x" and "y" happens to be (0,1) as in Traditional Propositional Logic (TPL), then we get the same result as in TPL.

By using a generic Free Algebra formula, the Truth Table now works for Domains with multiple Atoms as well.

We start to see, however, that for Domains with more than one Atom, a "Truth Table" is not really about the Attribute "Truth" at all. It is simply a reflection of the rules of Free Algebras, governing Sets and their Complements.

Fig. 7-7

The rewritten Truth Table in **Fig. 7-7** does not actually tell us the Value of the Boolean Formula, but it gives us the formula for performing the calculation for any pair of Elements "x" and "y" from the Order 2 Domain for any given Boolean Operation. The 16 Truth Tables correspond to the Elements of a two-Variable Power Set Lattice of Logic Formula Atoms. The number of Elements in the Order 2 Domain of Propositions is irrelevant. (This is contrary to the view taken in most books on Traditional Propositional Logic!) The fact that a Binary Order 2 Domain gives rise to 16 Truth Tables (as set forth in **Table 7-1**) is really just a coincidence; no matter how many Atoms are in the Order 2 Domain, we always have 16 Truth Tables if there are two Propositional Variables in the Order 3 Universe of Discourse.

7.5. *Expressing Truth Tables as Logic Formulas*

In this Section, we demonstrate how to generate the four Atoms of DBNF Clauses in two Variables and the four Atoms of CBNF Clauses in two Variables from Truth Tables. Each Set of four Atoms can form the Base Set of a Boolean Algebra. The $2^4 = 16$ Elements of each Boolean Algebra correspond to the 16 Truth Tables that we examined previously in connection with Logic Formulas using two Variables.

We will demonstrate that a better way to interpret Truth Tables from a MWN perspective, is to understand that the only reason we have a two-valued Range is because Traditional Propositional Logic is working in the Order 2 Boolean Algebra "2" where there is one Atom, and therefore two Elements in the Power Set: X = 1, and $P(X) = (\emptyset, 1)$. The Boolean Expressions in CBNF and DBNF can return any Element in the Boolean Algebra; it just happens that there are only two Elements in the P_1 Boolean Algebra, *i.e.*, Lattice "1" and the Lattice "0". In the broader Mathematics of Ideas, however, we often use a Domain that has more than two Elements.

Therefore, a better interpretation of Truth Tables is that we are not in fact dealing with Truth Values at all. Rather, we are simply applying the rules of DBNF and CBNF, which are equivalent to the rules governing Canonical Representation of Elements of Free Algebras with "n" Generators, that apply to any Boolean Algebra with any number of Atoms. It is just a coincidence that there are only two values in the Range. The two values are not really "Truth Values," as we use the term in MWN.

To begin, we see that a Truth Table is essentially a representation in Normal Form (DBNF or CBNF) of a Boolean Function. *See*, [Quine 1982] at 73. The easiest way to see this is to use a Truth Table to construct a formula in DBNF. For example, we can use the Truth Table for $(x \lor y)$ as an example. *See,* **Table 7-2**.

Table 7-2

x	y	$x \lor y$
T	T	T
T	F	T
F	T	T
F	F	F

For each row that is "True" in the final column, we create a term reflecting the Values for x and y. In this first example, the first three rows are True, so our Boolean Expression "OR" expressed in DBNF will have three Clauses:

OR $_{DBNF}$:
(Row 1) OR (Row 2) OR (Row 3) =
$(x \land y) \lor (x \land \neg y) \lor (\neg x \land y)$

Each Clause corresponds to one of the first three rows of the Truth Table.

Similarly, we can calculate the Boolean Expression "OR" expressed in CBNF from a Truth Table. For each row that is "False" in the final column of the Truth Table, we create a term reflecting the Values for "x" and "y". In this example, the last row is False, so our Boolean Expression in CBNF will have one term:

OR $_{CBNF}$:
Not Row 4 =
$\neg (\neg x \land \neg y) =$
$(x \lor y)$

In this manner, we can calculate the applicable Boolean Expression in DBNF and CBNF for each of the 16 Truth Tables relating to Formulas involving two Propositional Variables. *See,* **Table 7-3**.

Table 7-3

Name	Boolean Structure (Object)	DBNF = ¬ (Complement of CBNF)	CBNF = ¬ (Complement of DBNF)	Boolean Structure (Attribute)
Contradiction	$\varnothing$	$\varnothing$ **Contradiction :** $(x \wedge \neg x)$	$(x \vee y) \wedge$ $(x \vee \neg y) \wedge$ $(\neg x \vee y) \wedge$ $(\neg x \vee \neg y)$	[4321]
AND	(a)	$(x \wedge y)$	$(x \vee y) \wedge$ $(x \vee \neg y) \wedge$ $(\neg x \vee y)$	[432]
1st Difference	(b)	$(x \wedge \neg y)$	$(x \vee y) \wedge$ $(x \vee \neg y) \wedge$ $(\neg x \vee \neg y)$	[431]
2nd Difference	(c)	$(\neg x \wedge y)$	$(x \vee y) \wedge$ $(\neg x \vee y) \wedge$ $(\neg x \vee \neg y)$	[421]
Joint Denial	(d)	$(\neg x \wedge \neg y)$	$(x \vee \neg y) \wedge$ $(\neg x \vee y) \wedge$ $(\neg x \vee \neg y)$	[321]
Not p	(ab)	$(x \wedge y) \vee$ $(x \wedge \neg y)$	$(x \vee y) \wedge$ $(x \vee \neg y)$	[43]
Not q	(ac)	$(x \wedge y) \vee$ $(\neg x \wedge y)$	$(x \vee y) \wedge$ $(\neg x \vee y)$	[42]
Equivalence	(ad)	$(x \wedge y) \vee$ $(\neg x \wedge \neg y)$	$(x \vee \neg y) \wedge$ $(\neg x \vee y)$	[32]
Symmetric Difference	(bc)	$(x \wedge \neg y) \vee$ $(\neg x \wedge y)$	$(x \vee y) \wedge$ $(\neg x \vee \neg y)$	[41]
2nd Selector	(bd)	$(x \wedge \neg y) \vee$ $(\neg x \wedge \neg y)$	$(x \vee \neg y) \wedge$ $(\neg x \vee \neg y)$	[31]
1st Selector	(cd)	$(\neg x \wedge y) \vee$ $(\neg x \wedge \neg y)$	$(\neg x \vee y) \wedge$ $(\neg x \vee \neg y)$	[21]
Scheffer Stroke	(bcd)	$(x \wedge \neg y) \vee$ $(\neg x \wedge y) \vee$ $(\neg x \wedge \neg y)$	$(\neg x \vee \neg y)$	[1]
Implication-R	(cda)	$(\neg x \wedge y) \vee$ $(\neg x \wedge \neg y) \vee$ $(x \wedge y)$	$(\neg x \vee y)$	[2]
Implication-L	(dab)	$(\neg x \wedge \neg y) \vee$ $(x \wedge y) \vee$ $(x \wedge \neg y)$	$(x \vee \neg y)$	[3]
OR	(abc)	$(x \wedge y) \vee$ $(x \wedge \neg y) \vee$ $(\neg x \wedge y)$	$(x \vee y)$	[4]
Tautology	(abcd)	$(x \wedge y) \vee$ $(x \wedge \neg y) \vee$ $(\neg x \wedge y) \vee$ $(\neg x \wedge \neg y) \vee$	$\varnothing$ **Tautology:** $(x \vee \neg x)$	$\varnothing$

From **Table 7-3**, we can readily see that the four Clauses of the DBNF Formulas: $(x \wedge y)$, $(x \wedge \neg y)$, $(\neg x \wedge y)$, and $(\neg x \wedge \neg y)$ create a Boolean Algebra. Similarly, the four Clauses of the CBNF Logic Formulas: $(x \vee y)$, $(x \vee \neg y)$, $(\neg x \vee y)$, and $(\neg x \vee \neg y)$ create an Inverse, Dual Boolean Algebra.

Also, note the relationship between the CBNF and the DBNF: the DBNF is equal to the Negation of the Complement of the CBNF; and the CBNF is equal to the Negation of the Complement of the DBNF. This is consistent with the Dual Power Set Lattice structure of Objects and Attributes in MWN generally. We view Attributes as the Negation of the Complement of the related Object. For example, the Element (ab) in a P_4 Power Set has the Attribute Signature [43] representing not-(cd) (sometimes written "~(cd)"). In terms of the Boolean Algebra of Logic Formulas for the corresponding Elements, we have the following:

- The Complement of (ab) is (cd).
- Element (cd) corresponds to $(\neg x \vee y) \wedge (\neg x \vee \neg y)$ in CBNF.
- The Negation of (cd) = ~(cd) corresponds to
  $\neg((\neg x \vee y) \wedge (\neg x \vee \neg y))$
  $= (x \wedge \neg y) \vee (x \wedge y)$ (in DBNF)
  $= (ab)$

As expected, to convert (ab) = "$(x \vee y) \wedge (x \vee \neg y)$" from CBNF to DBNF, we take the Negation of the Complement (cd) = "$\neg((\neg x \vee y) \wedge (\neg x \vee \neg y)) = (x \wedge \neg y) \vee (x \wedge y)$".

Note that even though MWN Propositional Logic uses a different method of assigning Truth Values as compared to Traditional Propositional Logic, we can still use Truth Tables to compare Boolean Expressions to see if they are the same.

7.6. *Creating a Lattice of Logic Formulas*

As noted earlier, we can use the Atoms in DBNF or CBNF to create a Boolean Lattice. We start with an Atomic Formula "x", representing a single Proposition and Create DBNF and CBNF Logic Formulas. There are $2^1 = 2$ Clauses in each formula. That leaves us with the following:

- DBNF Atoms: (x), $(\neg x)$
- CBNF Atoms: (x), $(\neg x)$

Note that the Atoms for DBNF and CBNF Atoms appear to be the same when we are looking at formulas with one Variable. This will not be the case, however, when we look at formulas with two or more Variables.

Using the two Clauses as "Atoms," we can create Boolean Equations:

- DBNF formula: $(x) \lor (\neg\ x) = $ True, *i.e.*, "Lattice 1"
- CBNF formula: $(x) \land (\neg\ x) = $ False, *i.e.*, "Lattice 0"

Viewing each Clause as an Atom, we see that we can form one Lattice with two Atoms and $2^2 = 4$ Elements. *See,* **Fig. 7-8**.

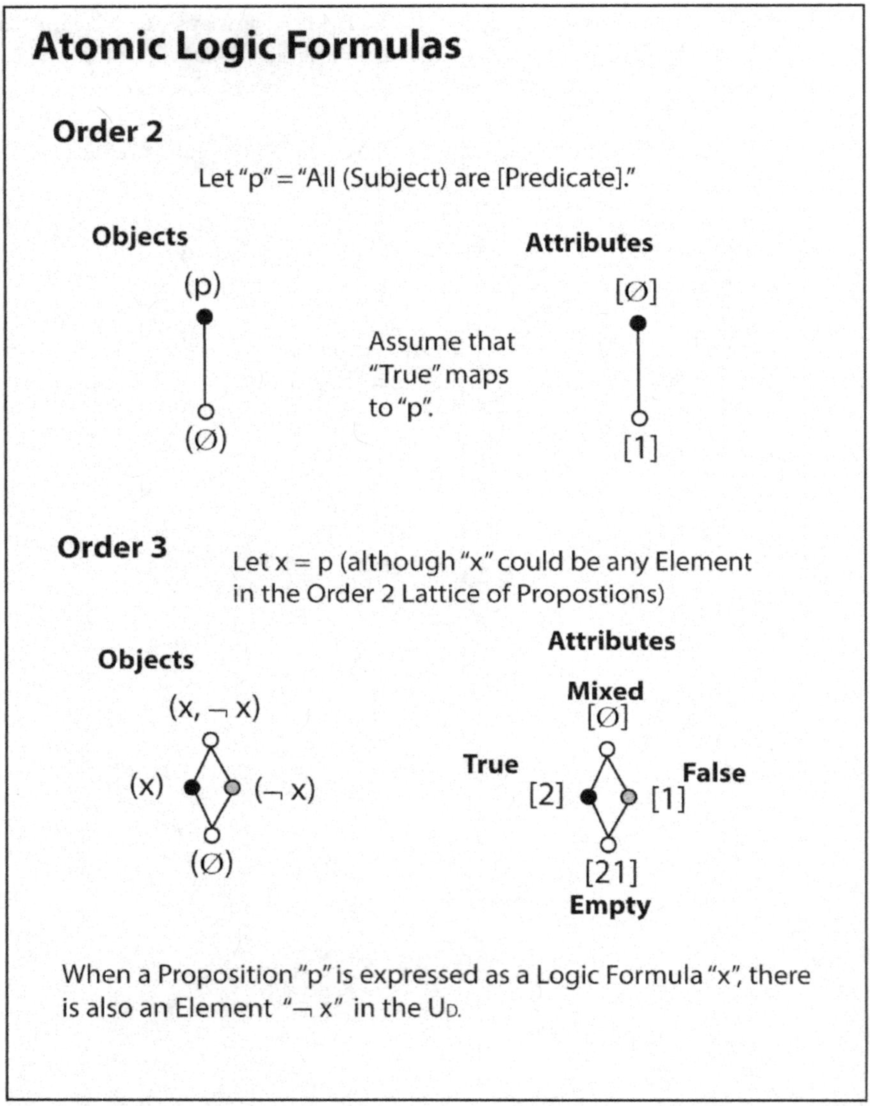

Atomic Logic Formulas

Order 2

Let "p" = "All (Subject) are [Predicate]."

Objects

(p)

(∅)

Assume that
"True" maps
to "p".

Attributes

[∅]

[1]

Order 3

Let x = p (although "x" could be any Element in the Order 2 Lattice of Propostions)

Objects

(x, ¬ x)

(x)   (¬ x)

(∅)

Attributes

Mixed
[∅]

True
[2]   [1] False

[21]
Empty

When a Proposition "p" is expressed as a Logic Formula "x", there is also an Element "¬ x" in the U$_D$.

Fig. 7-8

We can create an Order 3 Domain of two Variable Logic Formulas where there are $2^2 = 4$ Clauses in each of the DBNF and CBNF formulas. That leaves us with the following:

- **DBNF Clauses**: $(x \wedge y), (x \wedge \neg y), (\neg x \wedge y), (\neg x \wedge \neg y)$
- **CBNF Clauses**: $(x \vee y), (x \vee \neg y), (\neg x \vee y), (\neg x \vee \neg y)$

Viewing each Clause as an Atom, we see that we can form two Lattices with four Atoms and $2^4 = 16$ Elements each. *See*, **Fig. 7-9**.

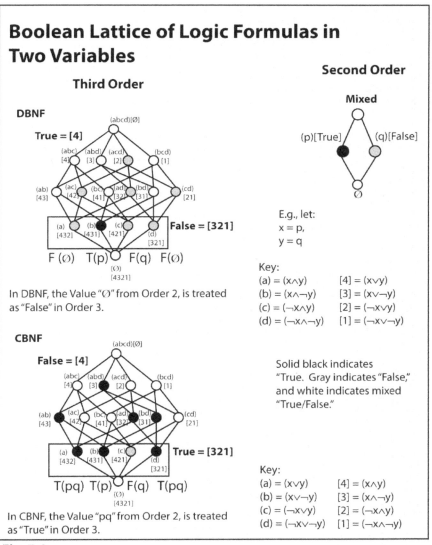

Boolean Lattice of Logic Formulas in Two Variables

Third Order

Second Order

Mixed

DBNF

In DBNF, the Value "()" from Order 2, is treated as "False" in Order 3.

E.g., let:
x = p,
y = q

Key:
(a) = (x∧y)   [4] = (x∨y)
(b) = (x∧¬y)   [3] = (x∨¬y)
(c) = (¬x∧y)   [2] = (¬x∨y)
(d) = (¬x∧¬y)   [1] = (¬x∨¬y)

CBNF

In CBNF, the Value "pq" from Order 2, is treated as "True" in Order 3.

Solid black indicates "True. Gray indicates "False," and white indicates mixed "True/False."

Key:
(a) = (x∨y)   [4] = (x∧y)
(b) = (x∨¬y)   [3] = (x∧¬y)
(c) = (¬x∨y)   [2] = (¬x∧y)
(d) = (¬x∨¬y)   [1] = (¬x∧¬y)

Fig. 7-9

Interestingly, there is another way to form a Boolean Lattice of Logic Formulas in two Variables. We can start with a Boolean Lattice of Logic Formulas in one Variable/two Atoms, and then Subdivide each of the two Atoms to take accommodate a second Variable. *See*, **Fig. 7-10**.

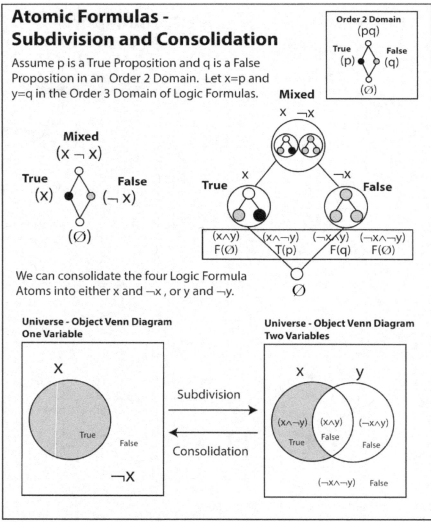

Fig. 7-10

The Venn Diagram in **Fig. 7-10** makes it easier to see how subdivision occurs.

We end this Section with **Fig. 7-11**, which illustrates how the Logic Formulas create a Boolean Lattice.

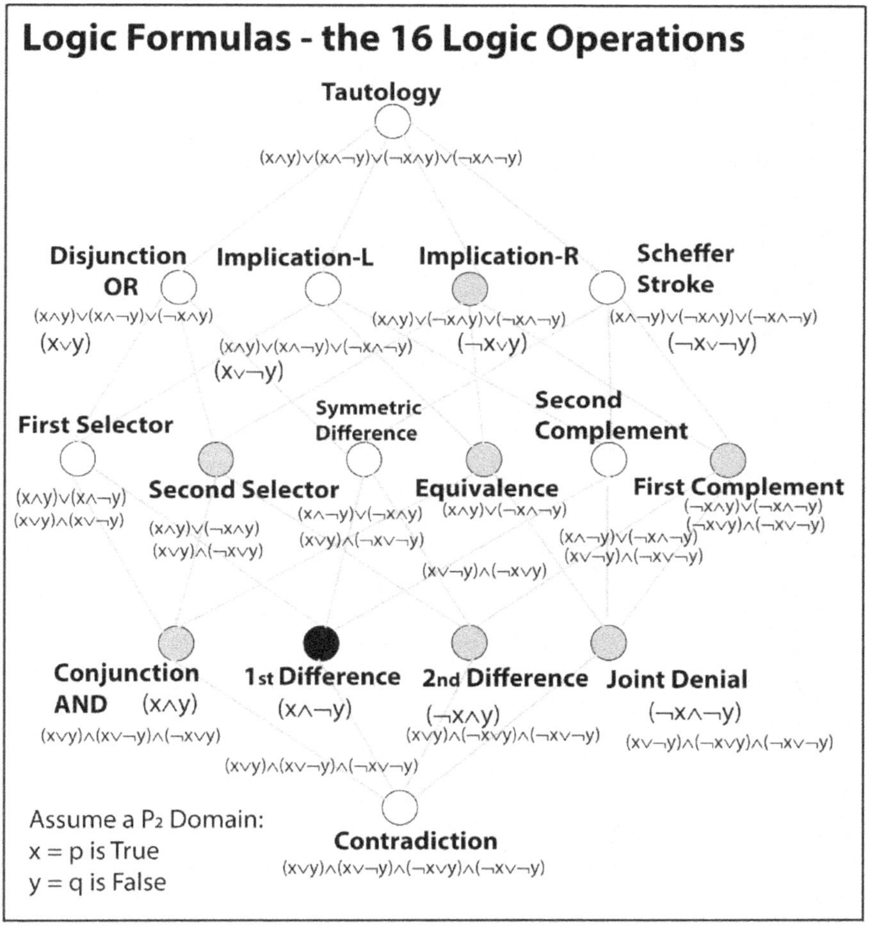

Logic Formulas - the 16 Logic Operations

Tautology
$(x\wedge y)\vee(x\wedge\neg y)\vee(\neg x\wedge y)\vee(\neg x\wedge\neg y)$

Disjunction OR
$(x\wedge y)\vee(x\wedge\neg y)\vee(\neg x\wedge y)$
$(x\vee y)$

Implication-L
$(x\wedge y)\vee(x\wedge\neg y)\vee(\neg x\wedge\neg y)$
$(x\vee\neg y)$

Implication-R
$(x\wedge y)\vee(\neg x\wedge y)\vee(\neg x\wedge\neg y)$
$(\neg x\vee y)$

Scheffer Stroke
$(x\wedge\neg y)\vee(\neg x\wedge y)\vee(\neg x\wedge\neg y)$
$(\neg x\vee\neg y)$

First Selector
$(x\wedge y)\vee(x\wedge\neg y)$
$(x\vee y)\wedge(x\vee\neg y)$

Symmetric Difference

Second Complement

Second Selector
$(x\wedge y)\vee(\neg x\wedge y)$
$(x\vee y)\wedge(\neg x\vee y)$

Equivalence
$(x\wedge y)\vee(\neg x\wedge y)$
$(x\vee y)\wedge(\neg x\vee\neg y)$
$(x\vee\neg y)\wedge(\neg x\vee y)$

First Complement
$(\neg x\wedge y)\vee(\neg x\wedge\neg y)$
$(\neg x\vee y)\wedge(\neg x\vee\neg y)$
$(x\wedge\neg y)\vee(\neg x\wedge\neg y)$
$(x\vee\neg y)\wedge(\neg x\vee\neg y)$

Conjunction AND $(x\wedge y)$
$(x\vee y)\wedge(x\vee\neg y)\wedge(\neg x\vee y)$

1st Difference
$(x\wedge\neg y)$
$(x\vee y)\wedge(x\vee\neg y)\wedge(\neg x\vee\neg y)$

2nd Difference
$(\neg x\wedge y)$
$(x\vee y)\wedge(\neg x\vee y)\wedge(\neg x\vee\neg y)$

Joint Denial
$(\neg x\wedge\neg y)$
$(x\vee\neg y)\wedge(\neg x\vee y)\wedge(\neg x\vee\neg y)$

Assume a P₂ Domain:
$x = p$ is True
$y = q$ is False

Contradiction
$(x\vee y)\wedge(x\vee\neg y)\wedge(\neg x\vee y)\wedge(\neg x\vee\neg y)$

Fig. 7-11

197

7.7. Boolean Functions: Disjunctive Boolean Normal Form (DBNF) and Conjunctive Boolean Normal Form (CBNF)

As we saw in **Chapter 3**, "Normal Form," and its variations DNF, CNF, DBNF, and CBNF, is an Attribute of every Boolean Algebra. Once we establish that the Order 3 Domain of Logic Formulas is a Boolean Algebra (essentially by equating $(\vee, \wedge, \neg)$ with $(\cup, \cap, \_')$, then we can apply the principles of Normal Form to Propositional Logic.

Definition: Disjunctive Boolean Normal Form (DBNF): A Disjunction of Conjunctions of Atomic Formulas and their negatives, where we impose the following additional requirements: (a) the Atomic Formulas are placed in alphabetical order, (b) each Clause is a Conjunction of each Atomic Formula or its Negation, and (c) the number of possible Clauses equals 2^n, where n = the number of Atomic Formulas:

Clauses in two Variables:
$$(x \wedge y), (x \wedge \neg y), (\neg x \wedge y), (\neg x \wedge \neg y)$$
Complete DBNF:
$$(x \wedge y) \vee (x \wedge \neg y) \vee (\neg x \wedge y) \vee (\neg x \wedge \neg y) = 1$$

Definition: Conjunctive Boolean Normal Form (CBNF): A Conjunction of Disjunctions of Atomic Formulas and their negatives, where we impose the following additional requirements: (a) the Atomic Formulas are placed in alphabetical order, (b) each Clause is a Disjunction of each Atomic Formula or its Negation, and (c) the number of possible Clauses equals 2^n, where n = the number of Atomic Formulas:

Clauses in two Variables:
$$(x \vee y), (x \vee \neg y), (\neg x \vee y), (\neg x \vee \neg y)$$
Complete CBNF:
$$(x \vee y) \wedge (x \vee \neg y) \wedge (\neg x \vee y) \wedge (\neg x \vee \neg y) = 0$$

7.8. Converting Boolean Functions to DBNF or CBNF

In this Section, we discuss how we can write every Formula of Propositional Logic, or Boolean Function, in either Disjunctive Boolean Normal Form (DBNF), or Conjunctive Boolean Normal Form (CBNF). (We looked at this in **Chapter 3** for Boolean Algebras generally, but here we focus on Propositional Logic.) This will be particularly useful in **Chapter 12** where we study the P_4 Lattice, because the four Atoms of DBNF Clauses or CBNF Clauses, as the case may be, along with the Operations of Union,

Intersection, and Complementation, form a Boolean Algebra and a related Boolean Lattice.

We start by defining four special types of Logic Formulas, each referred to as a "**Clause**":

- CNF Clause.
- DNF Clause.
- CBNF Clause.
- DBNF Clause.

A "**DNF Clause**" is a string of Conjunctions of Literals (*i.e.*, Atomic Formulas and their Negations), and can be of any length. For example, the following are DNF Clauses:

- (x)
- $(x \wedge y)$
- $(x \wedge y \wedge \neg x)$
- $(x \wedge y \wedge \neg x \wedge \neg y)$

A "**CNF Clause**" is a string of Disjunctions of Literals (*i.e.*, Atomic Formulas and their Negations), and can be of any length. For example, the following are CNF Clauses:

- (x)
- $(x \vee y)$
- $(x \vee y \vee \neg x)$
- $(x \vee y \vee \neg x \vee \neg y)$

(The labeling may seem backwards, but the reason for using these terms will become apparent.)

A "**DBNF Clause**" is a string of Conjunctions of Literals that uses each Atomic Formula or its Negation exactly one time. For Logic Formulas in two Variables, there are only $2^2 = 4$ DBNF Clauses:

- $(x \wedge y)$
- $(x \wedge \neg y)$
- $(\neg x \wedge y)$
- $(\neg x \wedge \neg y)$

A "**CBNF Clause**" is a string of Disjunctions of Literals that uses each Atomic Formula or its Negation exactly one time. For Logic Formulas in two Variables, there are only $2^2 = 4$ CBNF Clauses:

- $(x \lor y)$
- $(x \lor \neg y)$
- $(\neg x \lor y)$
- $(\neg x \lor \neg y)$

Now that we have defined the four types of Clauses, we need to define four types of Logic Formulas that use the four types of Clauses:

- Logic Formula in Disjunctive Normal Form (DNF).
- Logic Formula in Conjunctive Normal Form (CNF).
- Logic Formula in Disjunctive Boolean Normal Form (DBNF).
- Logic Formula in Conjunctive Boolean Normal Form (CBNF).

DNF and CNF contain only the following symbols (other than parentheses): Propositional Variables (x_1, x_2, x_3, ...) and their Negations ($\neg x_1$, $\neg x_2$, $\neg x_3$, ...), conjunction ($\land$), and disjunction ($\lor$). For a discussion of the Conjunctive Normal Form, *see* [Copi 1973] at 225 *et seq.* and 286 *et seq*, and [Hedman 2004] at 27 *et seq*.   In other words, a DNF Logic Formula is a Disjunction of DNF Clauses, and a CNF Logic Formula is a Conjunction of CNF Clauses. Similarly, a DBNF Logic Formula is a Disjunction of DBNF Clauses, and a CBNF Logic Formula is a Conjunction of CBNF Clauses.

Logic Formula in Disjunctive Normal Form (DNF): A Disjunction of DNF Clauses:

Two variables:
$$(x \land \neg y \land \neg x) \lor (\neg y \land y \land x) \lor (\neg x \land \neg y) \lor (\neg x \land x \land \neg y)$$

Logic Formula in Conjunctive Normal Form (CNF): A Conjunction of CNF Clauses:

Two variables:
$$(x \lor \neg y \lor \neg x) \land (\neg y \lor y \lor x) \land (\neg x \lor \neg y) \land (\neg x \lor x \lor \neg y)$$

Logic Formula in Disjunctive Boolean Normal Form (DBNF): A Disjunction of DBNF Clauses:

Two Propositional Variables:

- $(x \wedge y)$
- $(x \wedge y) \vee (x \wedge \neg y)$
- $(x \wedge y) \vee (x \wedge \neg y) \vee (\neg x \wedge y) \vee (\neg x \wedge \neg y)$

Logic Formula in Conjunctive Boolean Normal Form (CBNF):
A Conjunction of CBNF Clauses:

Two Propositional Variables:

- $(x \vee y)$
- $(x \vee y) \wedge (x \vee \neg y)$
- $(x \vee y) \wedge (x \vee \neg y) \wedge (\neg x \vee y) \wedge (\neg x \vee \neg y)$

(Now, the reason for naming the Clauses becomes apparent. DBNF Clauses are the Clauses used in a DBNF Logic Formula; CBNF Clauses are the Clauses used in a CBNF Logic Formula.)

Note that Logic Formulas in DNF or CNF can be comprised of long strings of Propositional Variables and their Negations. Logic Formulas in DBNF and CBNF, however, have a limited number of forms. For example, with two Propositional Variables, there are only four possible DBNF (or CBNF) Clauses. We can use these Clauses to form a Boolean Algebra with $2^4 = 16$ possible combinations of DBNF (or CBNF) Clauses. What this tells us is that for DBNF (or CBNF) Logic Formulas, there are only 16 possible Logic Formulas.

In this book, we demonstrate how to form a Boolean Algebra using either the following four Atoms in CBNF or DBNF:

DBNF Clauses: $((x \wedge y), (x \wedge \neg y), (\neg x \wedge y), (\neg x \wedge \neg y))$

CBNF Clauses: $((x \vee y), (x \vee \neg y), (\neg x \vee y), (\neg x \vee \neg y))$

There are a number of important facts about Formulas of Propositional Logic, including those listed below. We do not provide the proofs here, but the proofs are readily available in the refences listed below.

(1) Every Formula of Propositional Logic is equivalent to a Formula written in DNF, using only $\vee, \wedge$, and $\neg$.
(2) Every Formula of Propositional Logic is equivalent to a Formula written in CNF, using only $\vee, \wedge$, and $\neg$.

(3) Every Formula of Propositional Logic is equivalent to a Formula written in DBNF.

(4) Every Formula of Propositional Logic is equivalent to a Formula written in CBNF.

(5) The Negation of a DBNF Formula is a CBNF Formula.

(6) The Negation of a CBNF Formula is a DBNF Formula.

See, [Ackermann and Hilbert 1937] at 17, and [Hedman 2004] at 27 *et seq.*

7.9. *Value Map (Order 2) and Logic Formulas (Order 3)*

We know from our study of Boolean Algebras generally (*see*, **Chapter 3**), that the Operations of Union and Intersection (and OR an AND, to extent we treat them as being the same as Union and Intersection), are Closed with respect to the applicable Power Set Domain. Therefore, if we use Elements from an Order 2 Domain to fix the values of Propositional Variables in an Order 3 Lattice of Logic Formulas, then each Logic Formula will return one of the Elements from the Order 2 Domain. In this way, we can create a **"Value Map"** where each Boolean Expression in an Order 3 Lattice of Logic Formulas is replaced with an Element from the applicable Order 2 Lattice. *See*, **Fig. 7-12**, for examples using an Order 2 Lattice with one Atom $X = \{p\}$, and therefore two Elements $P(X) = (\varnothing, p)$. **Fig. 7-13**, **Fig. 7-14**, and **Fig. 7-15** cover Order 2 Lattices with two, three, and four Atoms, respectively, and **Fig. 7-16** provides a comparison of the Order 2 Domains with one, two, three, and four Atoms.

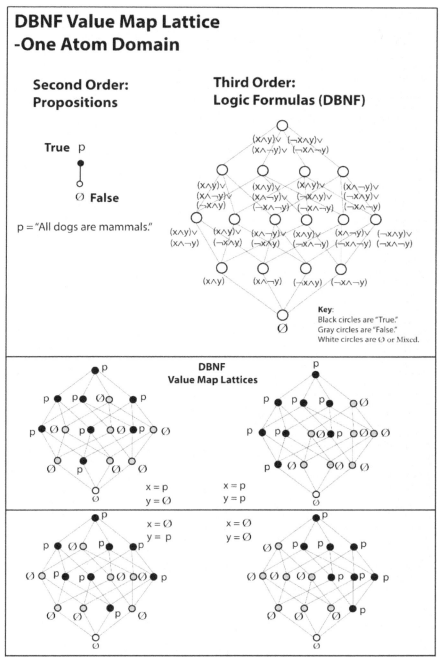

Fig. 7-12

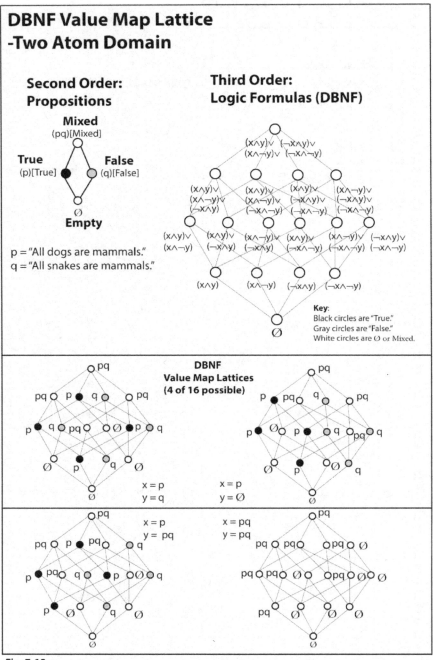

DBNF Value Map Lattice
-Two Atom Domain

Second Order: Propositions

Mixed
(pq)[Mixed]

True
(p)[True]

False
(q)[False]

∅
Empty

p = "All dogs are mammals."
q = "All snakes are mammals."

Third Order: Logic Formulas (DBNF)

(x∧y)∨ (¬x∧y)∨
(x∧¬y)∨ (¬x∧¬y)

(x∧y)∨   (x∧y)∨   (x∧y)∨   (x∧¬y)∨
(x∧¬y)∨   (x∧¬y)∨   (¬x∧y)∨   (¬x∧y)∨
(¬x∧y)   (¬x∧¬y)   (¬x∧¬y)   (¬x∧¬y)

(x∧y)∨   (x∧y)∨   (x∧¬y)∨ (x∧¬y)∨ (x∧¬y)∨ (¬x∧y)∨
(x∧¬y)   (¬x∧y)   (¬x∧y)   (¬x∧¬y) (¬x∧¬y) (¬x∧¬y)

(x∧y)   (x∧¬y)   (¬x∧y)   (¬x∧¬y)

∅

Key:
Black circles are "True."
Gray circles are "False."
White circles are ∅ or Mixed.

DBNF Value Map Lattices (4 of 16 possible)

pq

pq   p   q   pq

p   q   pq   ∅∅   p   q

∅   p   q   ∅

∅

x = p
y = q

pq

p   pq   q   pq

p   ∅∅   p   q   pq   q

∅   p   ∅∅   q

∅

x = p
y = ∅

pq

pq   p   pq   q

p   pq   q   p   ∅∅   q

p   ∅   q   ∅

∅

x = p
y = pq

x = pq
y = pq

pq

pq   pqq   pq   ∅

pq   pq   ∅∅   pq   ∅∅   ∅

pq   ∅   ∅   ∅

∅

Fig. 7-13

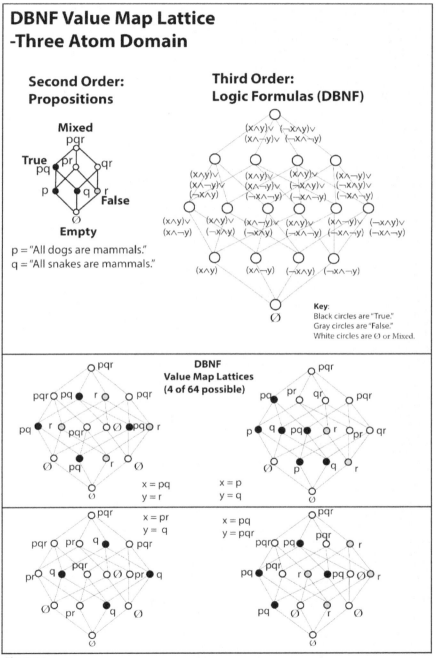

Fig. 7-14

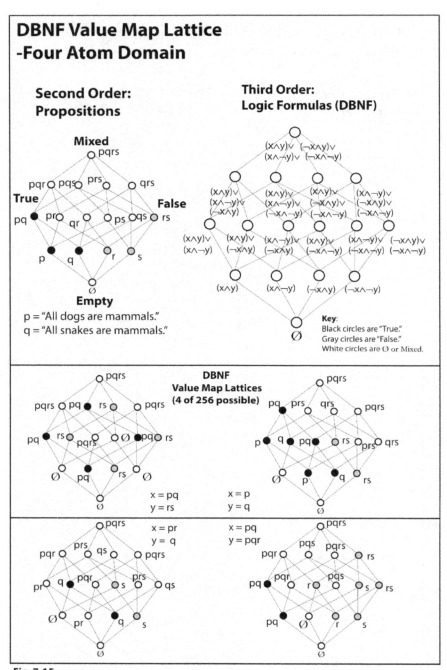

DBNF Value Map Lattice
-Four Atom Domain

Second Order: Propositions

Third Order: Logic Formulas (DBNF)

Fig. 7-15

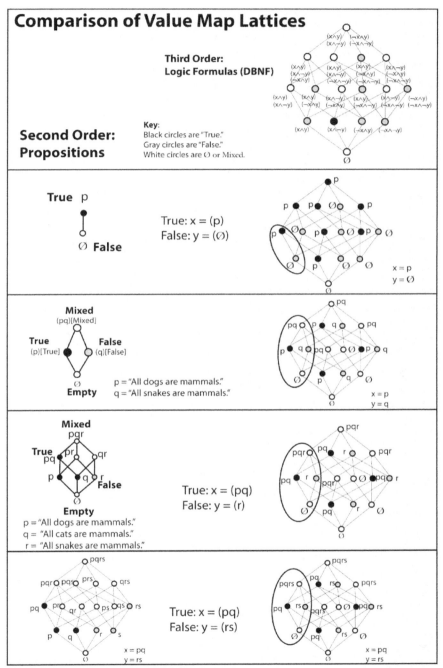

Fig. 7-16

Note that when there is an Order 2 Domain with a single Atom, *i.e.*, X = {p} and $P(X)$ = (Ø, p), then the Truth Values of the Elements of the Lattice in Order 3 are binary, *i.e.*, every Element in Order 3 Maps to either "Ø" or "p" in Order 2.

If there is more than one Atom, however, in the Order 2 Domain, then the Order 3 Elements will Map to one of four Truth Values: (Mixed, True, False, or Empty).

Traditional Propositional Logic uses the Value Map to determine the Truth Value of each Logic Formula in Order 3. MWN, however, takes a different approach to Truth Value. In MWN Propositional Logic, we use the Value Map to determine the Truth Value of Order 3 Atoms, and then we identify the "Attribute Element" as the sum of all "True" Atoms and the Complement represents the sum of all "False" Atoms. The remaining Elements, other than "(Ø)", have a Mixed Truth Value.

7.10. *The Meaning of Negation: Ideas v. Propositions v. Logic Formulas*

The term "Negation," and the word "not" that we use to implement Negation, have a variety of different meanings that depend upon the Domain and Universe of Discourse in which we are operating. In the Order 1 Universe of Discourse of "Ideas," the concept of "Negation" is interpreted as the Set Operation of Complementation, either Absolute or Relative. *See,* **Fig. 7-17**.

Negation - Order 1 - "Ideas"

Dimension 1 - Idea Atoms

$$X = \{ a, b, c \} \xrightarrow{\text{Map}} \{ \text{Yes, No} \}$$

If (a)={dog} and (bc)= {cat, crab}, then "not-Dog"= ~a = a' = (bc). The Complement of (a) is (bc). Here, the Complement is the "Relative Complement," i.e., relative to the Set X, which is the Base Set for our Universe of Discourse.

Dimension 2 - Power Set of Ideas

Mixed:
Some Yes, some No

We can form a Power Set from the same Base Set "X".

E.g.1: When we say "not-dog", we refer to the Complement: (a) '= (bc).
E.g. 2: "Not-mammal" = (ab)' = (c).

Fig. 7-17

In the Order 2 Domain of Propositions, Negation works exactly the same way as in the Order 1 Domain of Ideas. "Negation" is interpreted as Set Complementation, either Absolute or Relative. *See*, **Fig. 7-18**.

Negation - Order 2 - "Propositions"

Dimension 1 - Proposition Atoms

$$X = \{ p, q, r \} \xrightarrow{\text{Map}} \{ \text{True, False} \}$$

Let: p = "A dog is a mammal."
q = "A cat is a mammal."
r = "A crab is a mammal."

Propositions "p" and "q" Map to True; "r" Maps to False.

"Not-p" = {~p} = { q, r }. If we select a Proposition "p" from the Base Set X = { p, q, r }, then we have not selected "q" or "r".

Dimension 2 - Power Set of Propositions

Mixed:
Some True, some False

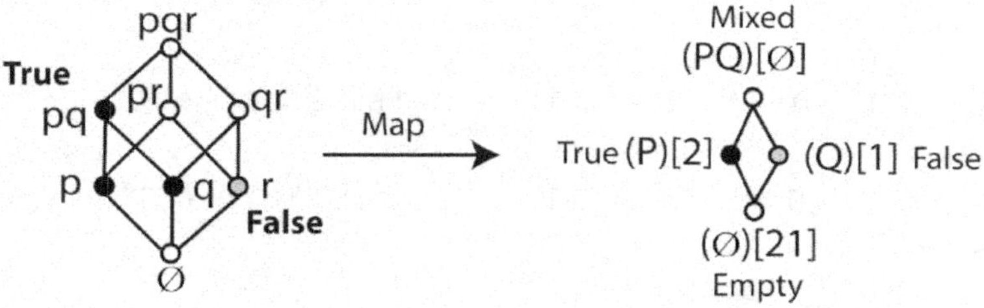

"Not-p" = (qr).

"Not-pq" = (r). In the context of a Dimension 2, Order 2 Power Set Lattice of Propositions, "not" is used to mean the unique Complement of an Element in the Power Set Lattice.

Fig. 7-18

"Negation" in the sense of "Sign Reversal" does not work well in the Order 2 Domain of Propositions. The reason is that Propositions may have more than one Negative, meaning that the Negative is not unique. For example, in **Fig. 7-18**, the Negative of the Element "r" using "Sign Reversal" is either "p" or "q" at the Atomic level, since they are each True. Also, Sign Reversal does not really make sense at all in the Order 2 Domain, because it would be tantamount to changing the Mapping of Attributes from the World of Ideas to the World of Abstract Sets.

In the Order 3 Domain of Logic Formulas, as a technical matter, we interpret Negation as Set Complementation that operates in the Boolean Algebra of Logic Formulas in exactly the same way as in the Order 1 and Order 2 Domains. *See*, **Fig. 7-19**. In one narrow case, we can interpret Negation as "Sign Reversal," *i.e.*, in Traditional Propositional Logic where the Order 2 Domain has a single Atom and provided that the subject matter is truly binary, like an electrical circuit, such that we are justified in using the Value Map as a proxy for Truth Value. In this narrow case, we can treat Negation as Sign Reversal, but we must exercise care because: (1) we do not want to inadvertently switch Domains (*see*, **Chapter 3**) and (2) the MWN approach to Truth Values is different from that used in Traditional Propositional Logic. As a general rule, however, it is better to think of Negation as being the same as Set Complementation.

Negation - Order 3 - "Logic Formulas: Lattices of CBNF and DBNF Clauses"

Dimension 1

DBNF Clauses
X = { (x∧y), (x∧¬y), (¬x∧y), (¬x∧¬y) } →Map→ { True, False }

CBNF Clauses
X = { (x∨y), (x∨¬y), (¬x∨y), (¬x∨¬y) } →Map→ { True, False }

Assume that "x=p" and "y=q" from a P₂ Domain where "p" is True and "q" is False.

Dimension 2

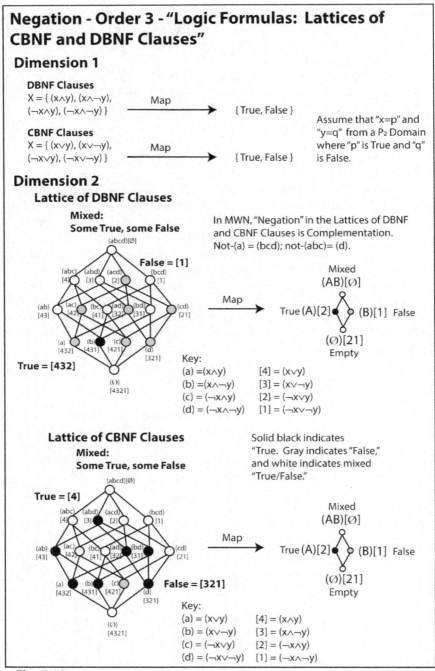

In MWN, "Negation" in the Lattices of DBNF and CBNF Clauses is Complementation. Not-(a) = (bcd); not-(abc)= (d).

Solid black indicates "True. Gray indicates "False," and white indicates mixed "True/False."

Lattice of DBNF Clauses

Key:
(a) =(x∧y)   [4] = (x∨y)
(b) =(x∧¬y)   [3] = (x∨¬y)
(c) = (¬x∧y)   [2] = (¬x∨y)
(d) = (¬x∧¬y) [1] = (¬x∨¬y)

Lattice of CBNF Clauses

Key:
(a) = (x∨y)   [4] = (x∧y)
(b) = (x∨¬y)   [3] = (x∧¬y)
(c) = (¬x∨y)   [2] = (¬x∧y)
(d) = (¬x∨¬y) [1] = (¬x∧¬y)

Fig. 7-19

7.11.   The MWN Approach to Assigning Truth Values in Lattices of Logic Formulas

We end this Chapter with a review of how we assign Truth Values to the Elements of a Boolean Lattice of Logic Formulas. We must start with the Order 1 Boolean Lattice of Ideas, however, which in turns gives rise to an Order 2 Boolean Lattice of Propositions. From there, we create an Order 3 Boolean Lattice of Logic Formulas, keeping in mind, however, that the Lattice of Logic Formulas is really a "Free Algebra with 'n' Generators," which could use *any* Boolean Lattice as its Domain, not just the Order 2 Boolean Lattice of Propositions.

As we saw in **Chapter 2**, we create an Order 1 Boolean Lattice of Ideas by creating a Map from the "World of Ideas" to Elements of a Boolean Lattice in the "World of Abstract Sets." Once we accept that an Idea is either an Atom (or Deemed Atom, really) or a Compound, then it follows that we can create a Boolean Lattice. In later books, we will explore in detail how we go about creating this Map, but it is largely through observation, experimentation, and Inductive Logic. Inductive Logic is inherently flawed in that it is based upon drawing conclusions about universal properties of Sets of Objects based upon an examination of a relatively small subset of Objects in most cases. We mention this here to emphasize that we must regularly revisit our assumptions, which in this case means revisiting our Map of the World of Ideas. A mistake in our Order 1 Lattice will lead to faulty conclusions in Orders 2 and 3.

In **Chapter 6**, we discussed how to create an Order 2 Boolean Lattice of Propositions, where each Atom is a Proposition, which by definition must be either True or False. We saw that the Truth Value of a Proposition is a statement of whether or not the Proposition accurately reflects the unique Two-Set Relationship of the Subject and Predicate when viewed in the Order 1 Lattice of Ideas. We refer to this as the "Logic of Lattices," because the Truth Value is determined by the Lattice position of the Subject and Predicate.

In **Chapter 4**, we examined in detail "Free Algebras with 'n' Generators," and saw that the structure of a Free Algebra reflects precisely the nature of Logic Formulas when expressed in Normal Form. We also saw, however, that Free Algebras are more accurately described as a means of generating Subalgebras, than as a means of generating Truth Values. It is true that if we assume a simple Order 2 Domain with a single True Proposition (representing the Consolidation of all True Propositions into a single Atom), then we end up with a Value Map that reflects the assignment of Truth Values as commonly understood in Traditional Propositional Logic. If, however, we add more Atoms to the Order 2 Domain (so as to allow us to sort Propositions by Attributes other than Truth Value), we see that the Value Map created by a Free Algebra has nothing to do with Truth Value. It is a means of creating a Subalgebra, but the Values in the Value Map do not reflect how we view Truth Value intuitively.

So, what do we do? How do we assign Truth Values to the Order 3 Logic Formulas? The solution that we use in MWN is to go back to our foundational principles, and apply the same rules that we applied to the Order 1 and Order 2 Lattices to determine Attribute Values. The steps are as follows:

- To assign Truth Values to Elements of Boolean Lattices of Logic Formulas, we apply the following rules:
    o Atoms, and only Atoms, have a binary Truth Value.
    o Once we Map the Truth Value of each Atom with respect to a particular Attribute, we can determine the Attribute Element in the Power Set, which is the Element consisting of all of the Atoms that exhibit the Attribute in question.
    o All Elements of the Boolean Lattice that are in the Down Set of the Attribute Element will also exhibit the Attribute. In other words, if the Set is Homogeneous, then we can say that the Set exhibits the Attribute, although technically only Atoms have binary Truth Values.
    o The Complement of the Attribute Element exhibits the "No" or "False" Attribute Value with respect to the Attribute in question.
    o All Elements of the Boolean Lattice that are in the Down Set of the Complement of the Attribute Element will also exhibit the "No" or "False" Attribute Value.
    o The remaining "Mixed" Elements (excluding the Empty Set, since it is empty and has no Objects in it) exhibit a mixture of "Yes/No" or "True/False" Atoms. We can apply a rule to assign a Truth Value to the Mixed Elements, but it is a judgment call that we make, not a result the characteristics of Boolean Algebras.

The key point is that we assume that Atoms have binary Yes/No Truth Values, so the question becomes: How do we assign Truth Values to the Atoms in the Order 3 Boolean Lattice? The general solution that we apply in MWN is to use the Value Map for the Atoms only, *i.e.*, we solve the Logic Formulas for a particular Order 2 Domain of Propositions with one special rule: in a DBNF Lattice we treat "(∅)" from Order 2 as "False" in Order 3. If we can live with this assumption, that Empty implies "not-True" and therefore "False," then we have a methodology for assigning Truth Values in an Order 3 Boolean Lattice. (Conversely, there is an Inverse, Dual rule for a CBNF Lattice.)

Are there other possible rules that we could apply to assign Truth Values to the "Mixed" Elements? The answer is "yes." Other possible rules include the following:

- **OR**: In a DBNF Lattice of Logic Formulas, we could apply an OR rule to classify the Mixed Elements as "True." The justification would be that connecting a string of False Propositions to a True Proposition by "OR" does not affect the Truth Value. (In fact, in MWN we go one step further and simplify the Mixed Elements by eliminating the False Clauses altogether.)
- **AND**: in a CBNF Lattice of Logic Formulas, we could apply an AND rule to classify the Mixed Elements as "False." The justification would be that connecting a string of True Propositions to a False Proposition by "AND" does not affect the Truth Value. (In fact, in MWN we go one step further and simplify the Mixed Elements by eliminating the True Clauses altogether.)
- **More than half**: in a voting situation, we often say that an action is "approved" if a simple majority vote in favor of the action.
- **More than two-thirds**: in other situation, we may require a two-thirds vote to approve a particularly controversial or important action.
- **Almost exclusively**: in yet other situations, we may allow for the so-called "exception that proves the rule," but otherwise require that the Mixed Set be almost exclusively "Yes" or "True" before assigning an Attribute Value or Truth Value.

A key point here is that we must exercise discretion to assign an Attribute Value or Truth Value to a Set of Atoms that contains a mixture of Yes/No or Truth/False Values. The rule that we choose to apply may vary depending upon the context. This may seem odd at first, but upon further reflection it is consistent with how we actually think. Answers to questions are not always black and white; we must exercise discretion and make judgment calls in the gray areas. In mathematical terms, we must come up with a rule for assigning an Attribute Value or Truth Value to Mixed Sets.

We end this Chapter with an example that highlights the differences between Traditional Propositional Logic and MWN Propositional Logic. Suppose we create an Order 2 Domain of Propositions as set forth in **Fig. 7-20**.

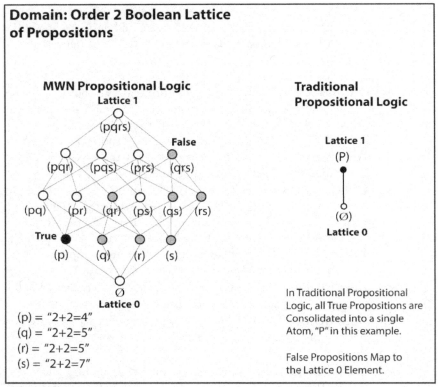

Domain: Order 2 Boolean Lattice of Propositions

MWN Propositional Logic
Lattice 1

(pqrs)

False

(pqr) (pqs) (prs) (qrs)

(pq) (pr) (qr) (ps) (qs) (rs)

True
(p) (q) (r) (s)

∅
Lattice 0

(p) = "2+2=4"
(q) = "2+2=5"
(r) = "2+2=5"
(s) = "2+2=7"

Traditional Propositional Logic

Lattice 1
(P)

(∅)
Lattice 0

In Traditional Propositional Logic, all True Propositions are Consolidated into a single Atom, "P" in this example.

False Propositions Map to the Lattice 0 Element.

Fig. 7-20

In MWN, the Order 2 Domain has four Proposition Atoms: p, q, r, and s, where only "p" is True. In Traditional Propositional Logic ("TPL"), however, all True Propositions are consolidated into a single Atom, and all False Propositions Map to Lattice 0. Therefore, in TPL the Order 2 Domain has one Proposition Atom "P".

Although MWN Propositional Logic and TPL have different Order 2 Domains, the one-Variable Order 3 Boolean Lattice of Logic Formulas is the same for both. *See,* **Fig. 7-21**.

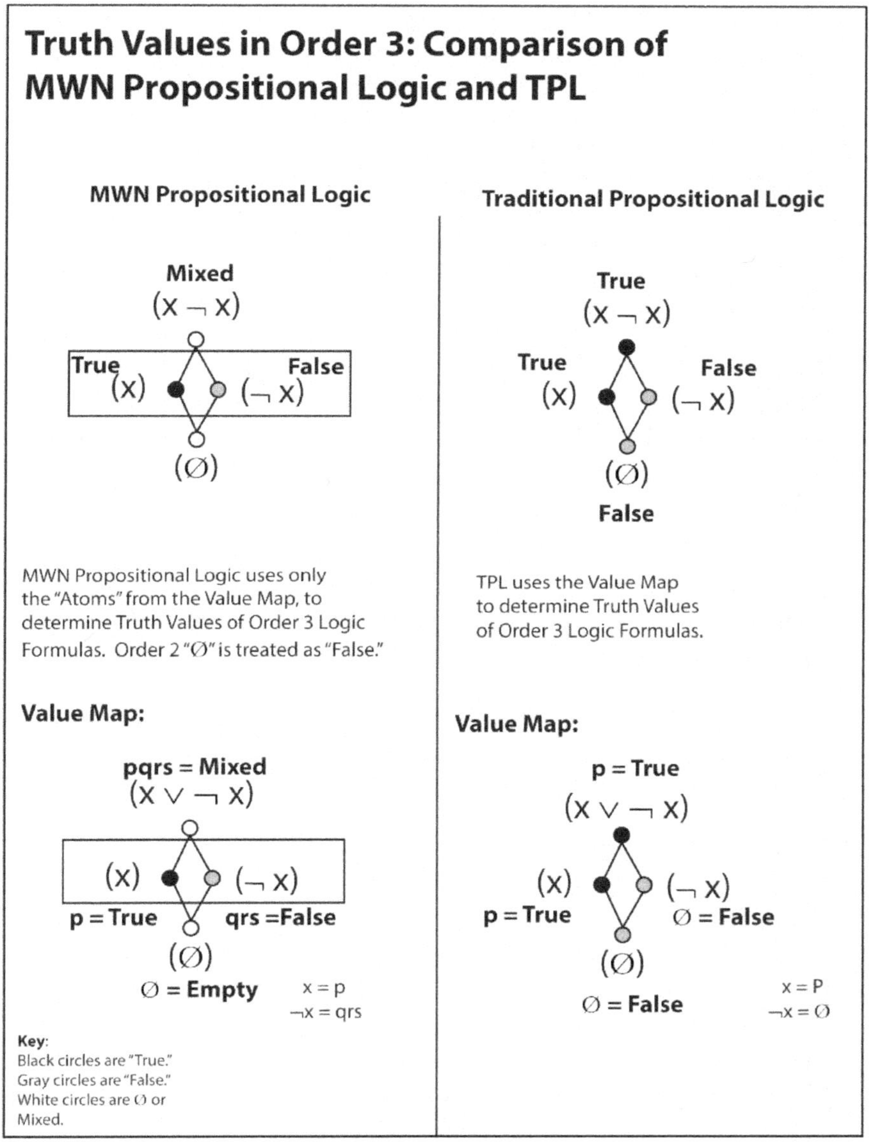

Truth Values in Order 3: Comparison of MWN Propositional Logic and TPL

MWN Propositional Logic

Traditional Propositional Logic

MWN Propositional Logic uses only the "Atoms" from the Value Map, to determine Truth Values of Order 3 Logic Formulas. Order 2 "Ø" is treated as "False."

TPL uses the Value Map to determine Truth Values of Order 3 Logic Formulas.

Value Map:

Value Map:

Key:
Black circles are "True."
Gray circles are "False."
White circles are Ø or Mixed.

Fig. 7-21

Although the Logic Formulas are the same for both TPL and MWN Propositional Logic, the approach to determining Truth Values in Order 3 is entirely different. In TPL, we simply use the Value Map to determine the Truth Values of all the Elements in the Lattice.

In MWN Propositional Logic, however, we take the position that only Atoms in the Order 3 Lattice have a binary Truth Value. The "Free Algebra with 'n' Generators," however, does not determine Truth Values in MWN Propositional Logic. Rather, it determines a Subalgebra based upon Elements chosen from a Boolean Algebra Domain. Specifically, we are left with a Set of two Atoms in the Value Map that constitute a Partition of Unity: (T, F).

Now, we come to the principal difference between Traditional Propositional Logic and MWN Propositional Logic. Rather than using the Value Map for the Truth Value of the remaining Elements, we use the standard MWN approach to Truth Value. The Union of True Atoms gives us the "Attribute Element," the Down Set of which represents "True"; the Complement of the Attribute Element (which is also the Union of False Atoms) gives us the "not-Attribute Element," the Down Set of which represents "False." The remaining Elements have a "Mixed" Truth Value.

Note from **Fig. 7-21**, that the principal difference is that in Traditional Propositional Logic, the Elements that are "Mixed" in MWN, are "True" in a DBNF Lattice. (The converse is the case in a CBNF Lattice, *i.e.*, the "Mixed" Elements in MWN are "False" in Traditional Propositional Logic.)

Now, to highlight the practical difference between the two systems of Propositional Logic, we look at some Boolean Expressions using our original Order 2 Domain of propositions:

- "p" = "2+2=4"
- "q" = "2+2=5"
- "r" = "2+2=5"
- "s" = "2+2=7"

Suppose we take the Logic Formula $(x) \vee (\neg x)$ and let "x" = "p". In Traditional Propositional Logic, we interpret "x" to be "1" and "$\neg$ x" to be "0", so the Formula becomes: $(x) \vee (\neg x) = (1) \vee (0) = 1$. In other words, in Traditional Propositional Logic the following sentence is considered to be True: (2+2=4) or (it is not the case that: 2+2=4).

In MWN Propositional Logic, however, we take a different approach. We view the Boolean Expression "$(x) \vee (\neg x)$" as having a "Mixed" Truth Value. In the context of Propositional Logic, we apply a rule stating that it adds nothing to a "True" Clause to add additional "False" Clauses with the Logic Operation "OR," so we can simplify any "Mixed" Expression in

DBNF by deleting any False Clauses. Therefore, in our example we can simplify the Expression to read as: "(x)" or simply (2+2=4).

Suppose two grade school students are taking a math exam and a question on the exam reads as follows: "Is 2+2=4?" Student A answers: "(2+2=4) or (it is not the case that: 2+2=4)"; Student B answers: (2+2=4). Which student answered the question correctly? The logician applying Traditional Propositional Logic would say that both students gave a "True" response. This seems like a bad result from a practical standpoint, because we cannot tell for sure whether Student A actually knew the correct answer. At best, it muddies the waters and leads to possible confusion, if we consider it to be correct to connect extraneous "False" Clauses to a "True" Clause and still consider the result to be "True." The MWN approach to Propositional Logic gives us a clear methodology for avoiding this confusion, by stating that we can delete any False Clauses in a Mixed Element when working in a DBNF Lattice. We refer to this as **"Simplification by Elimination."** (There is an Inverse, Dual rule for Mixed Elements in a CBNF Lattice.)

In some cases, we truly have a **"Binary Attribute Domain"** such that it makes sense every Element in the Power Set has a True or False Truth Value, rather than a "Mixed" Truth Value. An example of this is electric circuit design where a parallel circuit is represented by OR, and a series circuit is represented by AND. If any parallel path (OR) is closed (True), then the electricity will flow, and it is irrelevant that other parallel path is open (False). The issue for Propositional Logic, and Ideas generally, is that the way we think is not binary, or black and white, like an electrical circuit, because there are usually shades of gray representing judgment calls that we must make. In technical terms, our thought process is still "Boolean" in nature, but there are many Atoms in the Order 2 Domain, not just one Atom as in Traditional Propositional Logic.

From a MWN perspective, the only way to justify a truly binary approach is if there is only a single Atom. In MWN Propositional Logic, however, we prefer to view "True" Propositions as one Atom, and "False" Propositions as a second Atom.

We achieved our goal of articulating a new approach to demonstrating that Propositional Logic using the operations of OR, AND, and Negation, constitutes a Boolean Algebra. In fact, we demonstrated that there are several relevant Boolean Algebras. In Volume 2, we will review in detail more examples of relevant Boolean Algebras.

7.12.   *References, Historical Notes, and Further Reading*

For a discussion of CNF and DNF, see:

[Arnold 1962] at 102 *et seq.*

For a discussion of CBNF and DBNF, see:
[Quine 1982] at 73.

Negation
[Klenk 1994] at 56 *et seq.*

De Morgan Laws
[Hedman 2004] at 11.

[Klenk 1994] at 57.

[Couturat 1914] at 32.

BIBLIOGRAPHY

The year listed is the year of the latest revision by the author, but not necessarily the latest printing if no revisions were made. That way, the reader can get a sense of the historical perspective of the Book or article. (Note that the labels in the "Category" column form a valid Partition of the Book Titles!)

Abbreviation	Book	Category
[Aarts 2011]	Aarts, Bas, *Oxford Modern English Grammar*, Oxford University Press 2011.	Knowledge Base: English Grammar
[Abbott 1969]	Abbott, James C., *Sets, Lattices, and Boolean Algebras*, Boston, Allyn and Bacon, Inc. 1969.	Abstract Algebra
[Aristotle 350 BCE]	Richard McKeon (ed.), *The Basic Works of Aristotle*, New York, Random House 1941.	Classical Logic.
[Arnold 1962]	Arnold, Bradford Henry, *Logic and Boolean Algebra*, Mineola, New York Dover 2011.	Logic
[Auslander and Buchsbaum 1974]	Auslander, Maurice and David A. Buchsbaum, *Groups, Rings, Modules*, Mineola, New York, Dover 1974.	Group Theory, Ring Theory
[Bachhuber 1957]	Bachhuber, Andrew H., *Introduction to Logic*, New York Appleton-Century-Crofts, Inc. 1957,	Logic
[Baynes 1861]	Baynes, Thomas Spencer, *The Port-Royal Logic*, London, Hamilton, Adams, and Co. 1861. Reprinted by Kessinger Legacy Reprints.	Logic
[Beason and Lester 2013]	Beason, Larry, and Mark Lester, *English Grammar and Usage*, New York, McGraw Hill 2013.	Knowledge Base: English Grammar
[Bergman 2012]	Bergman, Clifford, *Universal Algebra – Fundamentals and Selected Topics*, New York, CRC Press, 2012.	Abstract Algebra
[Birkhoff 1995]	Birkhoff, Garrett, *Lattice Theory*, Providence, Rhode Island, American Mathematical Society 1995.	Lattice Theory
[Birkhoff and Mac Lane 1999]	Birkhoff, Garrett, and Saunders Mac Lane, *Algebra, 3d Ed.*, Providence Rhode Island, AMS Chelsea Publishing 1999.	Algebra
[Black 1952]	Black, Max, *Critical Thinking*, New Jersey, Prentice-Hall, 1952.	Logic
[Black 1968]	Black, Max, *The Labyrinth Of Language*, New York, Encyclopedia Britannica 1968.	Philosophy of Language
[Boole 1854]	Boole, George, *An Investigation of The Laws of Thought, On Which are Founded The Mathematical Theories of Logic and Probabilities*, New York, Dover Reprint of 1854 Ed.	Logic

Abbreviation	Book	Category
[Bourbaki 1968]	Bourbaki, Nicolas, *Elements of Mathematics, Theory of Sets*, Menlo Park, California, Addison-Wesley Publishing Co. 1968.	Set Theory
[Brachman and Levesque 2004]	Brachman, Ronald J. and Hector J. Levesque, *Knowledge Representation and Reasoning*, San Francisco, California, Elsevier 2004.	Knowledge Representation
[Burris 1998]	Burris, Stanley, *Logic for Mathematics and Computer Science*, New Jersey, Prentice Hall 1998.	Logic
[Burris and Sankappanavar 1981]	Burris, Stanley and H.P. Sankappanavar, *A Course in Universal Algebra*, New York, Springer 1981.	Universal Algebra
[Burton 1970]	Burton, David M., *A First Course in Rings and Ideals*, Menlo Park, California, Addison-Wesley Publishing Company, Inc. 1970.	Ring Theory
[CQ14 2014]	CQ Researcher, Issues for Debate in American Public Policy – Selections From CQ Researcher, 14th Edition (2014)	Knowledge Base: Current Issues
[CQ15 2015]	CQ Researcher, Issues for Debate in American Public Policy, 15th Ed. (CQ Press 2015)	Current Issues Knowledge Base:
[Carpineto and Romano 2004]	Carpineto, Claudio, and Giovanni Romano, *Concept and Data Analysis – Theory and Applications*, Chichester, West Sussex, England, John Wiley & Sons Inc. 2004.	Formal Concept Analysis
[Case, Funke, and Tortora 2016]	Case, Christine L., Berdell R. Funke, and Gerard J. Tortora, *Microbiology-An Introduction*, Essex, England, Pearson Education 2016.	Knowledge Base: Microbiology
[Caspard, Leclerc, and Monjardet 2012]	Caspard, Nathalie, Leclerc, Bruno, and Monjardet, Bernard, *Finite Ordered Sets*, New York, Cambridge University Press 2012.	Lattice Theory
[Chao ed. 1993]	Chao, Liu Hai, *Shaolin Gong-Fu – A Course in Tradition al Forms*, Henan Scientific and Technical Publishing House 1994.	Knowledge Base: Martial Arts
[Chen and Koh 1992]	Chen, Chuan-Chong and Koh, Khee-Meng, *Principles and Techniques in Combinatorics*, Singapore, World Scientific Publishing 1992.	Combinatorics
[Chilvers 2013]	Chilvers, Ian, Chief Consultant, *Art that Changed the World*, New York, Dorling Kindersley (DK) 2013.	Knowledge Base: Art
[CLA 2006]	Yahia, Sadok Ben, Engelbert Mephu Nguifo, Radim Belohlavek (Eds.), *Fourth International Conference, on Concept Lattices and Their Applications (CLA)*, New York, Springer 2008.	Lattice Theory
[Clark 1970]	Clark, Allan, *Elements of Abstract Algebra*, New York, Dover 1984.	Abstract Algebra
[Cogeval, Patry, and Guegan 2010]	Cogeval, Guy, Patry, Sylvie, and Guegan, Stephane, *Van Gogh, Gauguin, Cezanne, and Beyond*, New York, Del Monico Books -Prestel 2010.	Knowledge Base: Art
[Cogeval, Guegan, and Thomine-	Cogeval, Guy, Guegan, Stephane, and Thomine-Berrada, Alice, *Birth of Impressionism*, New York, Del Monico Books -Prestel 2010.	Knowledge Base: Art

Abbreviation	Book	Category
Barrada 2010]		
[Cohn 1999]	Cohn, Paul M., *An Introduction to Ring Theory*, New York, Springer 2000.	Ring Theory
[Coile 2005]	Coile, D. Caroline, *Encyclopedia of Dog Breeds*, New York, Barron's 2005.	Knowledge Base: Dogs
[Copi 1973]	Copi, Irving M., *Symbolic Logic*, New York, Macmillan Publishing Co., Inc. 1973.	Symbolic Logic
[Cori and Lascar 1993]	Cori, René, and Daniel Lascar, *Mathematical Logic*, Oxford, Oxford University Press 2000.	Mathematical Logic
[Cothran Book I 2000]	Cothran, Martin, *Traditional Logic – Introduction to Formal Logic*, Memoria Press 2000.	Logic
[Cothran Book II 2000]	Cothran, Martin, *Traditional Logic – Advanced Formal Logic*, Memoria Press 2000.	Logic
[Cothran 2006]	Cothran, Martin, *Material Logic*, Memoria Press 2006.	Logic
[Couturat 1914]	Couturat, Louis, *The Algebra of Logic*, Chicago, The Open Court Publishing Company 1914.	Algebraic Logic
[Crawley and Dilworth 1973]	Crawley, P. and Dilworth, R.., *Algebraic Theory of Lattices*, New Jersey, Prentice-Hall, Inc. 1973.	Lattice Theory
[Curry 1976]	Curry, Haskell B., *Foundations of Mathematical Logic*, New York, Dover 1977.	Mathematical Logic
[Davey and Priestley 2001]	Davey, B.A., and Priestley, H.A., *Introduction to Lattices and Order (2d Ed.)*, Cambridge University Press 2002.	Lattice Theory
[DeLong 1998]	DeLong, Howard, *A Profile of Mathematical Logic*, Mineola, New York, Dover 1998.	Mathematical Logic
[De Morgan 1847]	De Morgan, Augustus, *Formal Logic: or, The Calculus of Inference, Necessary and Probable*, London, Taylor and Walton 1847. Reprinted by Scholar Select, 2017.	Logic
[Denney, Duncan, and McKinney 1910]	Denney, Joseph Villiers, Carson S. Duncan, and Frank C. McKinney, *Argumentation and Debate*, New York, American Book Company 1910. Reprinted by Forgotten Books 2012.	Argumentation and Debate
[Devlin 1993]	Devlin, Keith, *The Joy of Sets*, New York, Springer 1993.	Set Theory
[Dugundji 1966]	Dugundji, James, *Topology*, Boston, Allyn and Bacon, Inc. 1966.	Topology
[Durant Vol.1 1935]	Durant, Will, *The Story of Civilization: 1, Our Oriental Heritage*, New York, Simon and Schuster 1935.	Knowledge Base: History
[Durant Vol.2 1939]	Durant, Will, *The Story of Civilization: 2, The Life of Greece*, New York, Simon and Schuster 1939.	Knowledge Base: History
[Durant Vol.3 1944]	Durant, Will, *The Story of Civilization: 3, Caesar and Christ*, New York, Simon and Schuster 1944.	Knowledge Base: History
[Durant Vol.4 1950]	Durant, Will, *The Story of Civilization: 4, The Age of Faith*, New York, Simon and Schuster 1950.	Knowledge Base: History

Abbreviation	Book	Category
[Durant Vol.5 1953]	Durant, Will, *The Story of Civilization: 5, The Rennaissance*, New York, Simon and Schuster 1953.	Knowledge Base: History
[Durant Vol.6 1957]	Durant, Will, *The Story of Civilization: 6, The Reformation*, New York, Simon and Schuster 1957.	Knowledge Base: History
[Durant Vol.7 1961]	Durant, Will and Ariel Durant, *The Story of Civilization: 7, The Age of Reason Begins*, New York, Simon and Schuster 1961.	Knowledge Base: History
[Durant Vol.8 1963]	Durant, Will and Ariel Durant, *The Story of Civilization: 8, The Age of Louis XIV*, New York, Simon and Schuster 1963.	Knowledge Base: History
[Durant Vol.9 1965]	Durant, Will and Ariel Durant, *The Story of Civilization: 9, The Age of Voltaire*, New York, Simon and Schuster 1965.	Knowledge Base: History
[Durant Vol. 10 1967]	Durant, Will and Ariel Durant, *The Story of Civilization: 10, Rousseau and Revolution*, New York, Simon and Schuster 1967.	Knowledge Base: History
[Durant Vol.11 1975]	Durant, Will and Ariel Durant, *The Story of Civilization: 11, The Age of Napoleon*, New York, MJF Books 1975.	Knowledge Base: History
[Ehrlich 1991]	Ehrlich, Gertrude, *Fundamental Concepts of Abstract Algebra*, Mineola, New York Dover 1991.	Abstract Algebra
[Enderton 1977]	Enderton, Herbert B., *Elements of Set Theory*, New York, Academic Press 1977.	Set Theory
[Evenden 1962]	Evenden, John. "A Lattice-Diagram for the Propositional Calculus." *The Mathematical Gazette*, vol. 46, no. 356, 1962, pp. 119–122. JSTOR, JSTOR, www.jstor.org/stable/3611637.	Lattice Theory
[Eves 1990]	Eves, Howard, *Foundations and Fundamental Concepts of Mathematics, 3rd ed.*, New York, Dover 1997.	Mathematics: Foundations
[Freeley and Steinberg 2009]	Freeley, Austin J., and David L. Steinberg, *Argumentation and Debate*, Boston, Massachusetts, Wadsworth Cengage Learning 2009.	Argumentation and Debate
[Frege 1879]	Frege, Gottlob, "Begriffsschrift, a formula language, modeled upon that of arithmetic, for pure thought" in *From Frege to Gödel, a Source Book in Mathematical Logic, 1879-1931*, Cambridge, Massachusetts, Harvard University Press 1967.	Mathematical Logic
[Frisch 1969]	Frisch, Joseph C., *Extension and Comprehension in Logic*, New York, Philosophical Library 1969.	Logic
[Funakoshi 1956]	Funakoshi, Gichin, *Karate-Do Kyohan – The Master Text*, New York, Kodansha International 1973.	Knowledge Base: Martial Arts
[Gamut 1991]	Gamut, L.T.F., *Logic, Language, and Meaning, Vol.1 Introduction to Logic*, Chicago, The University of Chicago Press 1991.	Logic
[Ganter and Wille 1999]	Ganter, Bernhard and Rudolf Wille, *Formal Concept Analysis*, New York, Springer 1999.	Formal Concept Analysis
[Ganter,	Ganter, Bernhard, Stumme, Gerd, and Wille,	Formal Concept

Abbreviation	Book	Category
Stumme, and Wille 2005]	Rudolf (Eds.), *Formal Concept Analysis – Foundations and Applications*, Springer 2005.	Analysis
[Gillie 1965]	Gillie, Angelo C., *Binary Arithmetic and Boolean Algebra*, New York, McGraw-Hill Book Company 1965.	Boolean Algebra
[Gindikin 1972]		
[Givant and Halmos 1998]	Givant, Steven and Paul Halmos, *Logic as Algebra*, The Mathematical Association of America 1998.	Logic
[Givant and Halmos 2009]	Givant, Steven and Paul Halmos, *Introduction to Boolean Algebras*, New York, Springer 2009.	Boolean Algebras and Rings
[Grätzer 2003]	Grätzer, George, *General Lattice Theory 2d Ed.*, Boston, Birkhäuser 2003.	Lattice Theory
[Grätzer 2008]	Grätzer, George, *Universal Algebra 2d Ed.*, New York, Springer 2008.	Universal Algebra
[Halmos 1960]	Halmos, Paul R., *Naive Set Theory*, Princeton, Van Nostrand 1960.	Set Theory
[Hamilton]	Hamilton, George Heard, *The Library of Art History: 19th and 20th Century Art*, New York, Harry N. Abrams, Inc.	Knowledge Base: Art
[Hedman 2004]	Hedman, Shawn, *A First Course in Logic*, Oxford, Oxford University Press 2004.	Logic
[Hilbert and Ackermann 1938]	Hilbert, D. and W. Ackermann, *Principles of Mathematical Logic*, Providence, Rhode Island, AMS Chelsea Publishing 2008.	Mathematical Logic
[Hill and Leeman 1977]	Hill, Bill, and Richard W. Leeman, *The Art and Practice of Argumentation and Debate*, Mountain View, California Mayfield Publishing Company 1997.	Argumentation and Debate
[Hinman 2005]	Hinman, Peter G., *Fundamentals of Mathematical Logic*, Wellesley, Massachusetts, A K Peters 2005.	Mathematical Logic
[Hitzler and Schärfe 2009]	Hitzler, Pascal and Henrik Schärfe (Eds.), *Conceptual Structures in Practice*, Baca Raton, Florida, CRC Press 2009.	Formal Concept Analysis
[Hrbacek and Jech 1999]	Hrbacek, Karel, and Thomas Jech, *Introduction to Set Theory, 3d Ed.*, Boca Raton, Florida, CRC Press 1999.	Set Theory
[Huntington 1933]	Huntington, Edward V. "New Sets of Independent Postulates for the Algebra of Logic, With Special Reference to Whitehead and Russell's Principia Mathematica." *Transactions of the American Mathematical Society*, vol. 35, no. 1, 1933, pp. 274–304. *JSTOR*, JSTOR, www.jstor.org/stable/1989325.	Algebraic Logic
[Huntington 1937]	Huntington, Edward V. "Postulates for Assertion, Conjunction, Negation, and Equality." *Proceedings of the American Academy of Arts and Sciences*, vol. 72, no. 1, 1937, pp. 1–44. *JSTOR*, JSTOR, www.jstor.org/stable/20023279.	Algebraic Logic
[ICFCA 2004]	Eklund, Peter (Ed.), *Formal Concept Analysis, 2nd International Conference, International Conference on*	Formal Concept Analysis

Abbreviation	Book	Category
	Formal Concept Analysis (ICFCA), New York, Springer 2004.	
[ICFCA 2009]	Ferré, Sébastien, and Sebastian Rudolph (Eds.), *Formal Concept Analysis, 7th International Conference, ICFCA,* New York, Springer 2009.	Formal Concept Analysis
[ICFCA 2011]	Valtchev, Petko, and Robert Jäschke (Eds.), *Formal Concept Analysis, 9th International Conference, ICFCA,* New York, Springer 2011.	Formal Concept Analysis
[ICFCA 2012]	Domenach, Florent, Dmitry I. Ignatov, Jonas Poelmans (Eds.), *Formal Concept Analysis, 10th International Conference, ICFCA,* New York, Springer 2012.	Formal Concept Analysis
[ICFCA 2013]	Cellier, Peggy, Felix Distel, Bernhard Ganter (Eds.), *Formal Concept Analysis, 11th International Conference, ICFCA,* New York, Springer 2013.	Formal Concept Analysis
[ICFCA 2014]	Glodeanu, Cynthia Vera, Mehdi Kaytoue, Christian Sacarea (Eds.), *Formal Concept Analysis, 12th International Conference, ICFCA,* New York, Springer 2014.	Formal Concept Analysis
[Isaacs 2008]	Isaacs, I. Martin, *Finite Group Theory*, Providence, Rhode Island, American Mathematical Society 2008.	Group Theory
[Jech 2003]	Jech, Thomas, *Set Theory – 3d Millennium Ed.*, New York Springer 2003.	Set Theory
[Jevons 1877]	Jevons, W. S., *Elementary Lessons in Logic,* Macmillan and Co. 1877. Reprint by Forgotten Books.	Logic
[Kaburlasos 2006]	Kaburlasos, Vassilis G., *Towards a Unified Modeling and Knowledge-Representation based on Lattice Theory*, New York, Springer 2006.	Lattice Theory
[Kamke 1950]	Kamke, E., *Theory of Sets*, New York, Dover 1950.	Set Theory
[Klammer, Schulz, and Volpe 2013]	Klammer, Thomas P., Muriel R. Schulz, and Angela Della Volpe, *Analyzing English Grammar 7th Ed.*, New York, Pearson Education, Inc. 2013.	Knowledge Base: English Grammar
[Kleene 1967]	Kleene, Stephen Cole, *Mathematical Logic*, Mineola, New York, Dover 1967.	Mathematical Logic
[Klenk 1994]	Klenk, Virginia, *Understanding Symbolic Logic, 3d.*, Englewood Cliffs, New Jersey, Prentice Hall 1994.	Logic
[Kneale and Kneale 1971]	Kneale, William, and Martha Kneale, *The Development of Logic*, Oxford, Clarendon Press 1971.	Logic
[Kneebone 1963]	Kneebone, G. T., *Mathematical Logic and the Foundations of Mathematics*, New York, D. Van Nostrand Company Ltd. 1963.	Mathematical Logic
[Kolln, Gray, and Salvatore 2016]	Kolln, Martha, Loretta Gray, and Joseph Salvatore, *Understanding English Grammar*, New York, Pearson 2016.	Knowledge Base: English Grammar
[Kneebone 1963]	Kneebone, G.T., *Mathematical Logic and the Foundations of Mathematics*, New York, D. Van Nostrand Company Limited 1963.	Mathematical Logic

Abbreviation	Book	Category
[Kreeft 2010]	Kreeft, P., *Socratic Logic*, South Bend, Indiana, St Augustine's Press 2010.	Logic
[Kunen 2011]	Kunen, Kenneth, *Set Theory*, London, College Publications 2011.	Set Theory
[Langer 1966]	Langer, Susanne K., *An Introduction to Symbolic Logic*, New York, Dover 1967.	Logic
[Lawvere and Rosebrugh 2003]	Lawvere, F. William, and Rosebrugh, Robert, *Sets for Mathematics*, University of Cambridge 2003.	Set Theory
[Lee and Ricke 1999]	Lee, Soon Man and Ricke, Gaetane, *Modern Taekwondo*, New York, Sterling Publishing Co., Inc. 1999.	Knowledge Base: Martial Arts
[Levy 1979]	Levy, Azriel, *Basic Set Theory*, Mineola, New York, Dover 1979.	Set Theory
[Lipschutz 2012]	Lipschutz, Seymour, *General Topology*, New York, McGraw Hill 2012.	Topology
[Lukasiewicz 1957]	Lukasiewicz, Jan, *Aristotle's Syllogistic 2d Ed.*, Oxford, Clarendon Press 1957.	Logic
[Margaris 1967]	Margaris, Angelo, *First Order Mathematical Logic*, Waltham, Massachusetts, Blaisdell Publishing Company 1967.	Mathematical Logic
[Maritain 1946]	Maritain, Jacques, *Formal Logic*, New York, Seed & Ward 1946.	Logic
[Markman 1998]	Markman, Arthur B., *Knowledge Representation*, New York, Psychology Press 1998.	Knowledge Representation
[McInerny 2004]	McInerny, Dennis, *La Logique Facile*, Paris, Eyrolles 2004.	Logic
[Mill 1872]	Mill, John Stuart, *System of Logic Vol. II*, London, Longmans, Green, Reader, and Dyer 1872. Reprint by Forgotten Books 2012.	Logic
[Minto 1893]	Minto, William, *Logic – Inductive and Deductive*, Boston, Adamant Media 2005. (Unabridged facsimile of the edition published in 1893 by John Murray, London.)	Logic
[Moore 2013]	Moore, Gregory H., *Zermelo's Axiom of Choice*, Mineola, New York, Dover 2013.	Set Theory
[Monk 1969]	Monk, J. Donald, *Introduction to Set Theory*, New York McGraw-Hill, Inc. 1969.	Set Theory
[Monk 1989]	Monk, J. Donald Ed., *Handbook of Boolean Algebras*, Vol. 1-3, Elsevier Science Publishers B.V. 1989.	Boolean Algebra
[Nakayama, Fundamentals 1978]	Nakayama, M., *Best Karate 2 – Fundamentals*, New York, Kodansha International 1978.	Knowledge Base: martial arts
[Northcott 1968]	Northcott, D.G., *Ideal Theory*, Cambridge University Press 1968.	Ring Theory, Ideal Theory
[Parker and Veatch 1959]	Parker, Francis H. and Henry B. Veatch, *Logic as a Human Instrument*, New York, Harper & Brothers 1959.	Logic
[Parrochia and Neuville 2013]	Parrochia, Daniel and Neuville, Pierre, *Towards a General Theory of Classifications*, Springer Basel, 2013.	Universal Logic, Classification

Abbreviation	Book	Category
		Theory
[Pinter 1990]	Pinter, Charles C., *A Book of Abstract Algebra*, 2d ed., Mineola, New York, Dover, 1990.	Abstract Algebra
[Pinter 2014]	Pinter, Charles C., *A Book of Set Theory*, Mineola, New York, Dover 2014.	Set Theory
[Porphyry 260 C.E.]	Porphyry, *Introduction*, Translated by Jonathan Barnes, New York, Oxford University Press 2003.	Logic
[Potter 2009]	Potter, Michael, *Set Theory and its Philosophy*, Oxford University Press 2009.	Set Theory
[Quine 1969]	Quine, Willard Van Orman, *Set Theory and Its Logic*, Cambridge, Massachusetts, Harvard University Press 1969.	Set Theory, Logic
[Quine 1981]	Quine, Willard Van Orman, *Mathematical Logic*, Cambridge, Mass., Harvard University Press, 1981.	Mathematical Logic
[Quine 1982]	Quine, Willard Van Orman, *Methods of Logic*, Cambridge, Massachusetts, Harvard University Press 1982.	Logic
[Quine 1986]	Quine, Willard Van Orman, *Philosophy of Logic*, Cambridge, Massachusetts, Harvard University Press 1970.	Logic
[Read 1909]	Read, Carveth, *Logic – Deductive and Inductive*, London, Alexander Moring Limited 1909. Reprinted by Forgotten Books 2012.	Logic
[Rees 2012]	Rees, Martin Ed., *Universe*, New York, Dorling Kindersley (DK Smithsonian) 2012.	Knowledge Base: Space Science
[Rigdon 1903]	Rigdon, Jonathan, *Grammar of the English Sentence*, London, Forgotten Books 2013.	Knowledge Base: Astronomy and the Planets
[Roberts and Zweig 2012]	Roberts, Edgar V., and Robert Zweig, *Literature – An Introduction to Reading and Writing*, New York, Longman 5th Compact Ed. 2012.	Knowledge Base: literature
[Rodgers 2000]	Rodgers, Nancy, *Learning to Reason*, New York, John Wiley & Sons, Inc. 2000.	Set Theory, Logic
[Roman 2008]	Roman, Steven, *Lattices and Ordered Sets*, New York, Springer 2008.	Lattice Theory
[Russell 1920]	Russell, Bertrand, *Introduction to Mathematical Philosophy*, New York, Dover ed. 1993.	Philosophy
[Russell 1921]	Russell, Bertrand, *The Analysis of Mind*, Mineola, New York, Dover 2005.	Philosophy
[Russell and Whitehead 1910]	Russell, Bertrand, and Alfred North Whitehead, *Principia Mathematica Vol. 1-3*, Rough Draft Printing 2011.	Logic
[Schröder 2003]	Schröder, Bernd S. W., *Ordered Sets*, Boston, Birkhauser 2003.	Lattice Theory

Abbreviation	Book	Category
[Shenefelt and White 2013]	Shenefelt, Michael, and Heidi White, *If A, then B - How the World Discovered Logic*, New York, Columbia University Press 2013.	Logic
[Shertzer 1986]	Shertzer, Margaret D., *The Elements of Grammar*, New York, Macmillan Publishing Company 1986.	Knowledge Base: English Grammar
[Sikorski 1964]	Sikorski, Roman, *Boolean Algebras*, New York, Springer-Verlag 1964.	Boolean Algebra
[Sider 2010]	Sider, Theodore, *Logic for Philosophy*, Oxford, Oxford University Press 2010.	Logic
[Singh 1959]	Singh, Jagjit, *Great Ideas of Modern Mathematics: Their Nature and Use*, New York, Dover Publications 1959.	Mathematics
[Smullyan 1968]	Smullyan, Raymond M., *First-Order Logic*, New York, Dover Publications 1995.	Mathematical Logic
[Smullyan 2014]	Smullyan, Raymond M., *A Beginner's Guide to Mathematical Logic*, New York, Dover Publications 2014.	Mathematical Logic
[Solomon 1990]	Solomon, A. D., *The Essentials of Boolean Algebra*, 1990.	Boolean Algebra
[Sowa 1984]	Sowa, John F., *Conceptual Structures: Information Processing in Mind and Machine*, Menlo Park, California, Addison-Wesley Publishing Company 1984.	Knowledge Representation
[Sowa 2000]	Sowa, John F., *Knowledge Representation*, Pacific Grove, California, Brooks/Cole 2000.	Knowledge Representation
[Stewart 2004]	Stewart, Ian, *Galois Theory*, New York, Chapman & Hall/CRC 2004.	Galois Theory
[Stewart and Tall 1977]	Stewart, Ian and Tall, David, *The Foundations of Mathematics*, Oxford University Press 1977.	Set Theory
[Stoll 1963]	Stoll, R.R., *Set Theory and Logic*, New York, Dover 1963.	Set Theory
[Stone 1936]	Stone, M.H., "The Theory of Representation for Boolean Algebras," Trans. Amer. Math. Soc. **40**, 37-111 (1936).	Boolean Algebras
[Stone 1937]	Stone, M.H., "Applications of the Theory of Boolean Rings to General Topology," Trans. Amer. Math. Soc. **41**, 375-481 (1937).	Boolean Algebras
[Sullivan 2005]	Sullivan, Scott M., *An Introduction to Traditional Logic*, North Charleston, SC, Booksurge Publishing 2006.	Logic
[Suppes 1972]	Suppes, Patrick, *Axiomatic Set Theory*, New York, Dover 1972.	Set Theory
[Tall 2014]	Tall, Aliou, *From Mathematics in Logic, to Logic in Mathematics*, Boston, Docent Press 2014.	Logic
[Thurman 2003]	Thurman, Susan, *The Only Grammar Book You'll Ever Need*, Avon Massachusetts, Adams Media 2003.	Knowledge Base:

Abbreviation	Book	Category
		English Grammar
[Tiles 1989]	Tiles, Mary, *The Philosophy of Set Theory*, Mineola, New York, Dover 1989.	Set Theory
[Toulmin 2003]	Toulmin, Stephen E., *The Uses of Argument*, New York, Cambridge University Press 2008.	Argumentation
[Toulmin, Rieke, and Janik 1979]	Toulmin, Stephen, Richard Rieke, and Allan Janik, *An Introduction to Reasoning*, New York, Macmillan Publishing Co. 1979.	Argumentation
[van der Waerden 1966]	Van der Waerden, B.L., *Algebra Vol. I*, New York, Springer 1970.	Abstract Algebra
[van der Waerden 1967]	Van der Waerden, B.L., *Algebra Vol. II*, New York, Springer 1970.	Abstract Algebra
[Veatch 2016] or [MWN Vol. 1]	Veatch, William S., *Math Without Numbers: The Mathematics of Ideas, Vol. 1 Foundations*, Createspace (2016), available on Amazon.com.	Boolean Algebra, Logic
[Venn 1894]	Venn, John, *Symbolic Logic*, London, Macmillan and Co., Forgotten Books ed. 2012.	Logic
[Vladimirov 1994]	Vladimirov, D. A., *Boolean Algebras in Analysis*, Boston, Kluwer Academic Publishers 2002.	Boolean Algebra
[Wallace 1998]	Wallace, D.A.R., *Groups, Rings and Fields*, London, Springer 1998.	Group Theory, Ring Theory
[Walton 2016]	Walton, Douglas, *Argument Evaluation and Evidence*, New York, Springer 2016.	Argumentation
[Warren 2013]	Warren, Rebecca, Knowledge Encyclopedia, New York, Dorling Kindersley (DK Smithsonian) 2013.	Knowledge Base: General
[Whately 1836]	Whately, Richard, *Elements of Logic*, New York, William Jackson 1836.	Logic
[Whitesitt 1960]	Whitesitt, J. Eldon, *Boolean Algebra and Its Applications, Mineola, New York, Dover 2010.*	Boolean Algebra
[Whitney 1933]	Whitney, Hassler. "Characteristic Functions and the Algebra of Logic." *Annals of Mathematics*, vol. 34, no. 3, 1933, pp. 405–414. *JSTOR*, JSTOR, www.jstor.org/stable/1968168.	Algebraic Logic
[Willard 1970]	Willard, Stephen, *General Topology*, Mineola, New York, Dover 1970.	Topology

Index

Page numbers in parenthesis refer to pages in Volumes of the "Math Without Numbers" series of books. "MWN1" refers to *Math Without Numbers – Vol. 1 Foundations*.

ABOUT THE AUTHOR

William S. Veatch is a practicing attorney, living in San Francisco, California. He obtained his B.A. degree in History at the University of Winnipeg, Winnipeg, Manitoba, Canada (1985), where he also studied Mathematics and Philosophy; his LL.B. law degree at the University of Manitoba, Winnipeg, Canada (1985); and his J.D. law degree from the University of California, Hastings College of the Law, San Francisco, California (1987).

www.ingramcontent.com/pod-product-compliance
Lightning Source LLC
LaVergne TN
LVHW022306060326
832902LV00020B/3303